WINDMAKER™

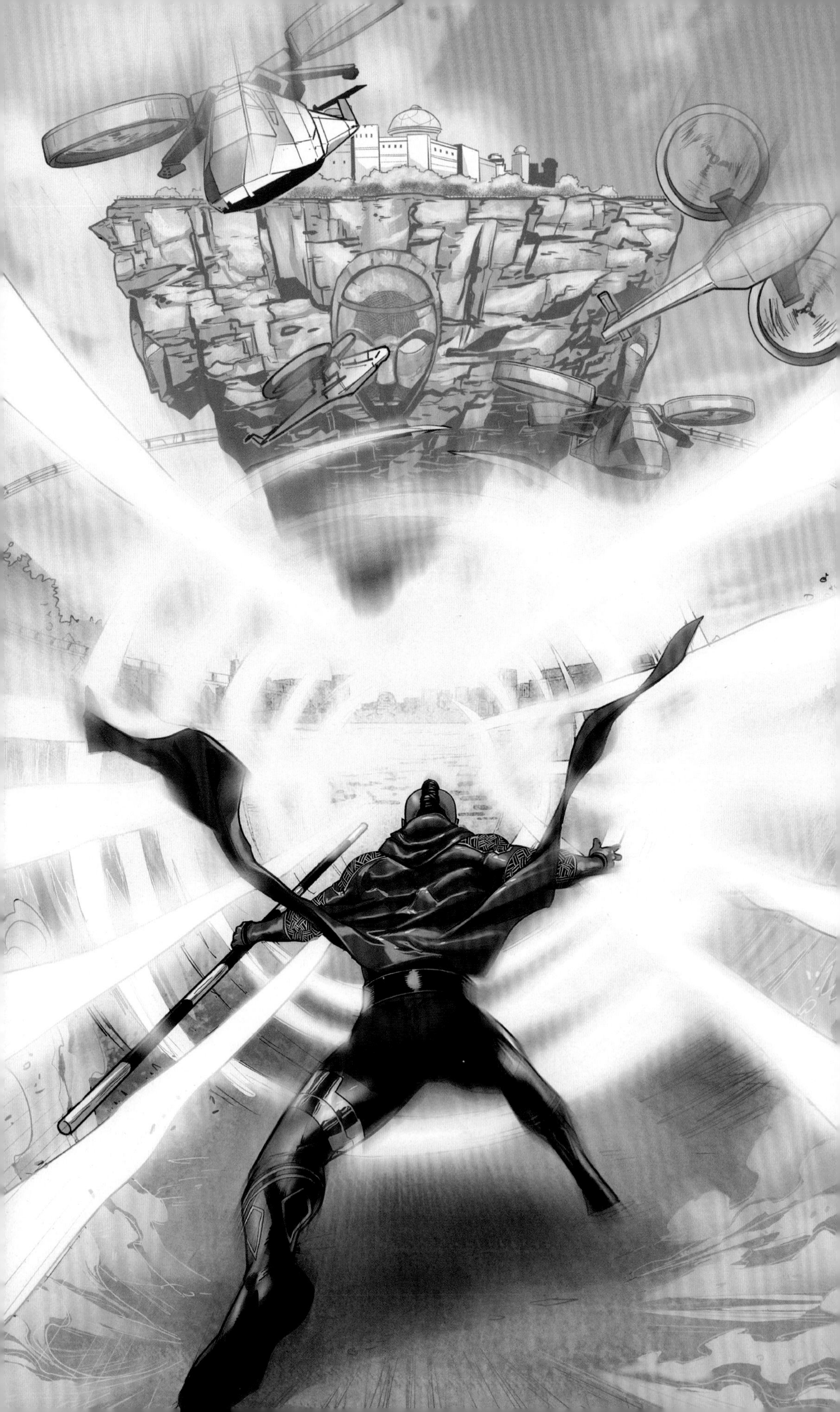

WINDMAKER™

VOLUME ONE

CREATOR AND WRITER
ROYE OKUPE

ART
SUNKANMI AKINBOYE

COLORS
TOYIN "MORBY" AJETUNMOBI

LETTERS
SPOOF ANIMATION

COVER ART
SUNKANMI AKINBOYE *with*
colors by GODWIN AKPAN

YOUNEEK
STUDIOS

DARK HORSE BOOKS

PUBLISHER
MIKE RICHARDSON

SENIOR EDITOR
PHILIP R. SIMON

ASSOCIATE EDITOR
JUDY KHUU

ASSISTANT EDITOR
ROSE WEITZ

DESIGNER
KATHLEEN BARNETT

DIGITAL ART TECHNICIAN
ADAM PRUETT

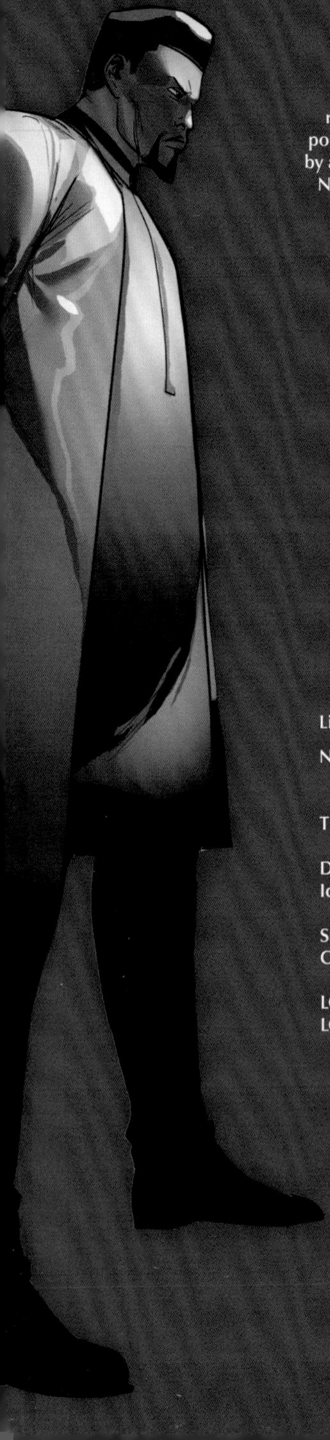

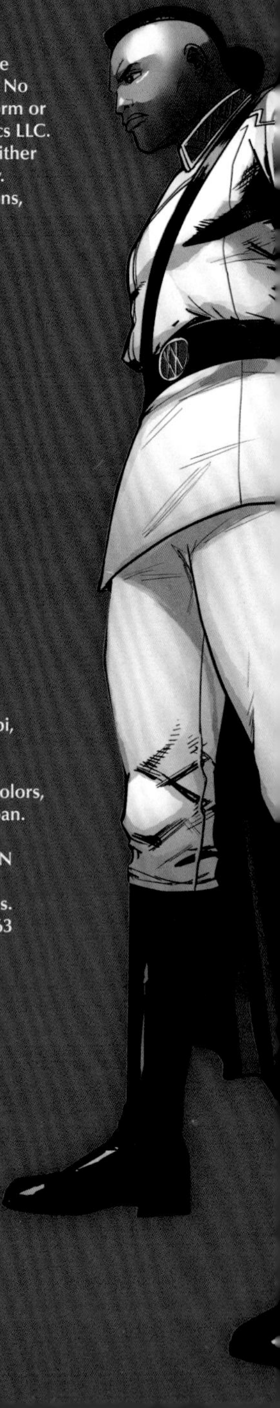

WINDMAKER VOLUME 1

Published by
Dark Horse Books
A division of Dark Horse Comics LLC
10956 SE Main Street
Milwaukie, OR 97222

DarkHorse.com

To find a comics shop in your area, visit comicshoplocator.com

First edition: April 2022

Ebook ISBN: 978-1-50672-321-1
Trade Paperback ISBN: 978-1-50672-311-2

1 3 5 7 9 10 8 6 4 2

Printed in China

Library of Congress Cataloging-in-Publication Data

Names: Okupe, Roye, writer. | Akinboye, Sunkanmi, artist. | Ajetunmobi, Toyin, colourist. | Spoof Animation, letterer. | Akpan, Godwin, cover artist.
Title: Windmaker / writer, Roye Okupe ; artist, Sunkanmi Akinboye ; colors, Toyin Ajetunmobi ; letters, Spoof Animation ; cover art, Godwin Akpan.
Description: Milwaukie, OR : Dark Horse Books, 2022.
Identifiers: LCCN 2021044933 (print) | LCCN 2021044934 (ebook) | ISBN 9781506723112 (trade paperback) | ISBN 9781506723211 (ebook)
Subjects: LCGFT: Afrofuturist comics. | Fantasy comics. | Graphic novels.
Classification: LCC PN6790.N563 O589 2022 (print) | LCC PN6790.N563 (ebook) | DDC 741.5/9669--dc23/eng/20211001
LC record available at https://lccn.loc.gov/2021044933
LC ebook record available at https://lccn.loc.gov/2021044934

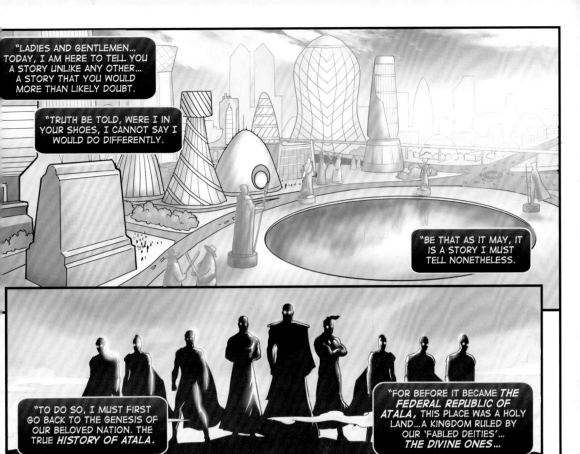

"LADIES AND GENTLEMEN... TODAY, I AM HERE TO TELL YOU A STORY UNLIKE ANY OTHER... A STORY THAT YOU WOULD MORE THAN LIKELY DOUBT.

"TRUTH BE TOLD, WERE I IN YOUR SHOES, I CANNOT SAY I WOULD DO DIFFERENTLY.

"BE THAT AS IT MAY, IT IS A STORY I MUST TELL NONETHELESS.

"TO DO SO, I MUST FIRST GO BACK TO THE GENESIS OF OUR BELOVED NATION. THE TRUE *HISTORY OF ATALA*.

"FOR BEFORE IT BECAME *THE FEDERAL REPUBLIC OF ATALA*, THIS PLACE WAS A HOLY LAND...A KINGDOM RULED BY OUR 'FABLED DEITIES'... *THE DIVINE ONES*...

"...A KINGDOM NAMED AFTER THE GREATEST OF THEM ALL, *ATALA, THE FIRST FATHER*.

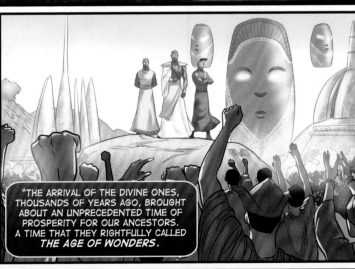

"THE ARRIVAL OF THE DIVINE ONES, THOUSANDS OF YEARS AGO, BROUGHT ABOUT AN UNPRECEDENTED TIME OF PROSPERITY FOR OUR ANCESTORS. A TIME THAT THEY RIGHTFULLY CALLED *THE AGE OF WONDERS*.

"UNFORTUNATELY, PEACE AND PROSPERITY WERE SOON REPLACED BY CHAOS AND TREACHERY AS THE *OLON JIN*...

"A SECT OF THE DIVINE ONES WHO CRAVED THE IMMENSE POWER DARK MAGIC HAD TO OFFER, CORRUPTED THE HEARTS OF MANY WITH A VERY *POWERFUL WEAPON*. THUS, THE DIVINE WARS BEGAN.

"AND EVEN THOUGH THEY WERE DEFEATED, CURSED, AND *BANISHED* TO AN *ISLAND* NO ONE KNOWS WHERE, NEVER TO SET FOOT ON ATALIAN SOIL AGAIN, THEIR TREACHERY STILL PLAGUES US TO THIS VERY DAY.

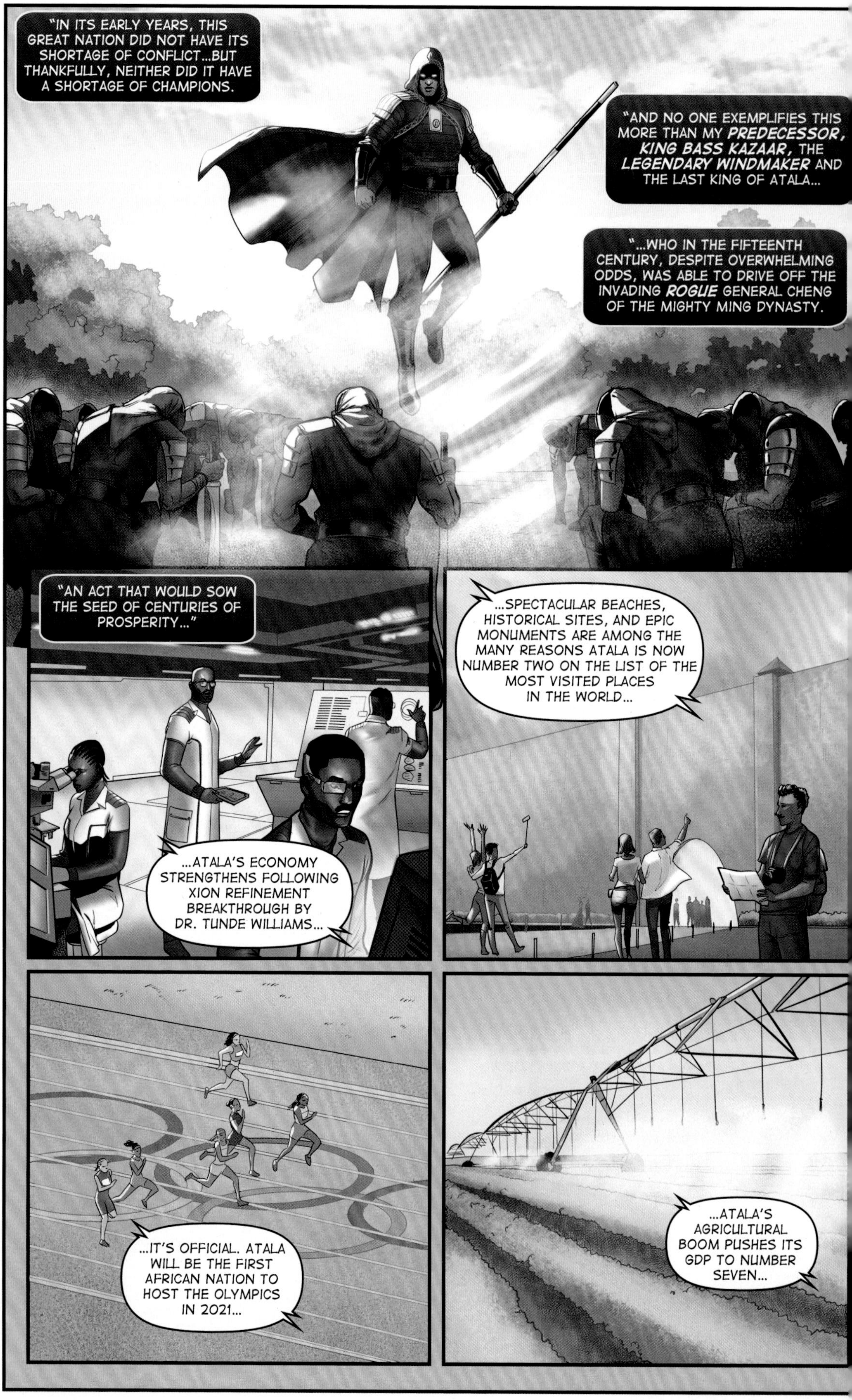
"IN ITS EARLY YEARS, THIS GREAT NATION DID NOT HAVE ITS SHORTAGE OF CONFLICT...BUT THANKFULLY, NEITHER DID IT HAVE A SHORTAGE OF CHAMPIONS.
"AND NO ONE EXEMPLIFIES THIS MORE THAN MY *PREDECESSOR, KING BASS KAZAAR,* THE *LEGENDARY WINDMAKER* AND THE LAST KING OF ATALA...
"...WHO IN THE FIFTEENTH CENTURY, DESPITE OVERWHELMING ODDS, WAS ABLE TO DRIVE OFF THE INVADING *ROGUE* GENERAL CHENG OF THE MIGHTY MING DYNASTY.
"AN ACT THAT WOULD SOW THE SEED OF CENTURIES OF PROSPERITY..."
...ATALA'S ECONOMY STRENGTHENS FOLLOWING XION REFINEMENT BREAKTHROUGH BY DR. TUNDE WILLIAMS...
...SPECTACULAR BEACHES, HISTORICAL SITES, AND EPIC MONUMENTS ARE AMONG THE MANY REASONS ATALA IS NOW NUMBER TWO ON THE LIST OF THE MOST VISITED PLACES IN THE WORLD...
...IT'S OFFICIAL. ATALA WILL BE THE FIRST AFRICAN NATION TO HOST THE OLYMPICS IN 2021...
...ATALA'S AGRICULTURAL BOOM PUSHES ITS GDP TO NUMBER SEVEN...

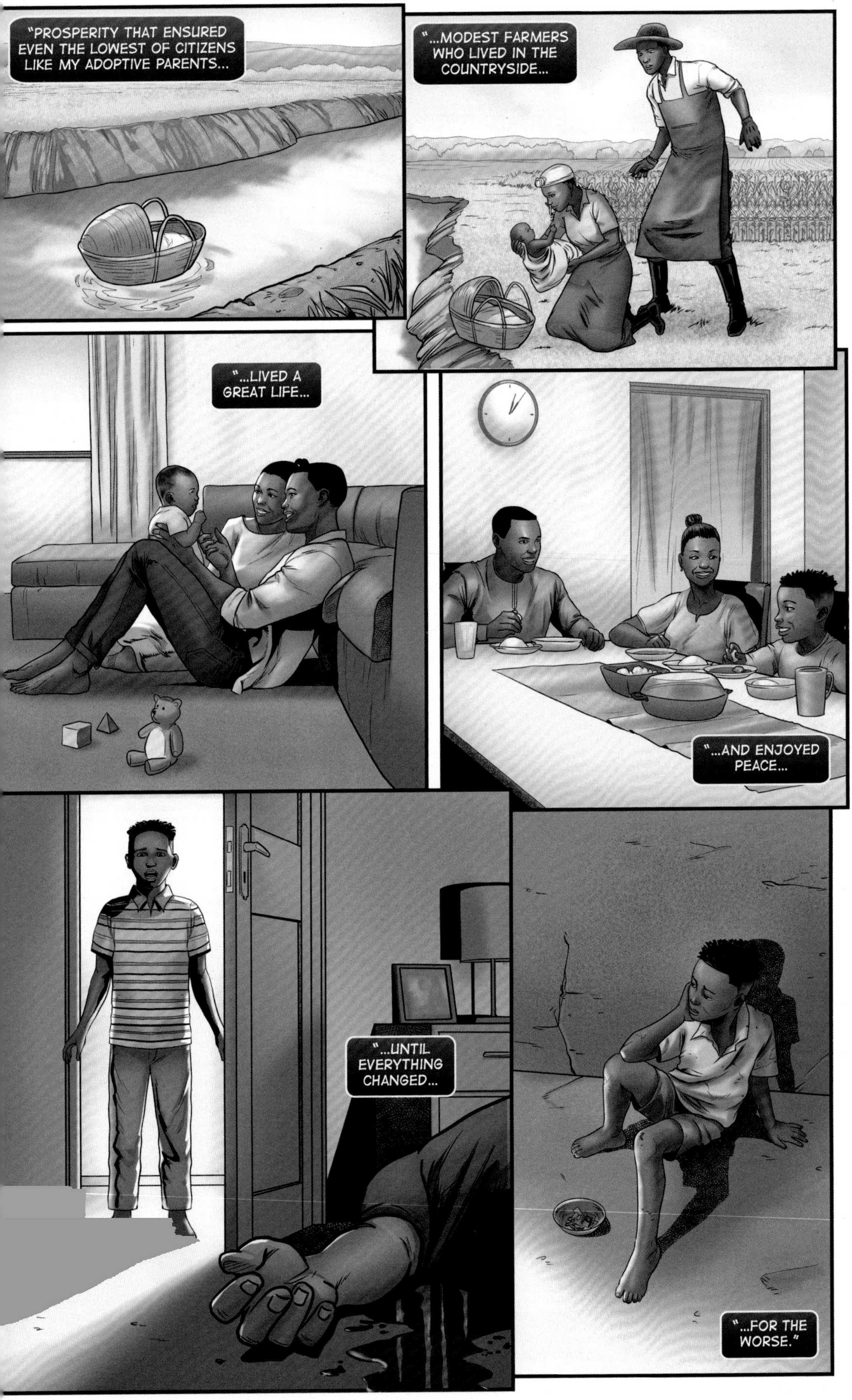
"PROSPERITY THAT ENSURED EVEN THE LOWEST OF CITIZENS LIKE MY ADOPTIVE PARENTS...
"...MODEST FARMERS WHO LIVED IN THE COUNTRYSIDE...
"...LIVED A GREAT LIFE...
"...AND ENJOYED PEACE...
"...UNTIL EVERYTHING CHANGED...
"...FOR THE WORSE."

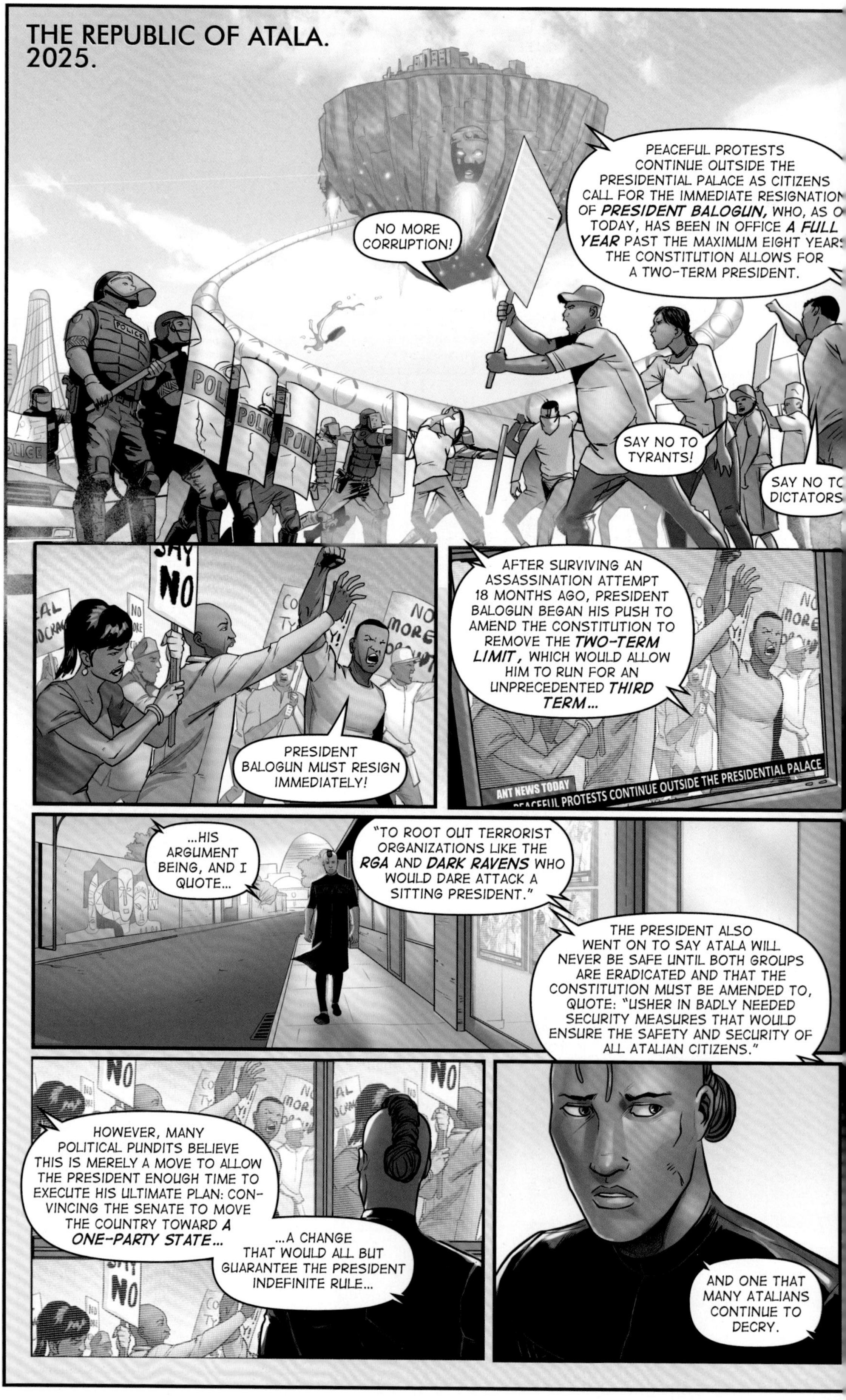

THE REPUBLIC OF ATALA. 2025.
NO MORE CORRUPTION!
PEACEFUL PROTESTS CONTINUE OUTSIDE THE PRESIDENTIAL PALACE AS CITIZENS CALL FOR THE IMMEDIATE RESIGNATIO OF PRESIDENT BALOGUN, WHO, AS O TODAY, HAS BEEN IN OFFICE A FULL YEAR PAST THE MAXIMUM EIGHT YEAR THE CONSTITUTION ALLOWS FOR A TWO-TERM PRESIDENT.
POLICE
SAY NO TO TYRANTS!
SAY NO T DICTATORS
SAY NO
PRESIDENT BALOGUN MUST RESIGN IMMEDIATELY!
AFTER SURVIVING AN ASSASSINATION ATTEMPT 18 MONTHS AGO, PRESIDENT BALOGUN BEGAN HIS PUSH TO AMEND THE CONSTITUTION TO REMOVE THE TWO-TERM LIMIT, WHICH WOULD ALLOW HIM TO RUN FOR AN UNPRECEDENTED THIRD TERM...
ANT NEWS TODAY
PROTESTS CONTINUE OUTSIDE THE PRESIDENTIAL PALACE
...HIS ARGUMENT BEING, AND I QUOTE...
"TO ROOT OUT TERRORIST ORGANIZATIONS LIKE THE RGA AND DARK RAVENS WHO WOULD DARE ATTACK A SITTING PRESIDENT."
THE PRESIDENT ALSO WENT ON TO SAY ATALA WILL NEVER BE SAFE UNTIL BOTH GROUPS ARE ERADICATED AND THAT THE CONSTITUTION MUST BE AMENDED TO, QUOTE: "USHER IN BADLY NEEDED SECURITY MEASURES THAT WOULD ENSURE THE SAFETY AND SECURITY OF ALL ATALIAN CITIZENS."
HOWEVER, MANY POLITICAL PUNDITS BELIEVE THIS IS MERELY A MOVE TO ALLOW THE PRESIDENT ENOUGH TIME TO EXECUTE HIS ULTIMATE PLAN: CONVINCING THE SENATE TO MOVE THE COUNTRY TOWARD A ONE-PARTY STATE...
...A CHANGE THAT WOULD ALL BUT GUARANTEE THE PRESIDENT INDEFINITE RULE...
AND ONE THAT MANY ATALIANS CONTINUE TO DECRY.

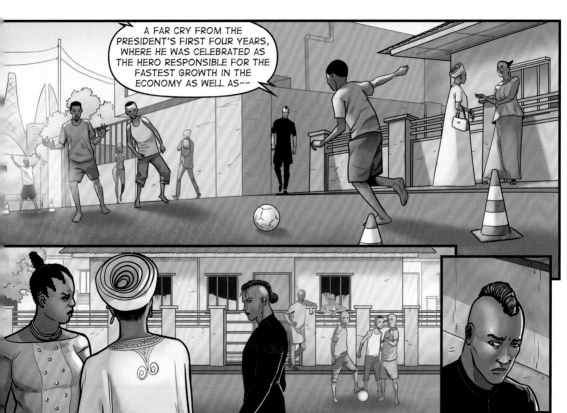

A FAR CRY FROM THE PRESIDENT'S FIRST FOUR YEARS, WHERE HE WAS CELEBRATED AS THE HERO RESPONSIBLE FOR THE FASTEST GROWTH IN THE ECONOMY AS WELL AS--

DING DONG

COMING!

BO! IT'S SO GOOD TO SEE YOU!

YOU TOO, SOLA.

COME IN!

9

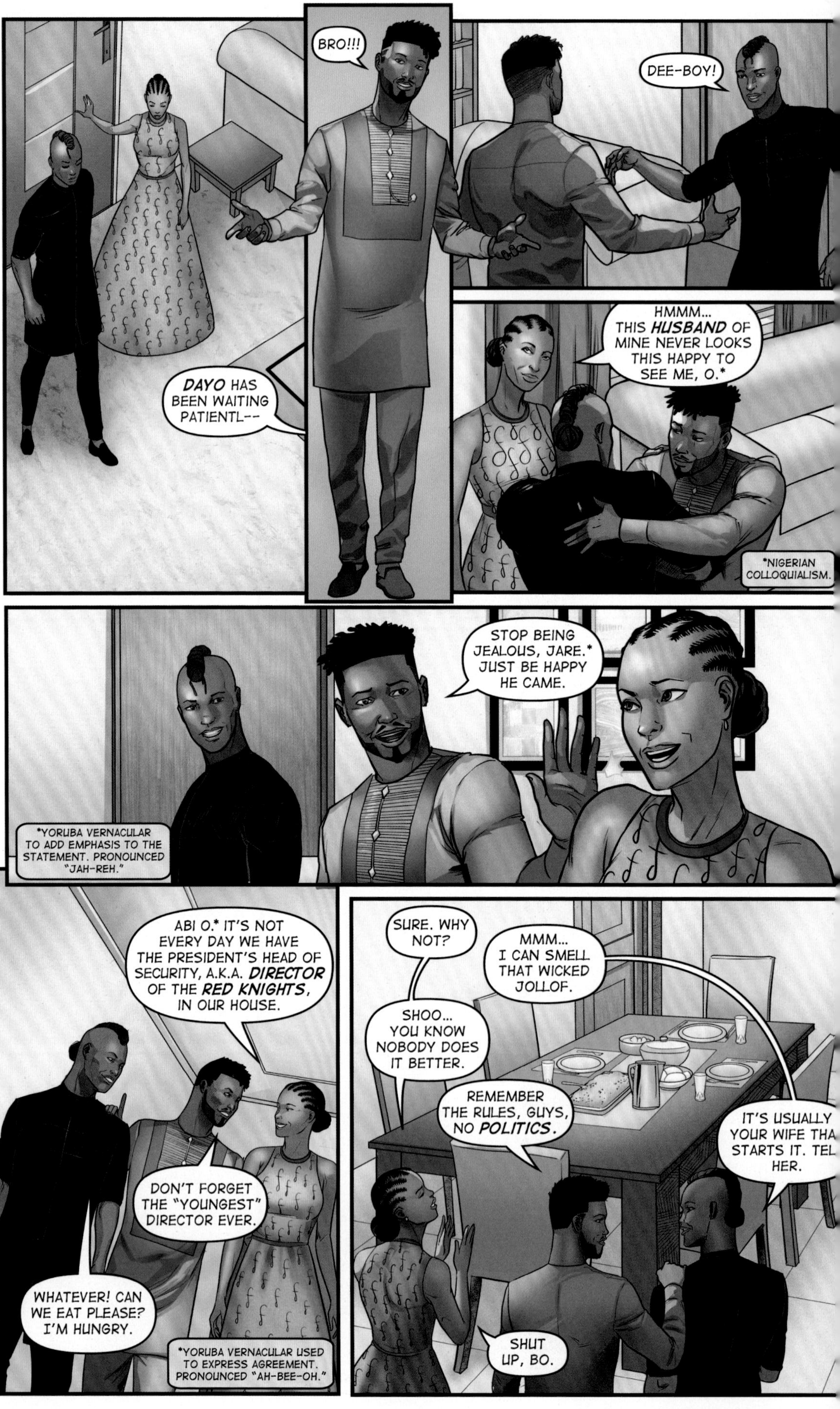
BRO!!!
DEE-BOY!
DAYO HAS BEEN WAITING PATIENTL--
HMMM... THIS HUSBAND OF MINE NEVER LOOKS THIS HAPPY TO SEE ME, O.*
*NIGERIAN COLLOQUIALISM.
STOP BEING JEALOUS, JARE.* JUST BE HAPPY HE CAME.
*YORUBA VERNACULAR TO ADD EMPHASIS TO THE STATEMENT. PRONOUNCED "JAH-REH."
ABI O.* IT'S NOT EVERY DAY WE HAVE THE PRESIDENT'S HEAD OF SECURITY, A.K.A. DIRECTOR OF THE RED KNIGHTS, IN OUR HOUSE.
DON'T FORGET THE "YOUNGEST" DIRECTOR EVER.
WHATEVER! CAN WE EAT PLEASE? I'M HUNGRY.
*YORUBA VERNACULAR USED TO EXPRESS AGREEMENT. PRONOUNCED "AH-BEE-OH."
SURE. WHY NOT?
MMM... I CAN SMELL THAT WICKED JOLLOF.
SHOO... YOU KNOW NOBODY DOES IT BETTER.
REMEMBER THE RULES, GUYS, NO POLITICS.
IT'S USUALLY YOUR WIFE THA STARTS IT. TEL HER.
SHUT UP, BO.

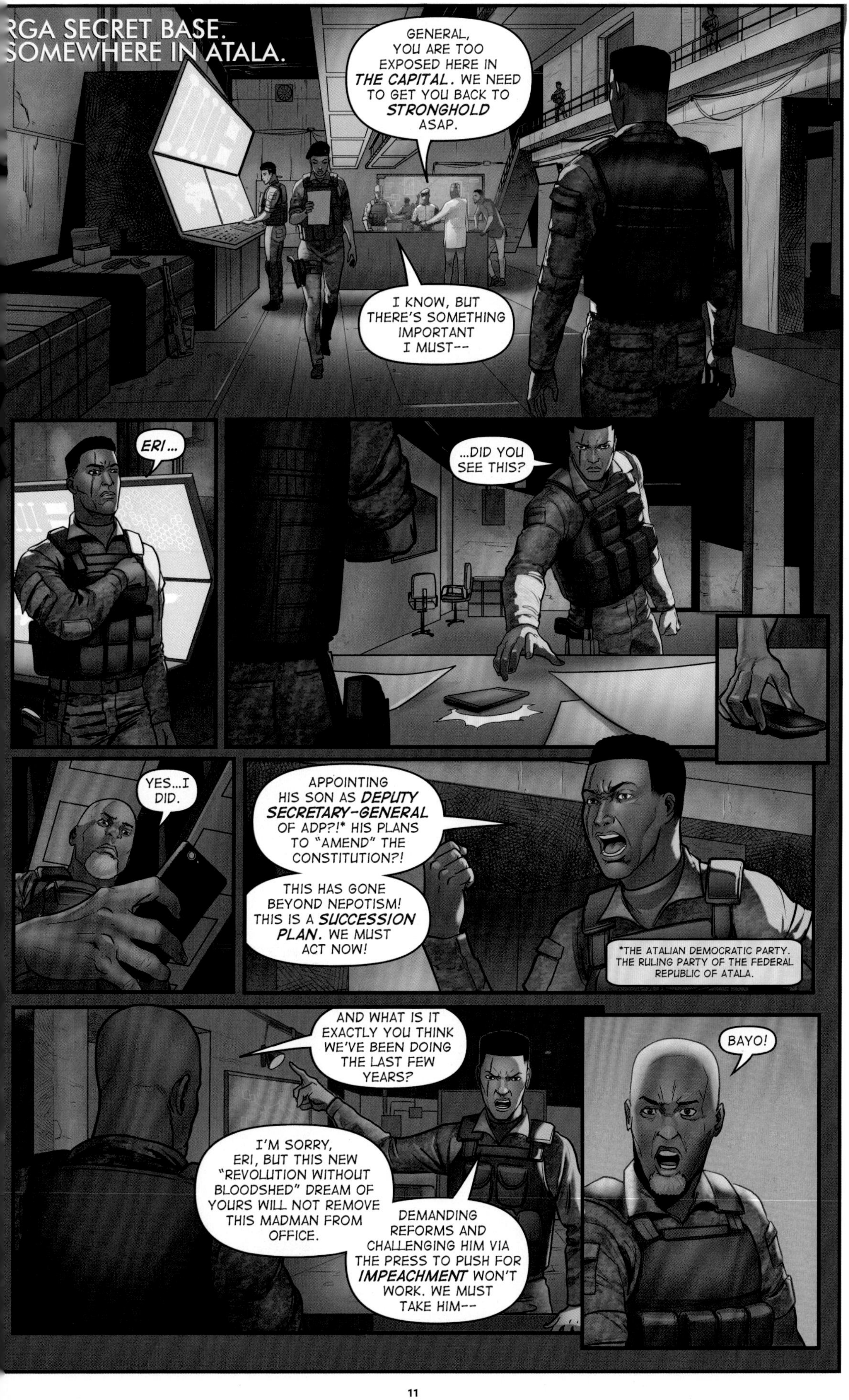
RGA SECRET BASE. SOMEWHERE IN ATALA.
GENERAL, YOU ARE TOO EXPOSED HERE IN THE CAPITAL. WE NEED TO GET YOU BACK TO STRONGHOLD ASAP.
I KNOW, BUT THERE'S SOMETHING IMPORTANT I MUST--
ERI...
...DID YOU SEE THIS?
YES...I DID.
APPOINTING HIS SON AS DEPUTY SECRETARY-GENERAL OF ADP?!* HIS PLANS TO "AMEND" THE CONSTITUTION?!
THIS HAS GONE BEYOND NEPOTISM! THIS IS A SUCCESSION PLAN. WE MUST ACT NOW!
*THE ATALIAN DEMOCRATIC PARTY. THE RULING PARTY OF THE FEDERAL REPUBLIC OF ATALA.
AND WHAT IS IT EXACTLY YOU THINK WE'VE BEEN DOING THE LAST FEW YEARS?
I'M SORRY, ERI, BUT THIS NEW "REVOLUTION WITHOUT BLOODSHED" DREAM OF YOURS WILL NOT REMOVE THIS MADMAN FROM OFFICE.
DEMANDING REFORMS AND CHALLENGING HIM VIA THE PRESS TO PUSH FOR IMPEACHMENT WON'T WORK. WE MUST TAKE HIM--
BAYO!

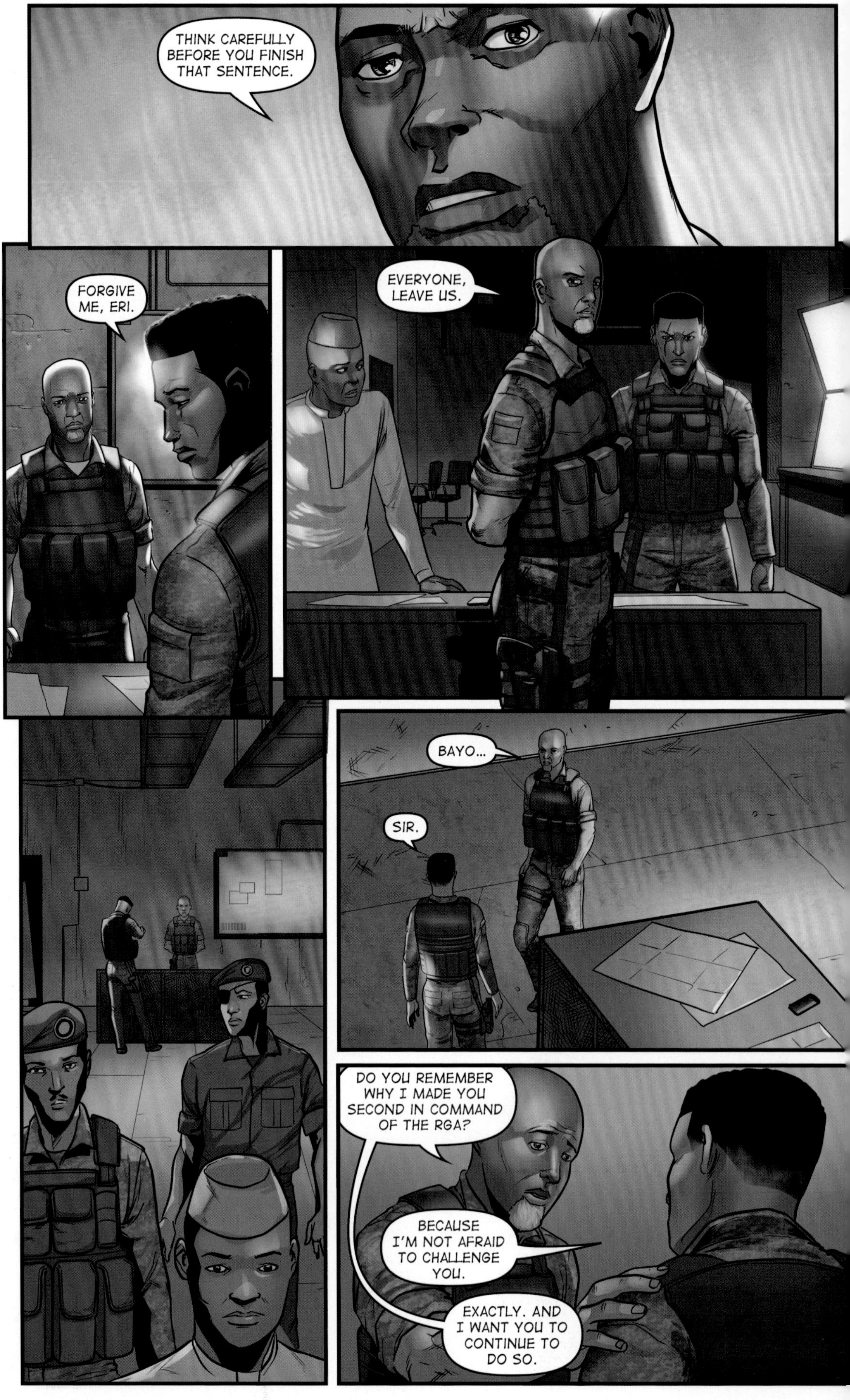
THINK CAREFULLY BEFORE YOU FINISH THAT SENTENCE.
FORGIVE ME, ERI.
EVERYONE, LEAVE US.
BAYO...
SIR.
DO YOU REMEMBER WHY I MADE YOU SECOND IN COMMAND OF THE RGA?
BECAUSE I'M NOT AFRAID TO CHALLENGE YOU.
EXACTLY. AND I WANT YOU TO CONTINUE TO DO SO.

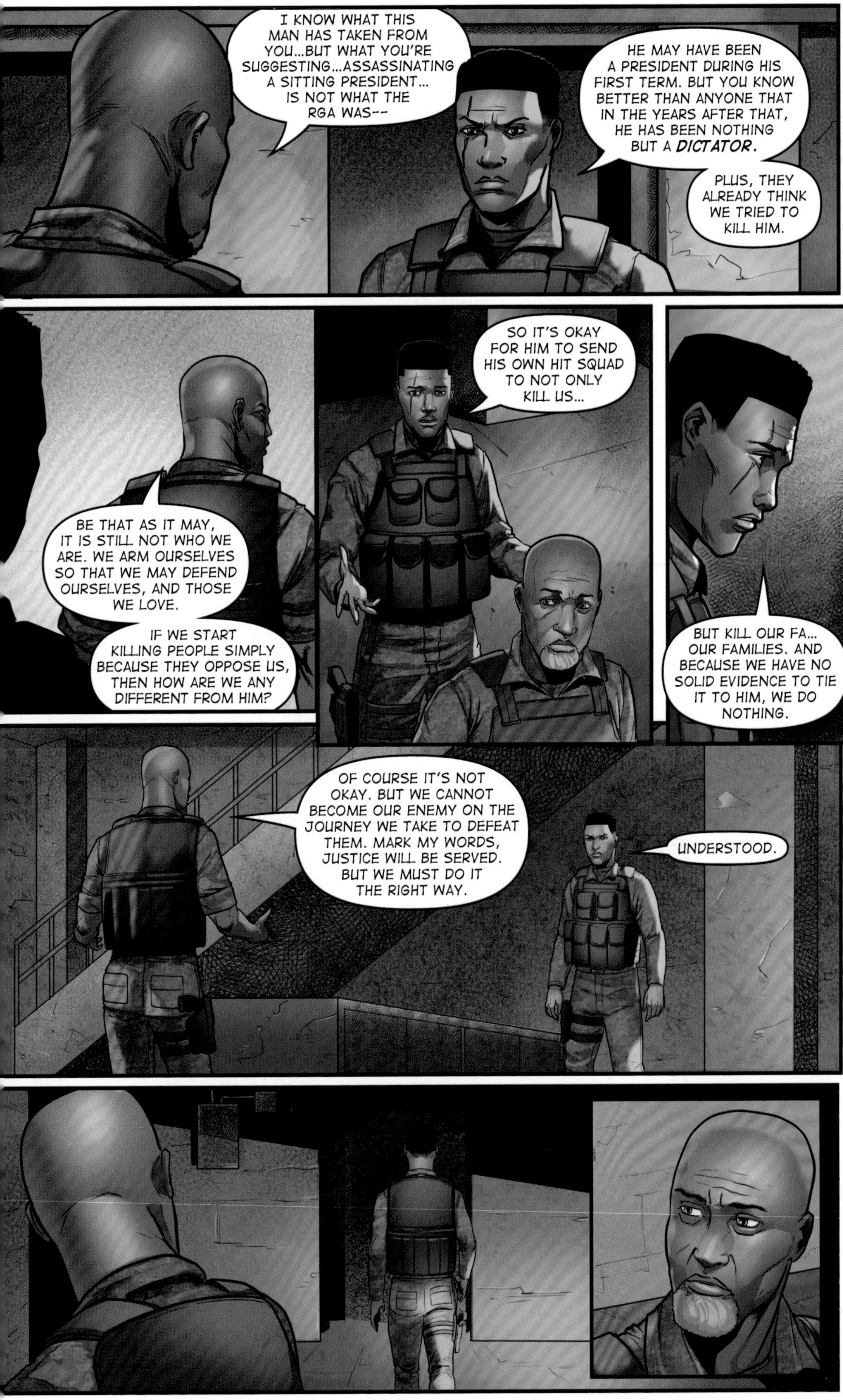
I KNOW WHAT THIS MAN HAS TAKEN FROM YOU...BUT WHAT YOU'RE SUGGESTING...ASSASSINATING A SITTING PRESIDENT... IS NOT WHAT THE RGA WAS--
HE MAY HAVE BEEN A PRESIDENT DURING HIS FIRST TERM. BUT YOU KNOW BETTER THAN ANYONE THAT IN THE YEARS AFTER THAT, HE HAS BEEN NOTHING BUT A *DICTATOR.*
PLUS, THEY ALREADY THINK WE TRIED TO KILL HIM.
BE THAT AS IT MAY, IT IS STILL NOT WHO WE ARE. WE ARM OURSELVES SO THAT WE MAY DEFEND OURSELVES, AND THOSE WE LOVE.
IF WE START KILLING PEOPLE SIMPLY BECAUSE THEY OPPOSE US, THEN HOW ARE WE ANY DIFFERENT FROM HIM?
SO IT'S OKAY FOR HIM TO SEND HIS OWN HIT SQUAD TO NOT ONLY KILL US...
BUT KILL OUR FA... OUR FAMILIES. AND BECAUSE WE HAVE NO SOLID EVIDENCE TO TIE IT TO HIM, WE DO NOTHING.
OF COURSE IT'S NOT OKAY. BUT WE CANNOT BECOME OUR ENEMY ON THE JOURNEY WE TAKE TO DEFEAT THEM. MARK MY WORDS, JUSTICE WILL BE SERVED. BUT WE MUST DO IT THE RIGHT WAY.
UNDERSTOOD.

ARE YOU EVER NOT GOING TO TELL THAT JOKE, SOLA?

HONESTLY, THE FUNNIEST PART ISN'T THAT YOU NEARLY PEED YOURSELF A LITTLE WHILE TRYING TO ASK ME...

IT'S HOW YOU SAID IT.

"SO... SOLA...WILL... WILL YOU VE MY BALENTINE?"

SHUT UP, STUPID IDIOT. I WAS NINE YEARS OLD AND DIDN'T KNOW ANYTHING!

≥SIGH≥ GROWING UP AT THAT ORPHANAGE... THOSE WERE THE GOOD OLD DAYS.

YUP.

BUT MEHN, WE CAUSED A LOT OF TROUBLE, THOUGH.

WE SURE DID. REMEMBER WHAT MRS. OMONIYI USED TO CALL SOLA?

ONIJOGBON.*

*TROUBLEMAKER.

BETTER THAN WHAT SHE CALLED YOU: OLORI NLA.*

*BIG HEAD.

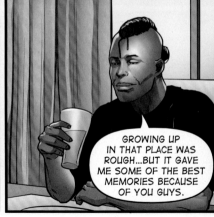

GROWING UP IN THAT PLACE WAS ROUGH...BUT IT GAVE ME SOME OF THE BEST MEMORIES BECAUSE OF YOU GUYS.

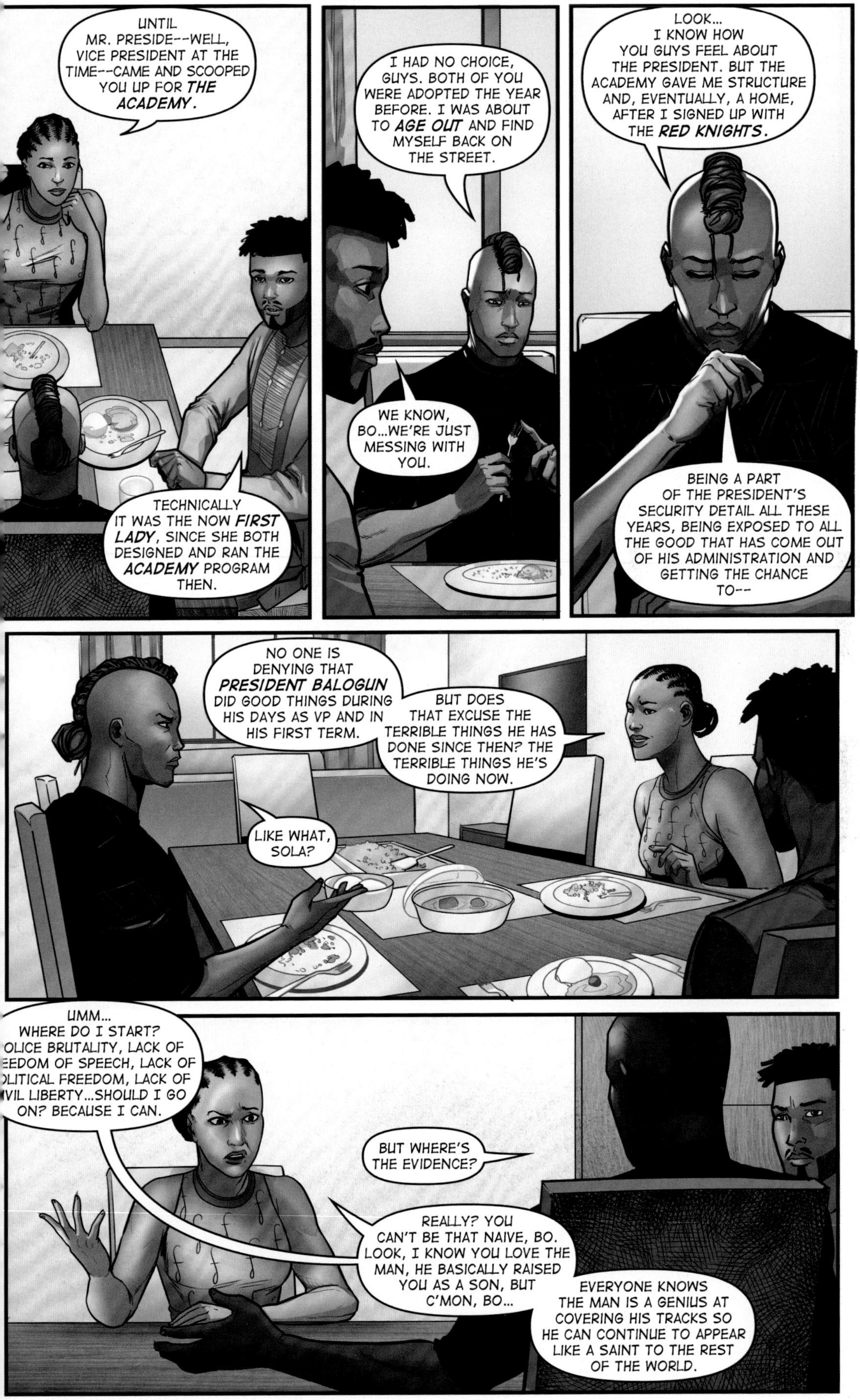
UNTIL MR. PRESIDE--WELL, VICE PRESIDENT AT THE TIME--CAME AND SCOOPED YOU UP FOR THE ACADEMY.
TECHNICALLY IT WAS THE NOW FIRST LADY, SINCE SHE BOTH DESIGNED AND RAN THE ACADEMY PROGRAM THEN.
I HAD NO CHOICE, GUYS. BOTH OF YOU WERE ADOPTED THE YEAR BEFORE. I WAS ABOUT TO AGE OUT AND FIND MYSELF BACK ON THE STREET.
WE KNOW, BO...WE'RE JUST MESSING WITH YOU.
LOOK... I KNOW HOW YOU GUYS FEEL ABOUT THE PRESIDENT. BUT THE ACADEMY GAVE ME STRUCTURE AND, EVENTUALLY, A HOME, AFTER I SIGNED UP WITH THE RED KNIGHTS.
BEING A PART OF THE PRESIDENT'S SECURITY DETAIL ALL THESE YEARS, BEING EXPOSED TO ALL THE GOOD THAT HAS COME OUT OF HIS ADMINISTRATION AND GETTING THE CHANCE TO--
NO ONE IS DENYING THAT PRESIDENT BALOGUN DID GOOD THINGS DURING HIS DAYS AS VP AND IN HIS FIRST TERM.
BUT DOES THAT EXCUSE THE TERRIBLE THINGS HE HAS DONE SINCE THEN? THE TERRIBLE THINGS HE'S DOING NOW.
LIKE WHAT, SOLA?
UMM... WHERE DO I START? OLICE BRUTALITY, LACK OF EEDOM OF SPEECH, LACK OF OLITICAL FREEDOM, LACK OF VIL LIBERTY...SHOULD I GO ON? BECAUSE I CAN.
BUT WHERE'S THE EVIDENCE?
REALLY? YOU CAN'T BE THAT NAIVE, BO. LOOK, I KNOW YOU LOVE THE MAN, HE BASICALLY RAISED YOU AS A SON, BUT C'MON, BO...
EVERYONE KNOWS THE MAN IS A GENIUS AT COVERING HIS TRACKS SO HE CAN CONTINUE TO APPEAR LIKE A SAINT TO THE REST OF THE WORLD.

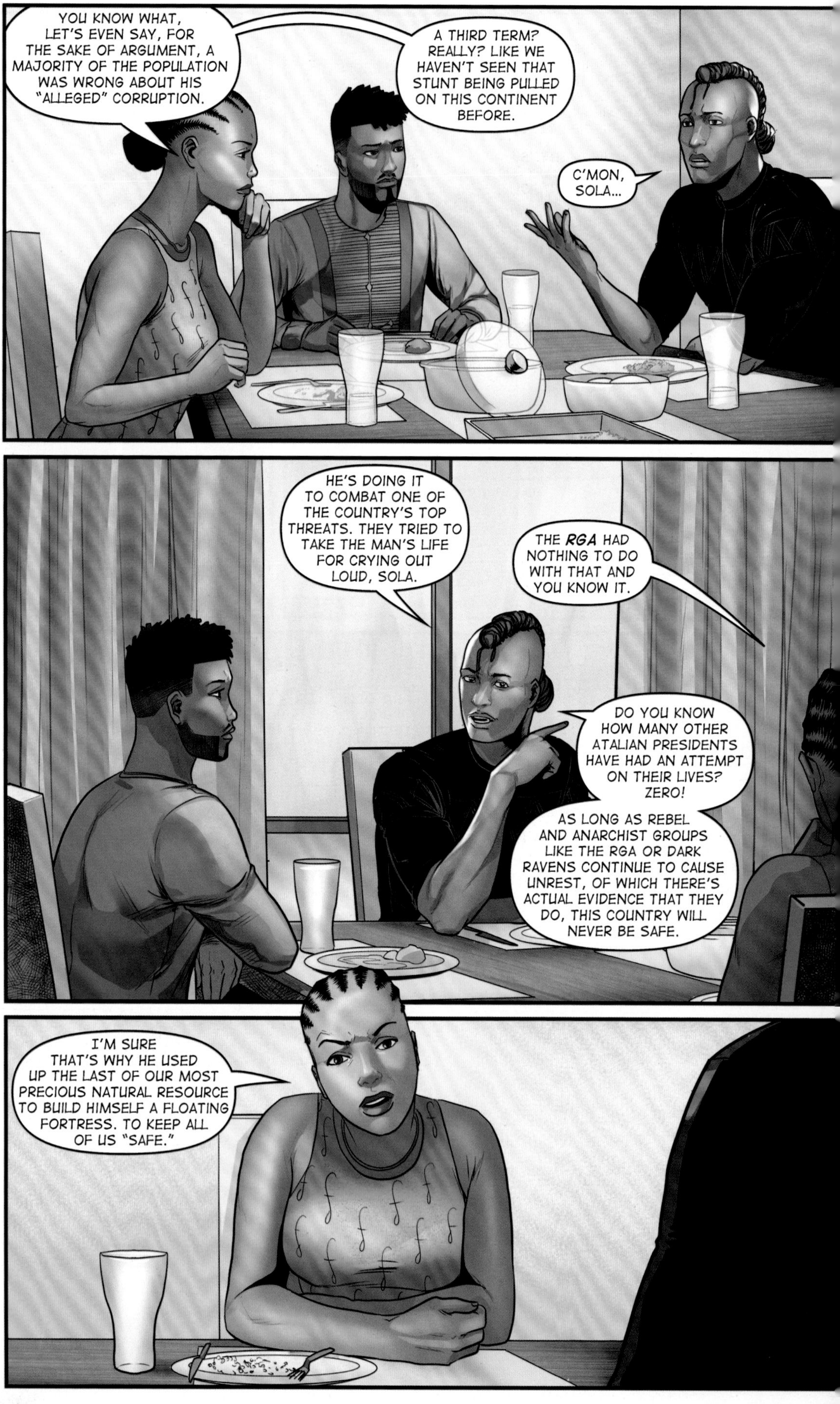
YOU KNOW WHAT, LET'S EVEN SAY, FOR THE SAKE OF ARGUMENT, A MAJORITY OF THE POPULATION WAS WRONG ABOUT HIS "ALLEGED" CORRUPTION.
A THIRD TERM? REALLY? LIKE WE HAVEN'T SEEN THAT STUNT BEING PULLED ON THIS CONTINENT BEFORE.
C'MON, SOLA...
HE'S DOING IT TO COMBAT ONE OF THE COUNTRY'S TOP THREATS. THEY TRIED TO TAKE THE MAN'S LIFE FOR CRYING OUT LOUD, SOLA.
THE *RGA* HAD NOTHING TO DO WITH THAT AND YOU KNOW IT.
DO YOU KNOW HOW MANY OTHER ATALIAN PRESIDENTS HAVE HAD AN ATTEMPT ON THEIR LIVES? ZERO!
AS LONG AS REBEL AND ANARCHIST GROUPS LIKE THE RGA OR DARK RAVENS CONTINUE TO CAUSE UNREST, OF WHICH THERE'S ACTUAL EVIDENCE THAT THEY DO, THIS COUNTRY WILL NEVER BE SAFE.
I'M SURE THAT'S WHY HE USED UP THE LAST OF OUR MOST PRECIOUS NATURAL RESOURCE TO BUILD HIMSELF A FLOATING FORTRESS. TO KEEP ALL OF US "SAFE."

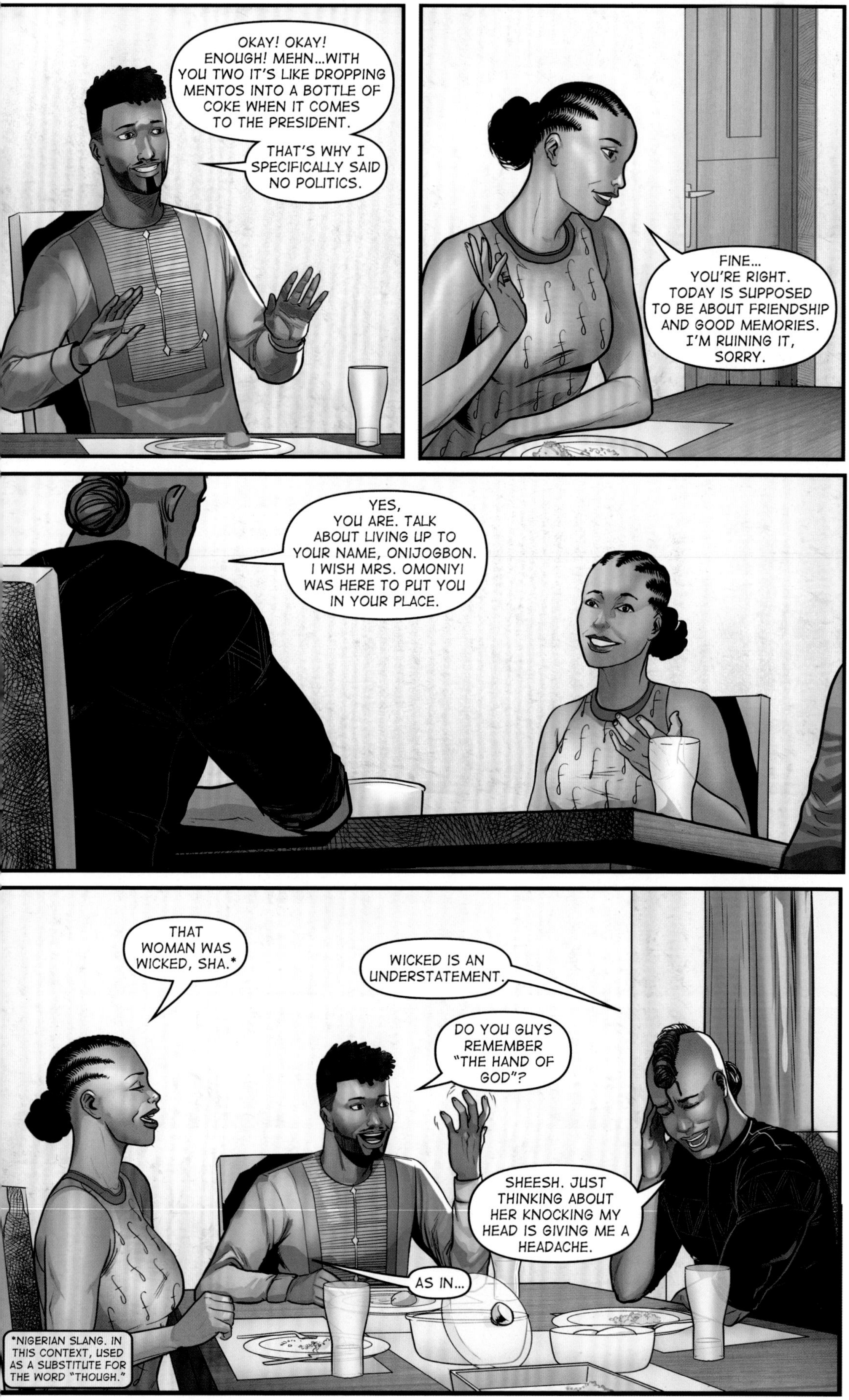
OKAY! OKAY! ENOUGH! MEHN...WITH YOU TWO IT'S LIKE DROPPING MENTOS INTO A BOTTLE OF COKE WHEN IT COMES TO THE PRESIDENT.
THAT'S WHY I SPECIFICALLY SAID NO POLITICS.
FINE... YOU'RE RIGHT. TODAY IS SUPPOSED TO BE ABOUT FRIENDSHIP AND GOOD MEMORIES. I'M RUINING IT, SORRY.
YES, YOU ARE. TALK ABOUT LIVING UP TO YOUR NAME, ONIJOGBON. I WISH MRS. OMONIYI WAS HERE TO PUT YOU IN YOUR PLACE.
THAT WOMAN WAS WICKED, SHA.*
WICKED IS AN UNDERSTATEMENT.
DO YOU GUYS REMEMBER "THE HAND OF GOD"?
SHEESH. JUST THINKING ABOUT HER KNOCKING MY HEAD IS GIVING ME A HEADACHE.
AS IN...
*NIGERIAN SLANG. IN THIS CONTEXT, USED AS A SUBSTITUTE FOR THE WORD "THOUGH."

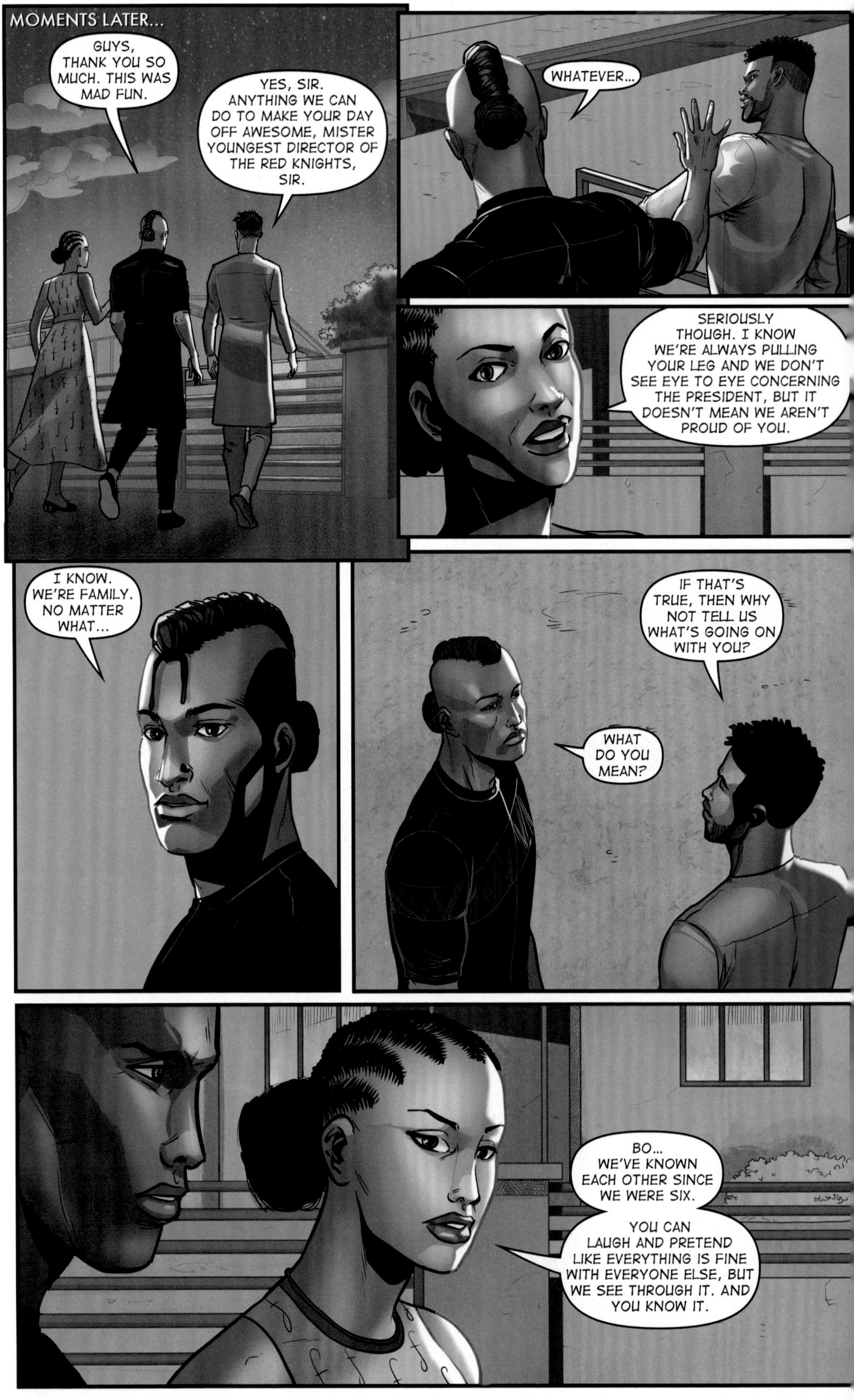
MOMENTS LATER...
GUYS, THANK YOU SO MUCH. THIS WAS MAD FUN.
YES, SIR. ANYTHING WE CAN DO TO MAKE YOUR DAY OFF AWESOME, MISTER YOUNGEST DIRECTOR OF THE RED KNIGHTS, SIR.
WHATEVER...
SERIOUSLY THOUGH. I KNOW WE'RE ALWAYS PULLING YOUR LEG AND WE DON'T SEE EYE TO EYE CONCERNING THE PRESIDENT, BUT IT DOESN'T MEAN WE AREN'T PROUD OF YOU.
I KNOW. WE'RE FAMILY. NO MATTER WHAT...
IF THAT'S TRUE, THEN WHY NOT TELL US WHAT'S GOING ON WITH YOU?
WHAT DO YOU MEAN?
BO... WE'VE KNOWN EACH OTHER SINCE WE WERE SIX.
YOU CAN LAUGH AND PRETEND LIKE EVERYTHING IS FINE WITH EVERYONE ELSE, BUT WE SEE THROUGH IT. AND YOU KNOW IT.

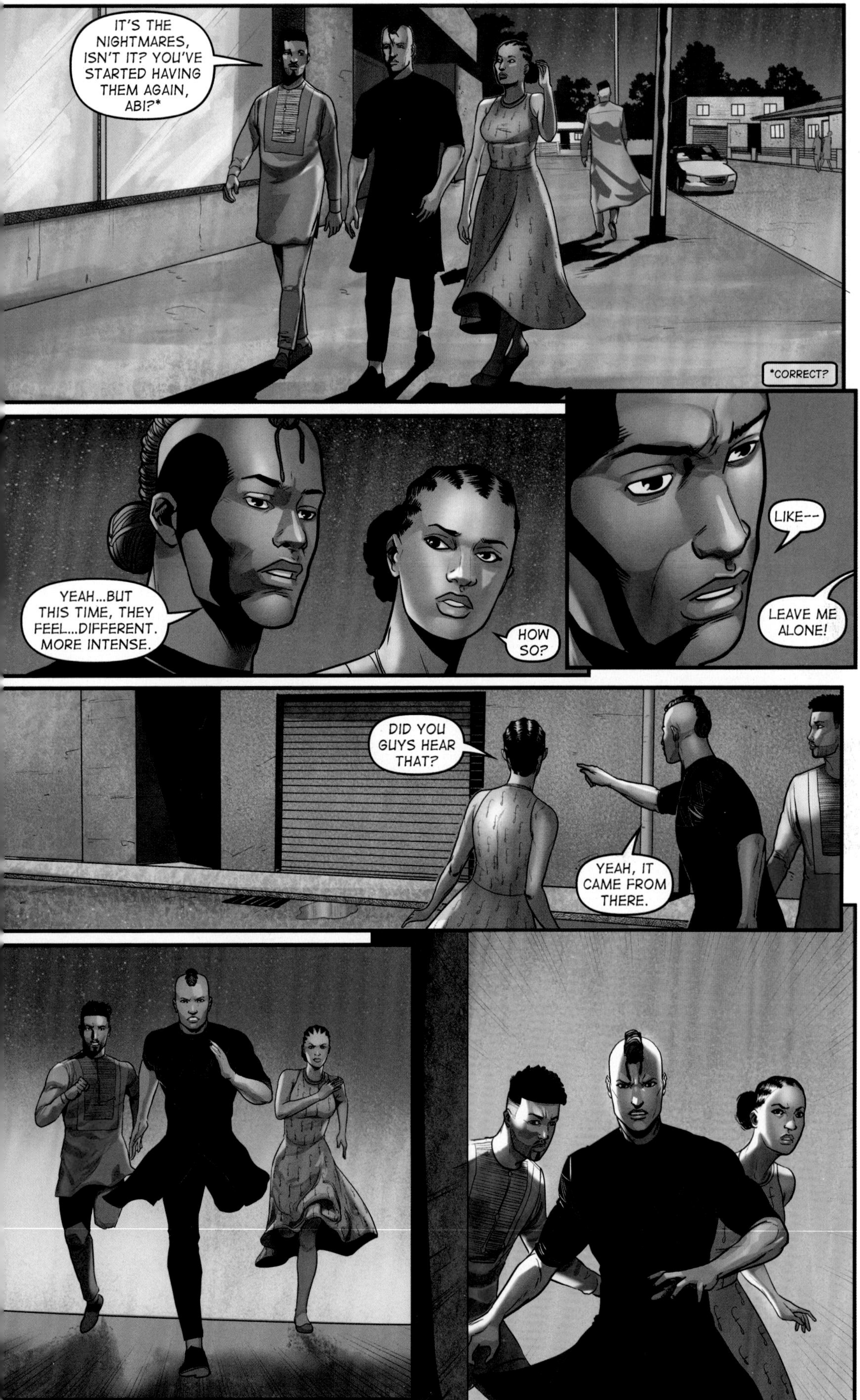
IT'S THE NIGHTMARES, ISN'T IT? YOU'VE STARTED HAVING THEM AGAIN, ABI?*
*CORRECT?
YEAH...BUT THIS TIME, THEY FEEL...DIFFERENT. MORE INTENSE.
HOW SO?
LIKE--
LEAVE ME ALONE!
DID YOU GUYS HEAR THAT?
YEAH, IT CAME FROM THERE.

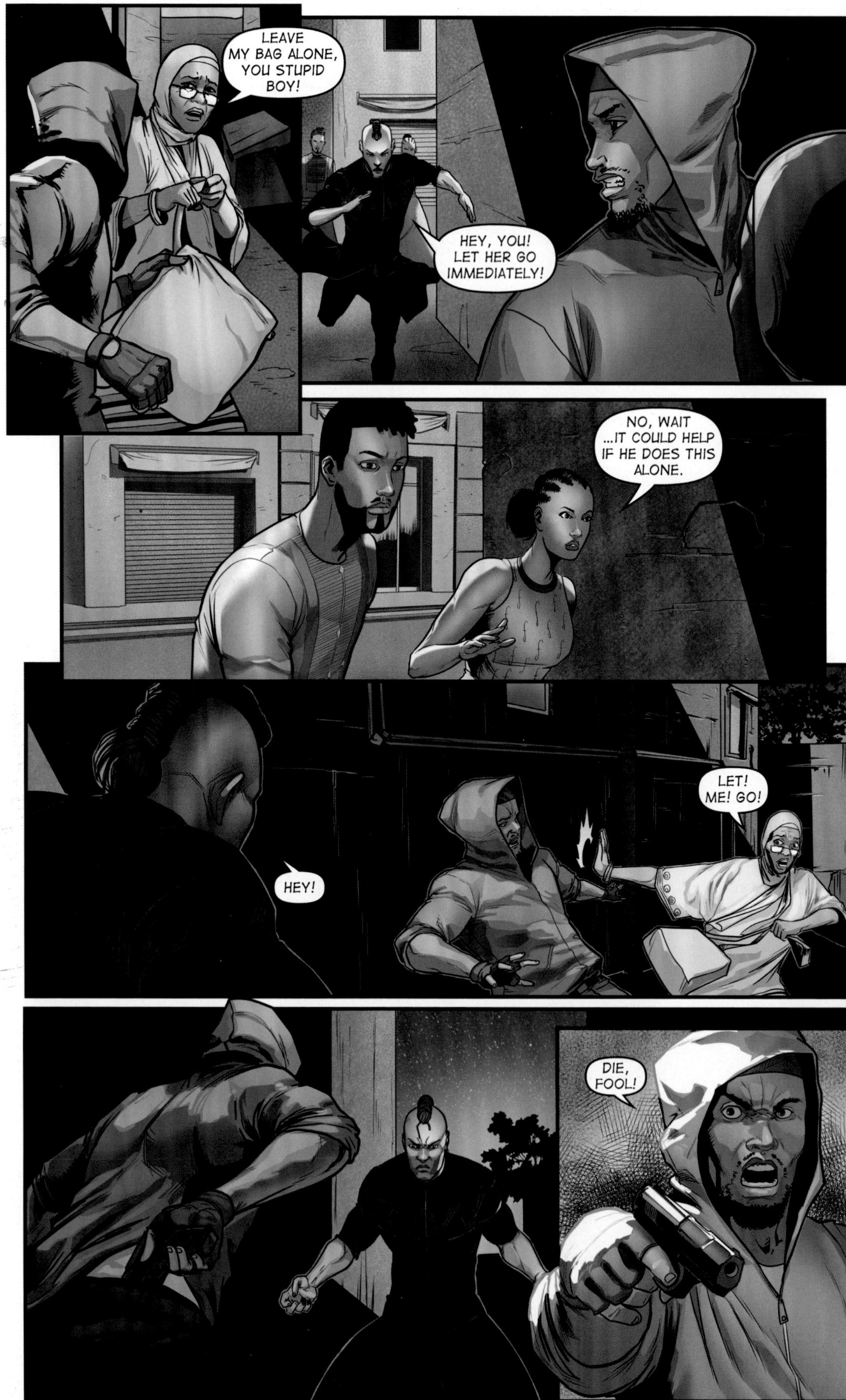

LEAVE MY BAG ALONE, YOU STUPID BOY!
HEY, YOU! LET HER GO IMMEDIATELY!
NO, WAIT ...IT COULD HELP IF HE DOES THIS ALONE.
LET! ME! GO!
HEY!
DIE, FOOL!

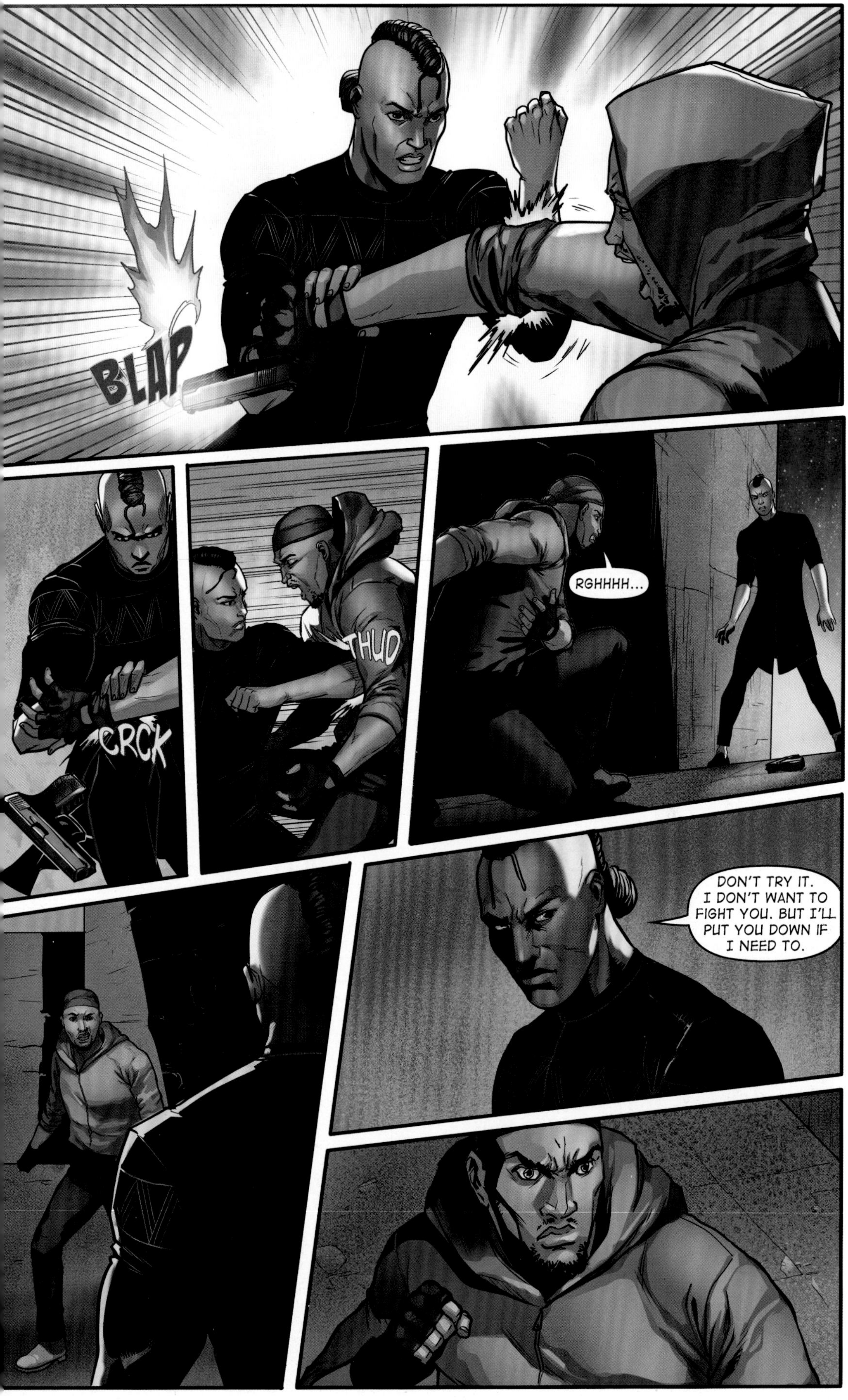
BLAP
CRCK
THUD
RGHHHH...
DON'T TRY IT. I DON'T WANT TO FIGHT YOU. BUT I'LL PUT YOU DOWN IF I NEED TO.

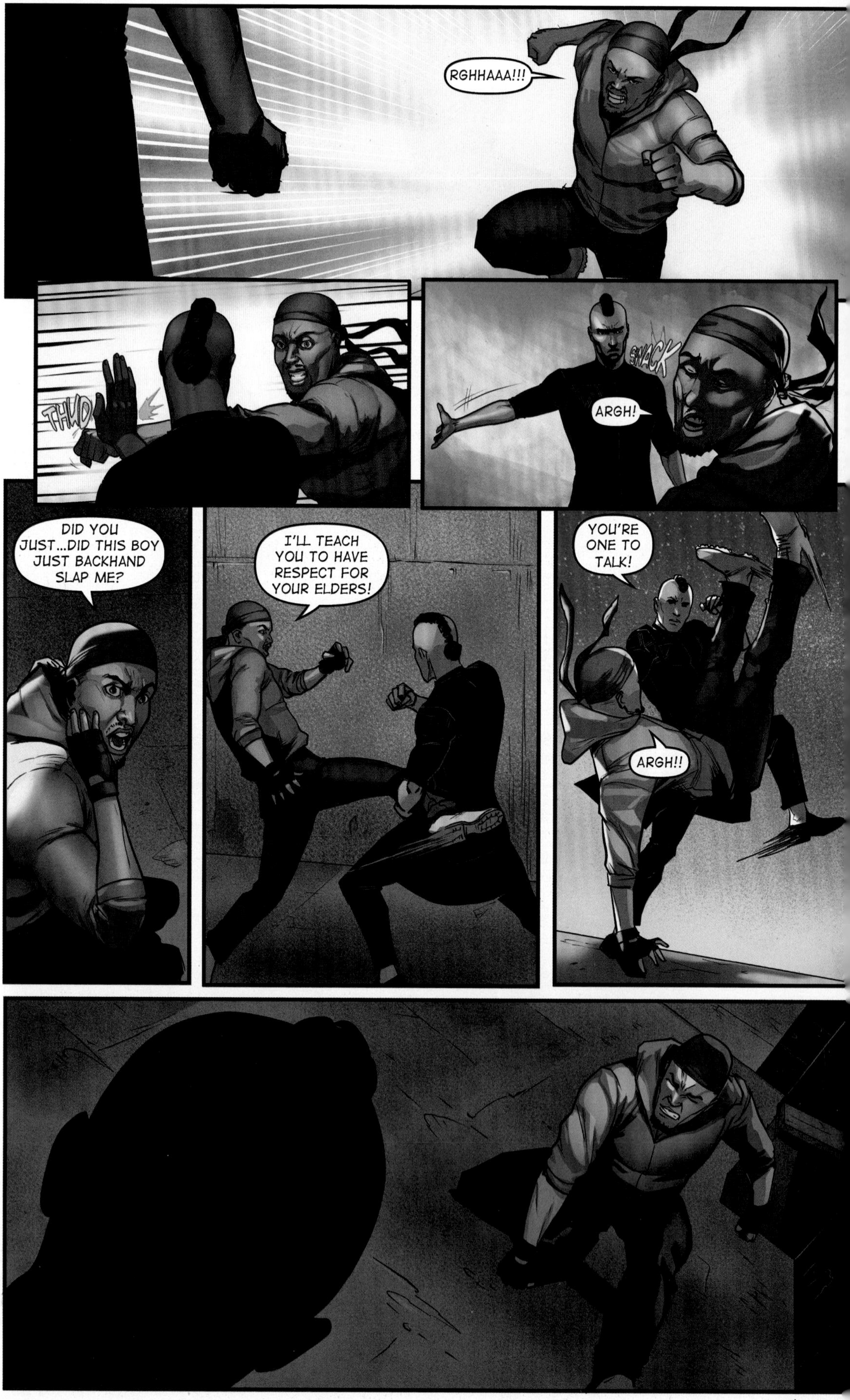
RGHHAAA!!!
THUD
SNACK
ARGH!
DID YOU JUST...DID THIS BOY JUST BACKHAND SLAP ME?
I'LL TEACH YOU TO HAVE RESPECT FOR YOUR ELDERS!
YOU'RE ONE TO TALK!
ARGH!!

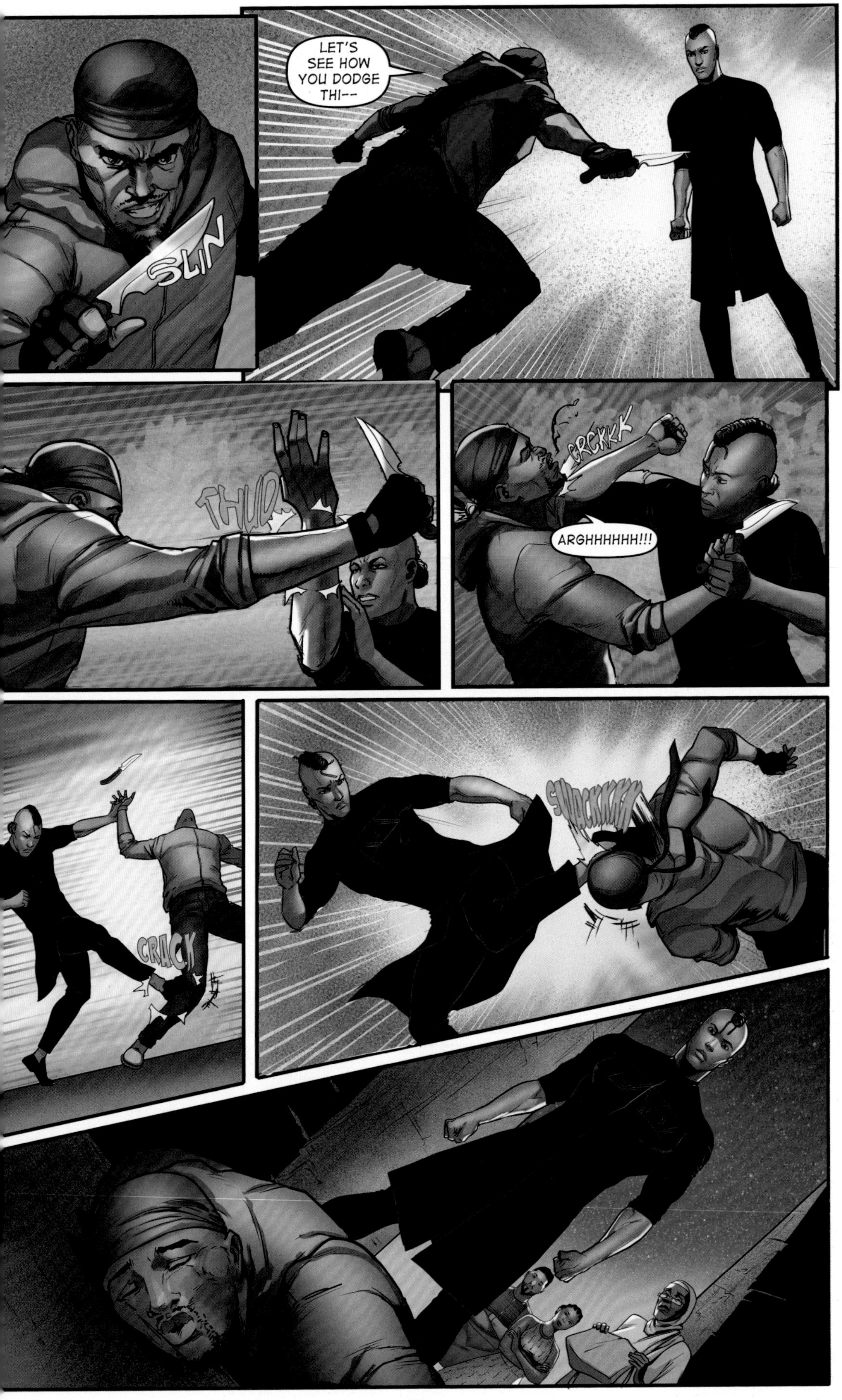
SLIN
LET'S SEE HOW YOU DODGE THI--
THUD
GRCKKK
ARGHHHHHH!!!
CRACK
SMACKKKK

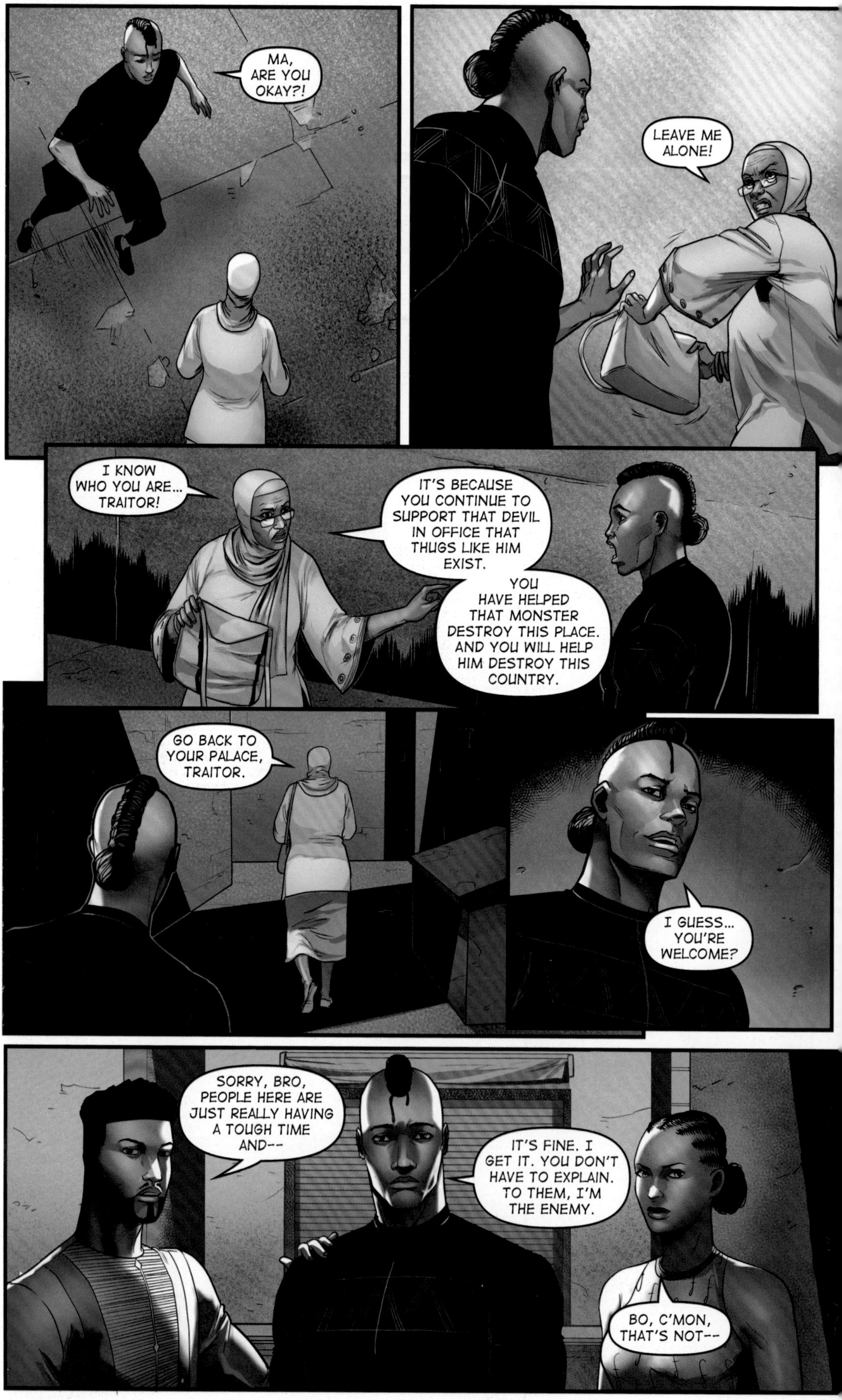
MA, ARE YOU OKAY?!
LEAVE ME ALONE!
I KNOW WHO YOU ARE... TRAITOR!
IT'S BECAUSE YOU CONTINUE TO SUPPORT THAT DEVIL IN OFFICE THAT THUGS LIKE HIM EXIST.
YOU HAVE HELPED THAT MONSTER DESTROY THIS PLACE. AND YOU WILL HELP HIM DESTROY THIS COUNTRY.
GO BACK TO YOUR PALACE, TRAITOR.
I GUESS... YOU'RE WELCOME?
SORRY, BRO, PEOPLE HERE ARE JUST REALLY HAVING A TOUGH TIME AND--
IT'S FINE. I GET IT. YOU DON'T HAVE TO EXPLAIN. TO THEM, I'M THE ENEMY.
BO, C'MON, THAT'S NOT--

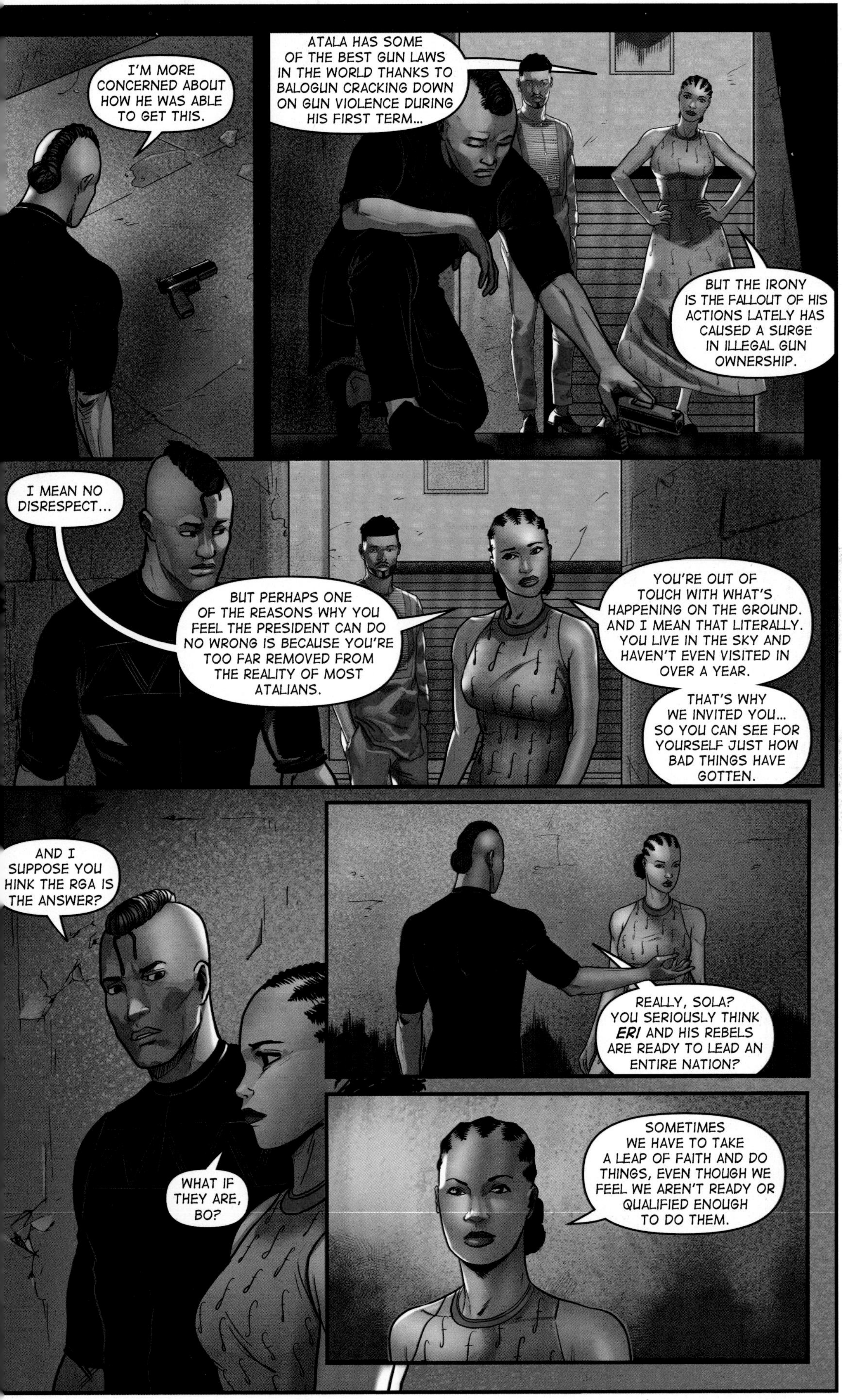
I'M MORE CONCERNED ABOUT HOW HE WAS ABLE TO GET THIS.
ATALA HAS SOME OF THE BEST GUN LAWS IN THE WORLD THANKS TO BALOGUN CRACKING DOWN ON GUN VIOLENCE DURING HIS FIRST TERM...
BUT THE IRONY IS THE FALLOUT OF HIS ACTIONS LATELY HAS CAUSED A SURGE IN ILLEGAL GUN OWNERSHIP.
I MEAN NO DISRESPECT...
BUT PERHAPS ONE OF THE REASONS WHY YOU FEEL THE PRESIDENT CAN DO NO WRONG IS BECAUSE YOU'RE TOO FAR REMOVED FROM THE REALITY OF MOST ATALIANS.
YOU'RE OUT OF TOUCH WITH WHAT'S HAPPENING ON THE GROUND. AND I MEAN THAT LITERALLY. YOU LIVE IN THE SKY AND HAVEN'T EVEN VISITED IN OVER A YEAR.
THAT'S WHY WE INVITED YOU... SO YOU CAN SEE FOR YOURSELF JUST HOW BAD THINGS HAVE GOTTEN.
AND I SUPPOSE YOU HINK THE RGA IS THE ANSWER?
REALLY, SOLA? YOU SERIOUSLY THINK ERI AND HIS REBELS ARE READY TO LEAD AN ENTIRE NATION?
WHAT IF THEY ARE, BO?
SOMETIMES WE HAVE TO TAKE A LEAP OF FAITH AND DO THINGS, EVEN THOUGH WE FEEL WE AREN'T READY OR QUALIFIED ENOUGH TO DO THEM.

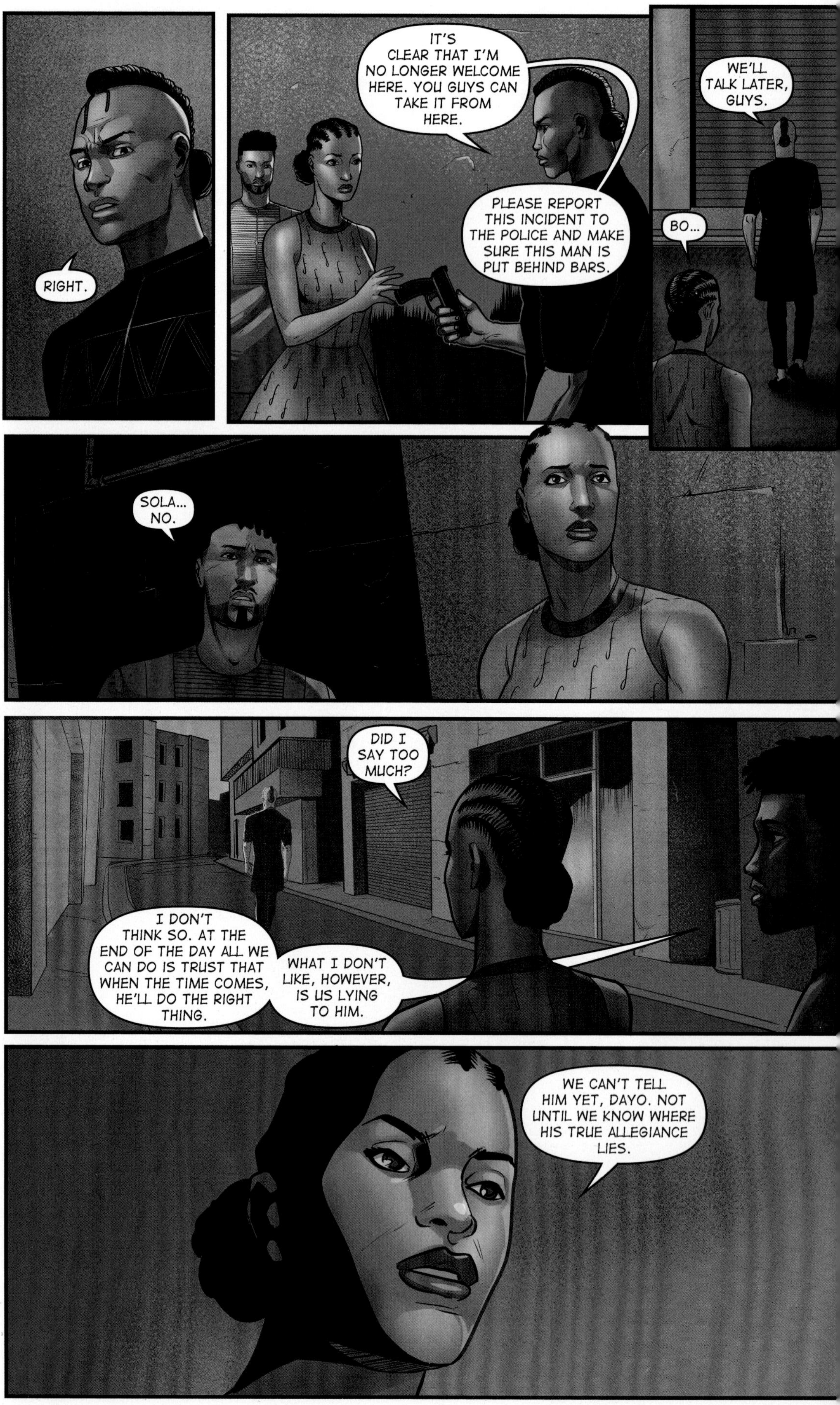
RIGHT.
IT'S CLEAR THAT I'M NO LONGER WELCOME HERE. YOU GUYS CAN TAKE IT FROM HERE.
PLEASE REPORT THIS INCIDENT TO THE POLICE AND MAKE SURE THIS MAN IS PUT BEHIND BARS.
WE'LL TALK LATER, GUYS.
BO...
SOLA... NO.
DID I SAY TOO MUCH?
I DON'T THINK SO. AT THE END OF THE DAY ALL WE CAN DO IS TRUST THAT WHEN THE TIME COMES, HE'LL DO THE RIGHT THING.
WHAT I DON'T LIKE, HOWEVER, IS US LYING TO HIM.
WE CAN'T TELL HIM YET, DAYO. NOT UNTIL WE KNOW WHERE HIS TRUE ALLEGIANCE LIES.

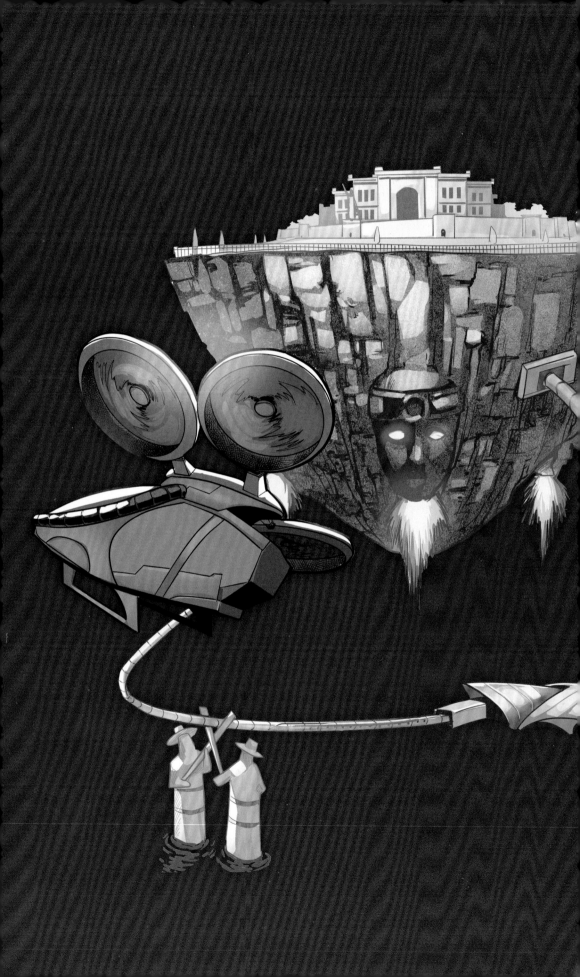

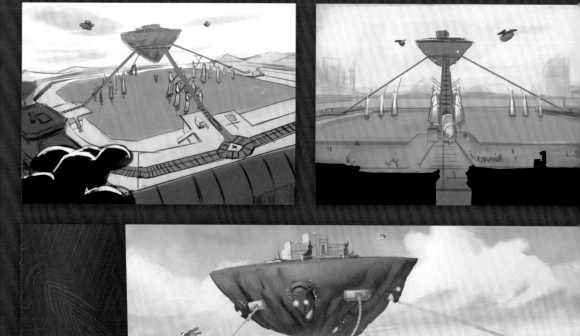

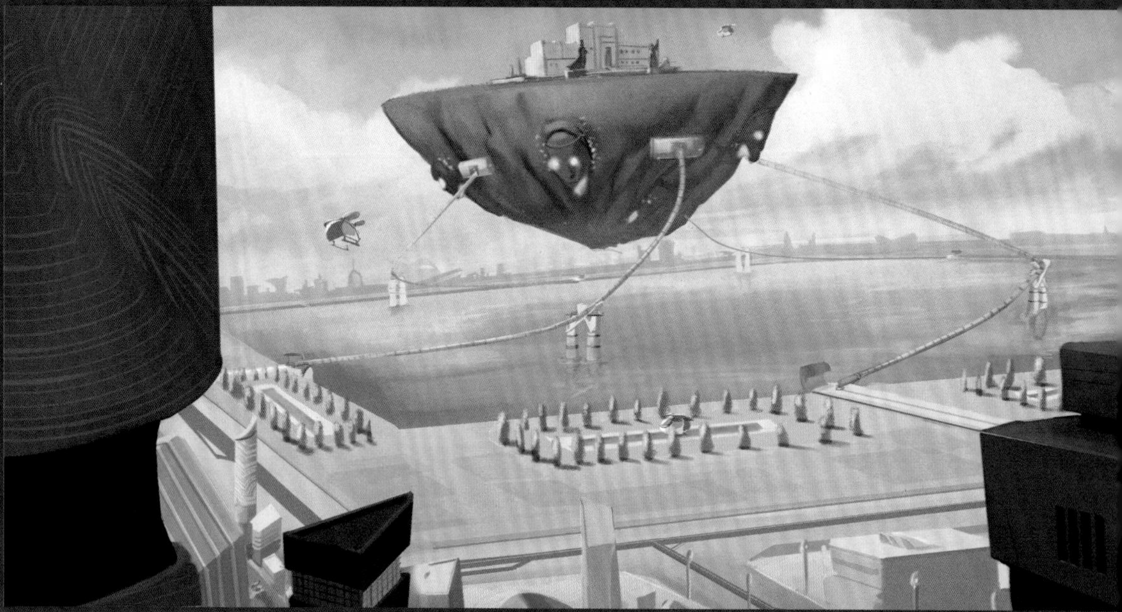

CHAPTER TWO

ART BY TOYIN "MORBY" AJETUNMOBI

I had a lot of fun working with my artists on this one. When I first started working on the story for *WindMaker*, I had this crazy idea of having the presidential villa be a floating structure. But I wanted to make sure I added some unique elements not only to support the physics of the structure but to also make it relevant to West African culture. If you've been reading the previous series in the YouNeek YouNiverse (*Malika: Warrior Queen, E.X.O.: The Legend of Wale Williams,* etc.), you'll know that the fictional Republic of Atala is a nation that is inspired by Yoruba people and culture.

As such, the statues in the water that hold up the tubes/rail-lines for the trains are actually modelled after the Eyo Masquerades. Eyo Masquerades are famous in the Eyo Festival, which is a Yoruba festival unique to Lagos, Nigeria.

The four large heads that serve as the jet-propulsion engines that keep the palace afloat are modelled after a variation of Yoruba facemasks and statue heads.

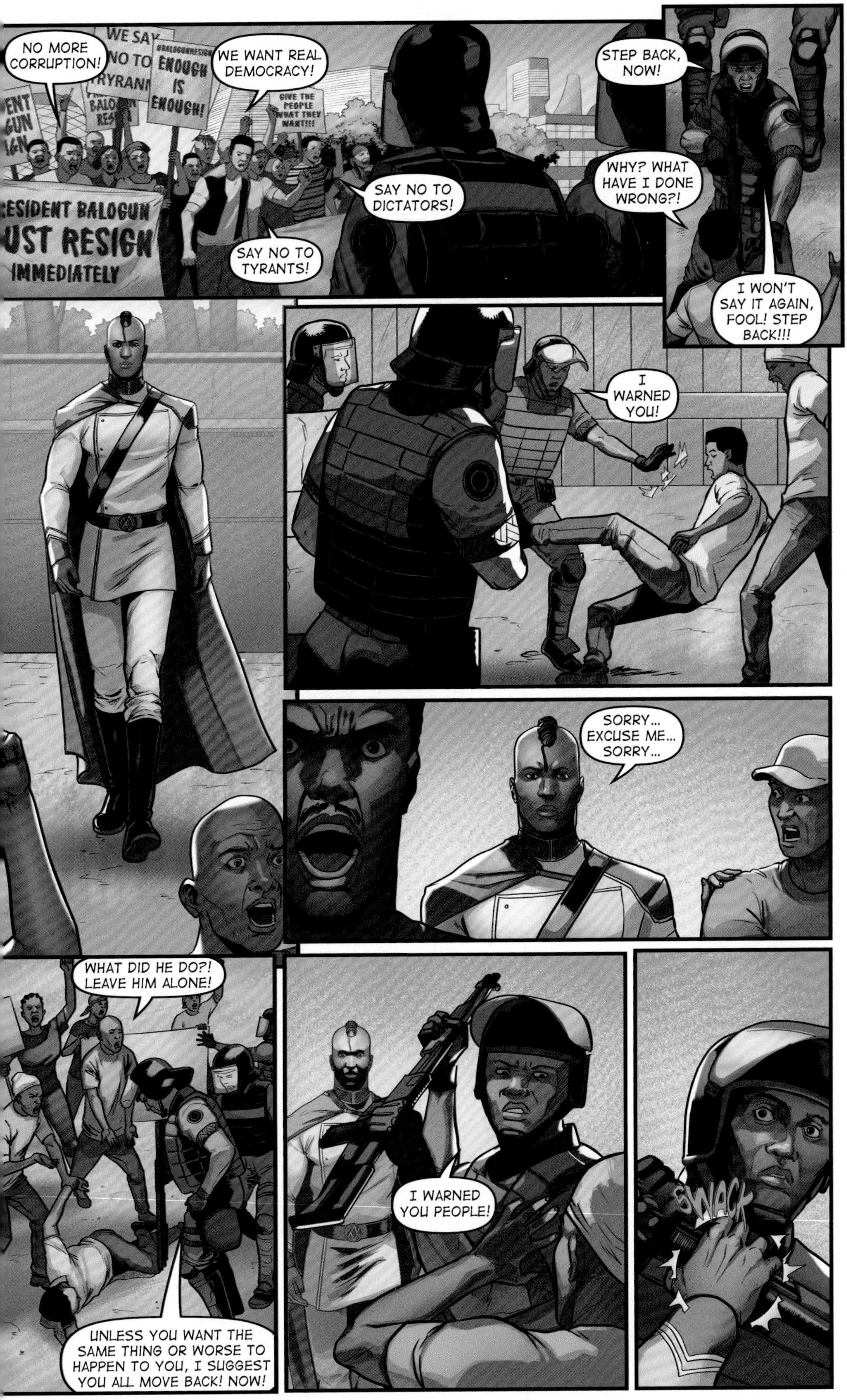

NO MORE CORRUPTION!
WE SAY NO TO TYRANN
#BALOGUNRESIGN ENOUGH IS ENOUGH!
WE WANT REAL DEMOCRACY!
GIVE THE PEOPLE WHAT THEY WANT!!!!
RESIDENT BALOGUN UST RESIGN IMMEDIATELY
SAY NO TO DICTATORS!
SAY NO TO TYRANTS!
STEP BACK, NOW!
WHY? WHAT HAVE I DONE WRONG?!
I WON'T SAY IT AGAIN, FOOL! STEP BACK!!!
I WARNED YOU!
SORRY... EXCUSE ME... SORRY...
WHAT DID HE DO?! LEAVE HIM ALONE!
UNLESS YOU WANT THE SAME THING OR WORSE TO HAPPEN TO YOU, I SUGGEST YOU ALL MOVE BACK! NOW!
I WARNED YOU PEOPLE!
SWACK

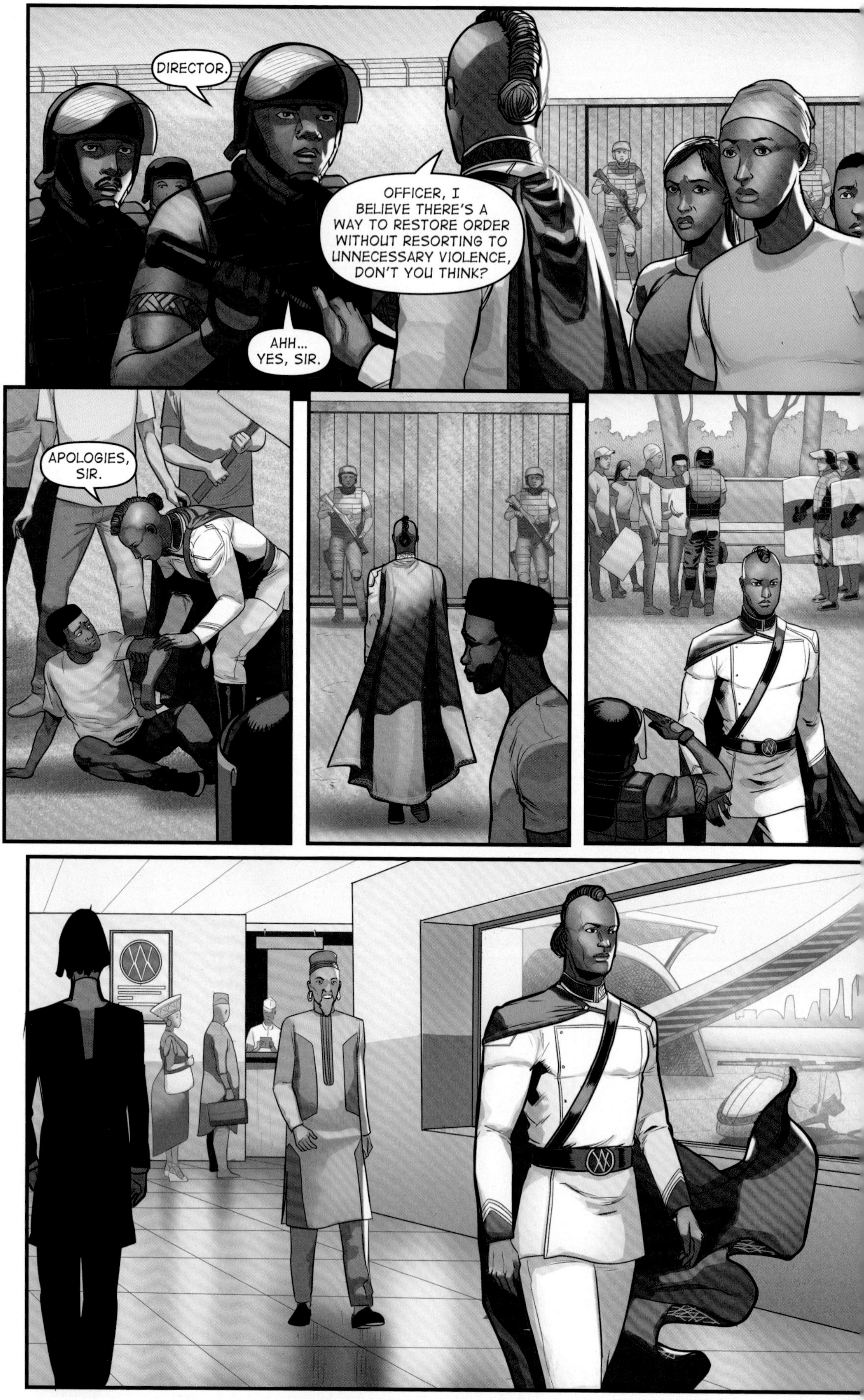
DIRECTOR.
OFFICER, I BELIEVE THERE'S A WAY TO RESTORE ORDER WITHOUT RESORTING TO UNNECESSARY VIOLENCE, DON'T YOU THINK?
AHH... YES, SIR.
APOLOGIES, SIR.

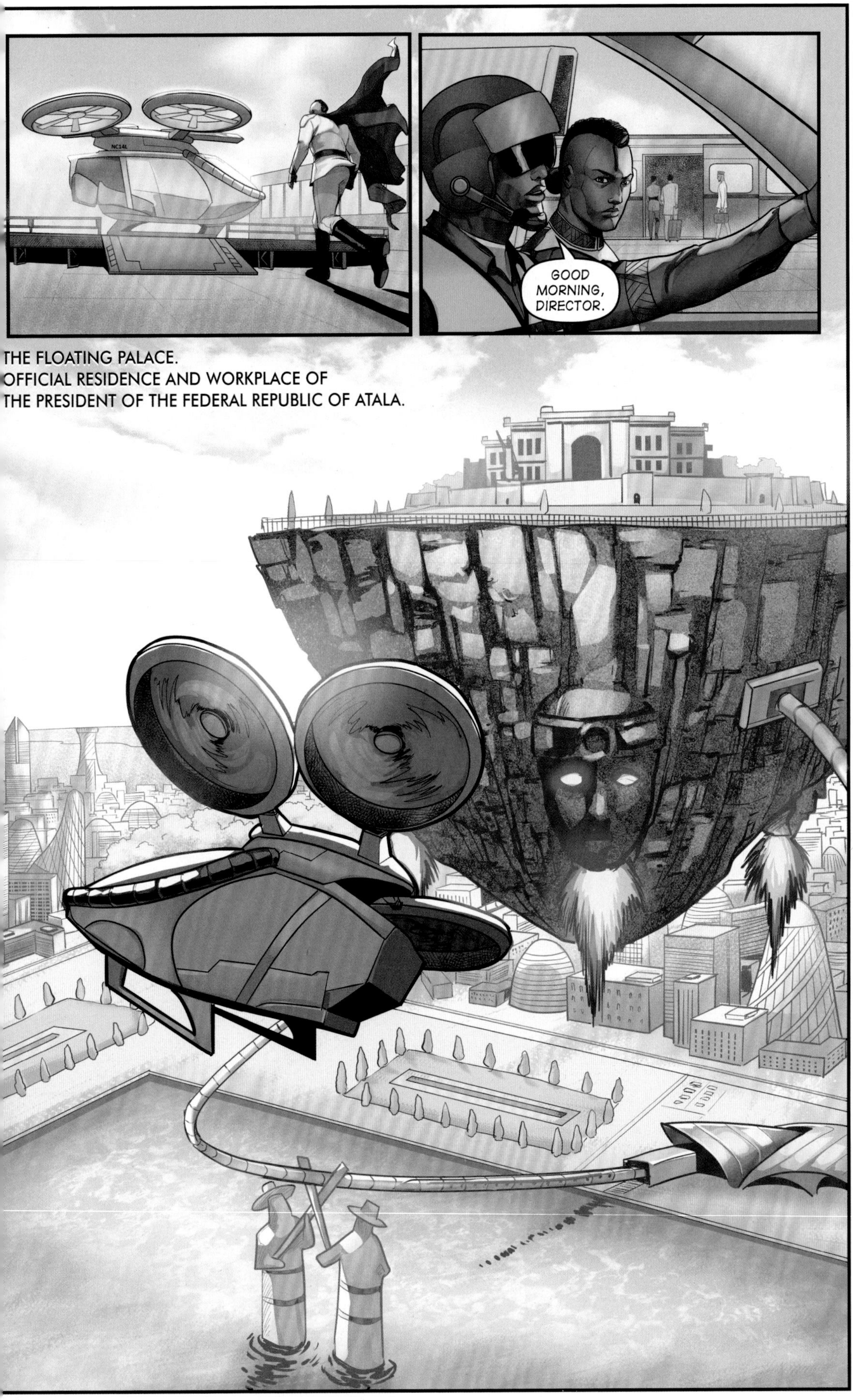
NC14L
GOOD MORNING, DIRECTOR.
THE FLOATING PALACE.
OFFICIAL RESIDENCE AND WORKPLACE OF
THE PRESIDENT OF THE FEDERAL REPUBLIC OF ATALA.

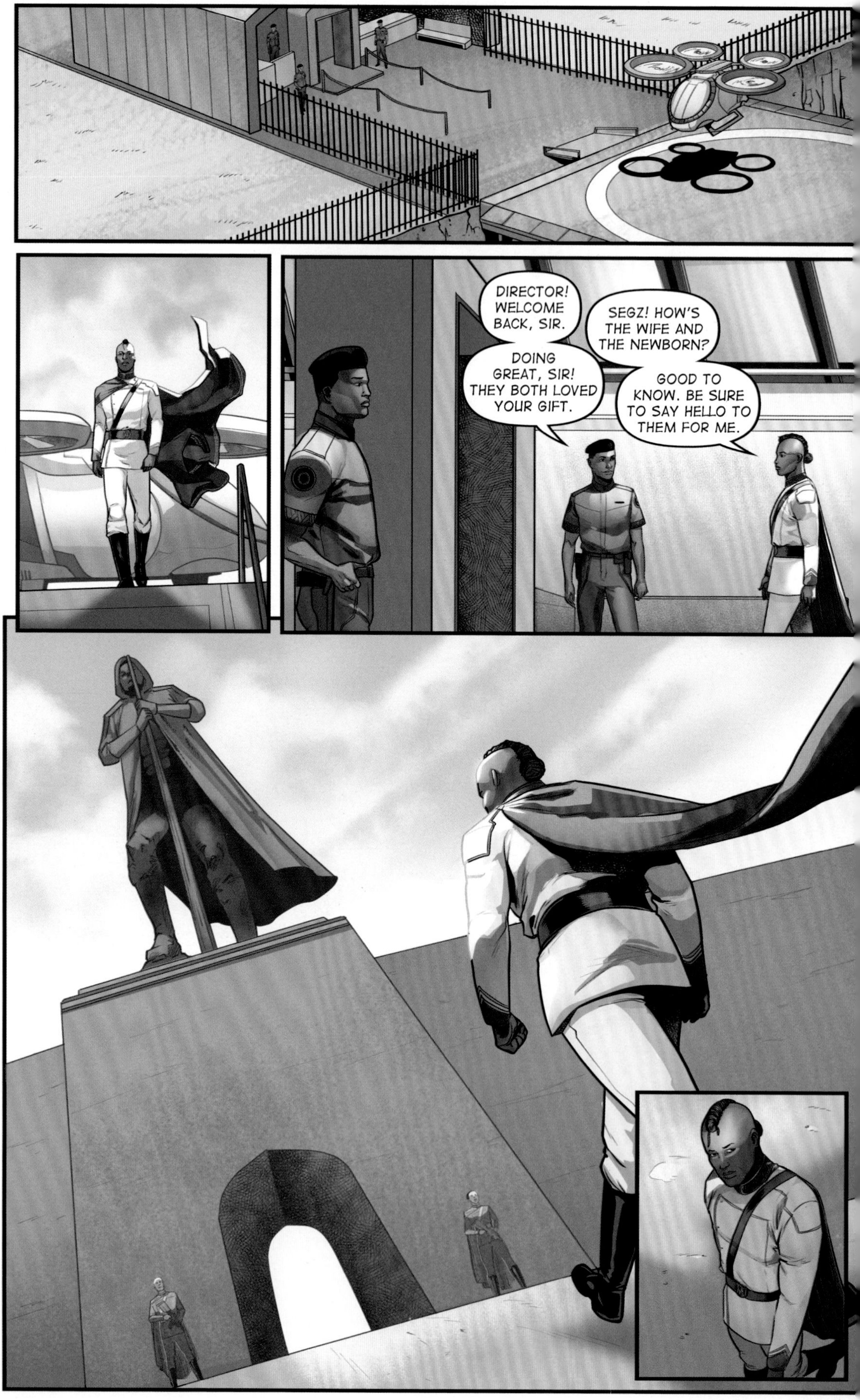
DIRECTOR! WELCOME BACK, SIR.
SEGZ! HOW'S THE WIFE AND THE NEWBORN?
DOING GREAT, SIR! THEY BOTH LOVED YOUR GIFT.
GOOD TO KNOW. BE SURE TO SAY HELLO TO THEM FOR ME.

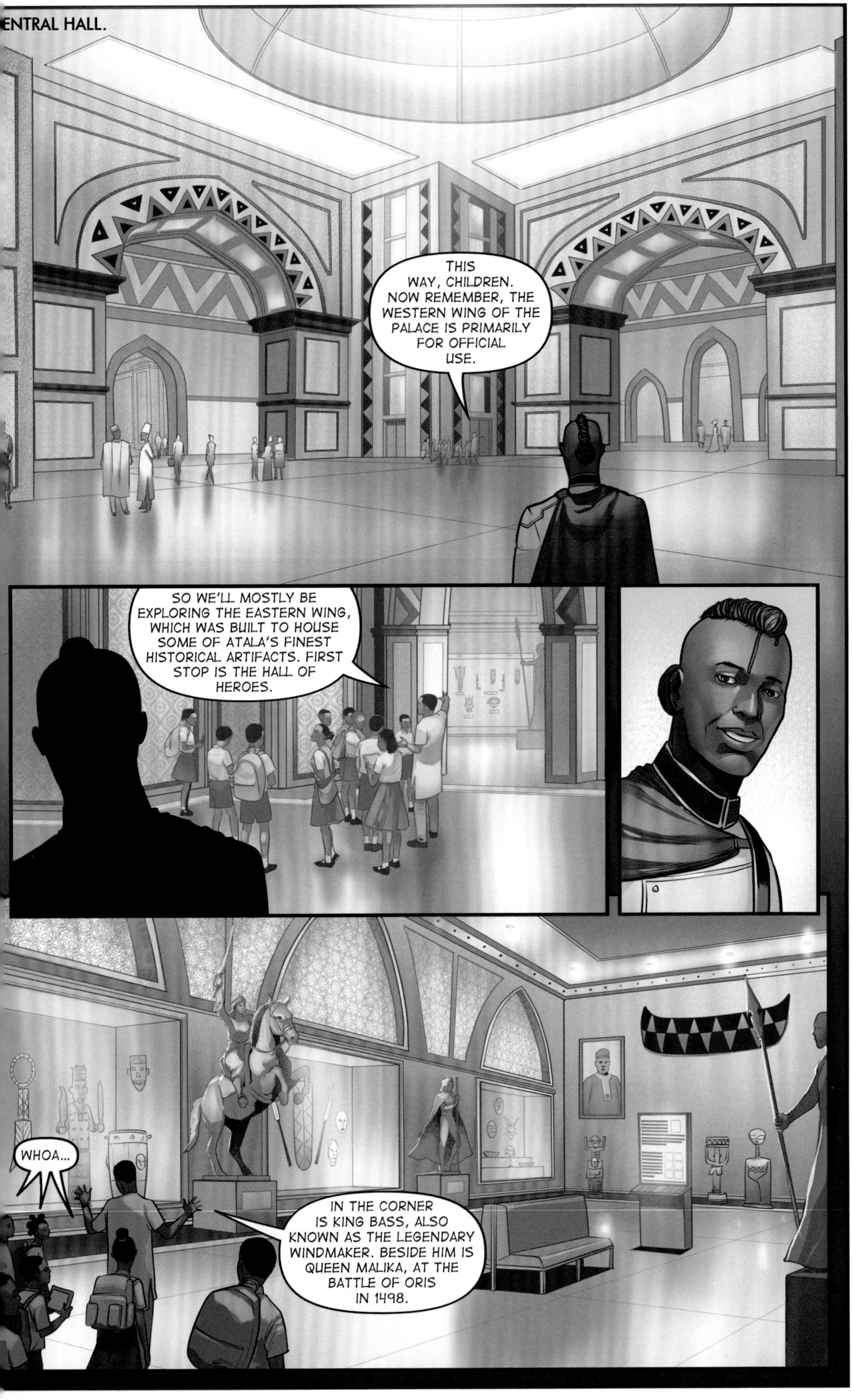
ENTRAL HALL.
THIS WAY, CHILDREN. NOW REMEMBER, THE WESTERN WING OF THE PALACE IS PRIMARILY FOR OFFICIAL USE.
SO WE'LL MOSTLY BE EXPLORING THE EASTERN WING, WHICH WAS BUILT TO HOUSE SOME OF ATALA'S FINEST HISTORICAL ARTIFACTS. FIRST STOP IS THE HALL OF HEROES.
WHOA...
IN THE CORNER IS KING BASS, ALSO KNOWN AS THE LEGENDARY WINDMAKER. BESIDE HIM IS QUEEN MALIKA, AT THE BATTLE OF ORIS IN 1498.

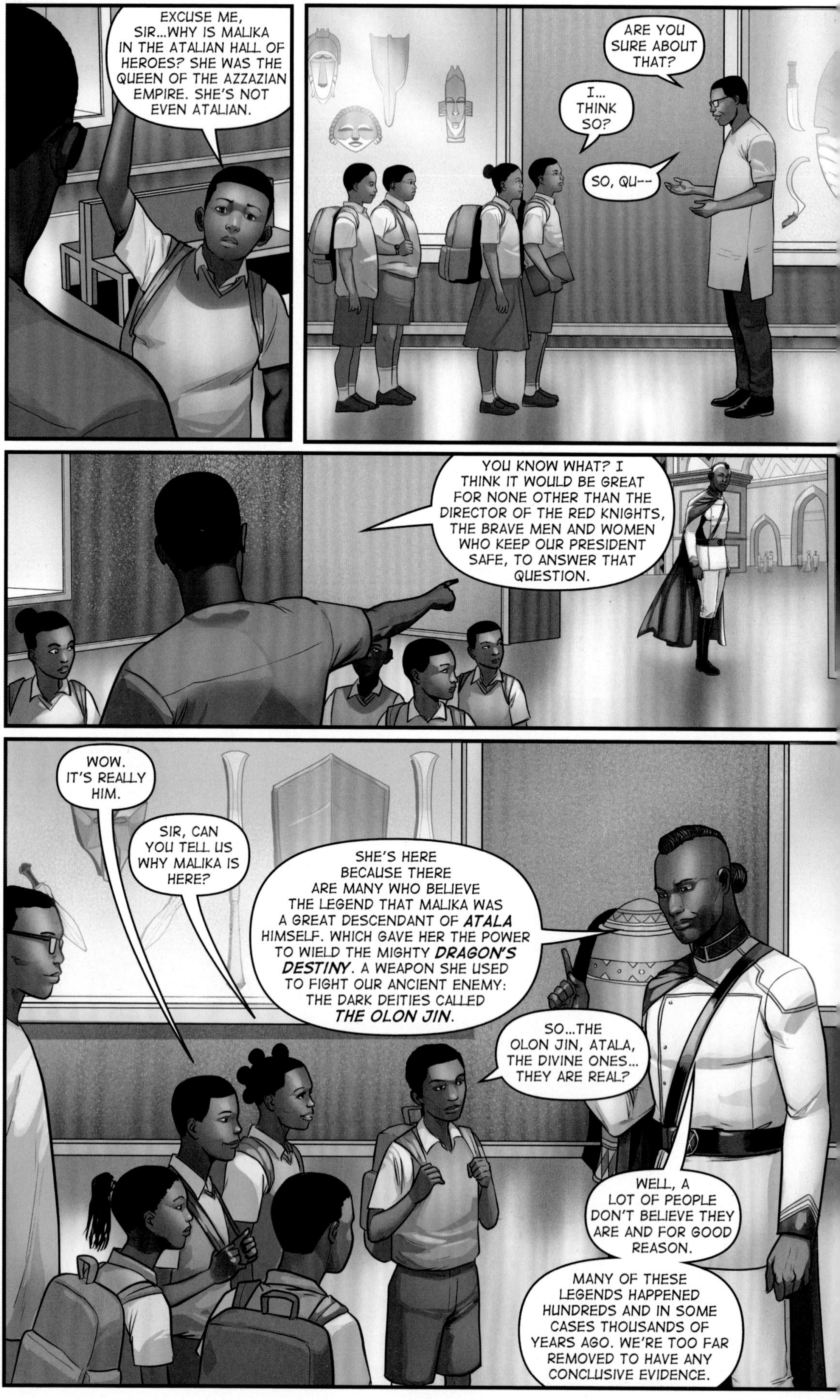
EXCUSE ME, SIR...WHY IS MALIKA IN THE ATALIAN HALL OF HEROES? SHE WAS THE QUEEN OF THE AZZAZIAN EMPIRE. SHE'S NOT EVEN ATALIAN.
ARE YOU SURE ABOUT THAT?
I... THINK SO?
SO, QU--
YOU KNOW WHAT? I THINK IT WOULD BE GREAT FOR NONE OTHER THAN THE DIRECTOR OF THE RED KNIGHTS, THE BRAVE MEN AND WOMEN WHO KEEP OUR PRESIDENT SAFE, TO ANSWER THAT QUESTION.
WOW. IT'S REALLY HIM.
SIR, CAN YOU TELL US WHY MALIKA IS HERE?
SHE'S HERE BECAUSE THERE ARE MANY WHO BELIEVE THE LEGEND THAT MALIKA WAS A GREAT DESCENDANT OF ***ATALA*** HIMSELF. WHICH GAVE HER THE POWER TO WIELD THE MIGHTY ***DRAGON'S DESTINY***. A WEAPON SHE USED TO FIGHT OUR ANCIENT ENEMY: THE DARK DEITIES CALLED ***THE OLON JIN***.
SO...THE OLON JIN, ATALA, THE DIVINE ONES... THEY ARE REAL?
WELL, A LOT OF PEOPLE DON'T BELIEVE THEY ARE AND FOR GOOD REASON.
MANY OF THESE LEGENDS HAPPENED HUNDREDS AND IN SOME CASES THOUSANDS OF YEARS AGO. WE'RE TOO FAR REMOVED TO HAVE ANY CONCLUSIVE EVIDENCE.

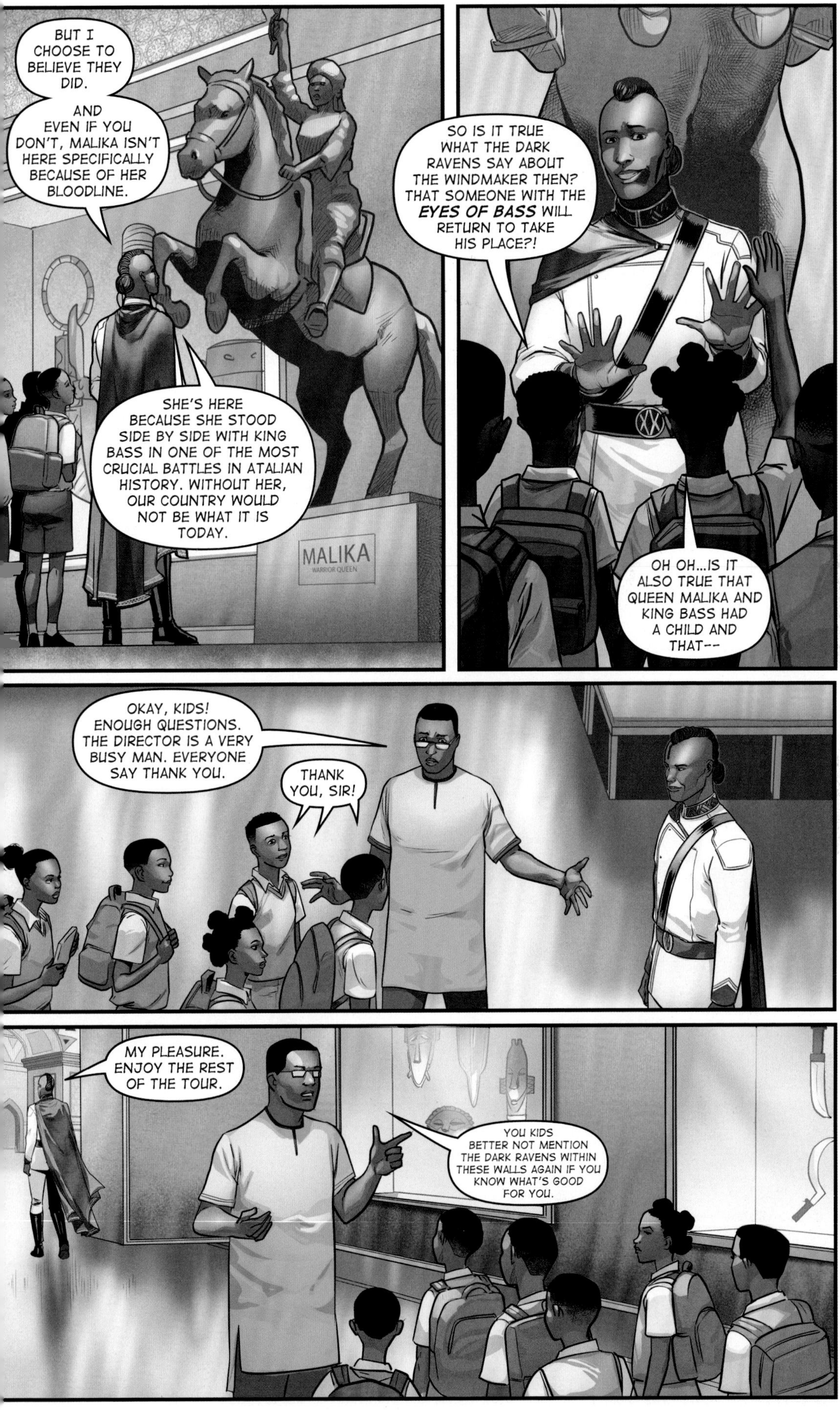
BUT I CHOOSE TO BELIEVE THEY DID.
AND EVEN IF YOU DON'T, MALIKA ISN'T HERE SPECIFICALLY BECAUSE OF HER BLOODLINE.
SHE'S HERE BECAUSE SHE STOOD SIDE BY SIDE WITH KING BASS IN ONE OF THE MOST CRUCIAL BATTLES IN ATALIAN HISTORY. WITHOUT HER, OUR COUNTRY WOULD NOT BE WHAT IT IS TODAY.
MALIKA
WARRIOR QUEEN
SO IS IT TRUE WHAT THE DARK RAVENS SAY ABOUT THE WINDMAKER THEN? THAT SOMEONE WITH THE *EYES OF BASS* WILL RETURN TO TAKE HIS PLACE?!
OH OH...IS IT ALSO TRUE THAT QUEEN MALIKA AND KING BASS HAD A CHILD AND THAT--
OKAY, KIDS! ENOUGH QUESTIONS. THE DIRECTOR IS A VERY BUSY MAN. EVERYONE SAY THANK YOU.
THANK YOU, SIR!
MY PLEASURE. ENJOY THE REST OF THE TOUR.
YOU KIDS BETTER NOT MENTION THE DARK RAVENS WITHIN THESE WALLS AGAIN IF YOU KNOW WHAT'S GOOD FOR YOU.

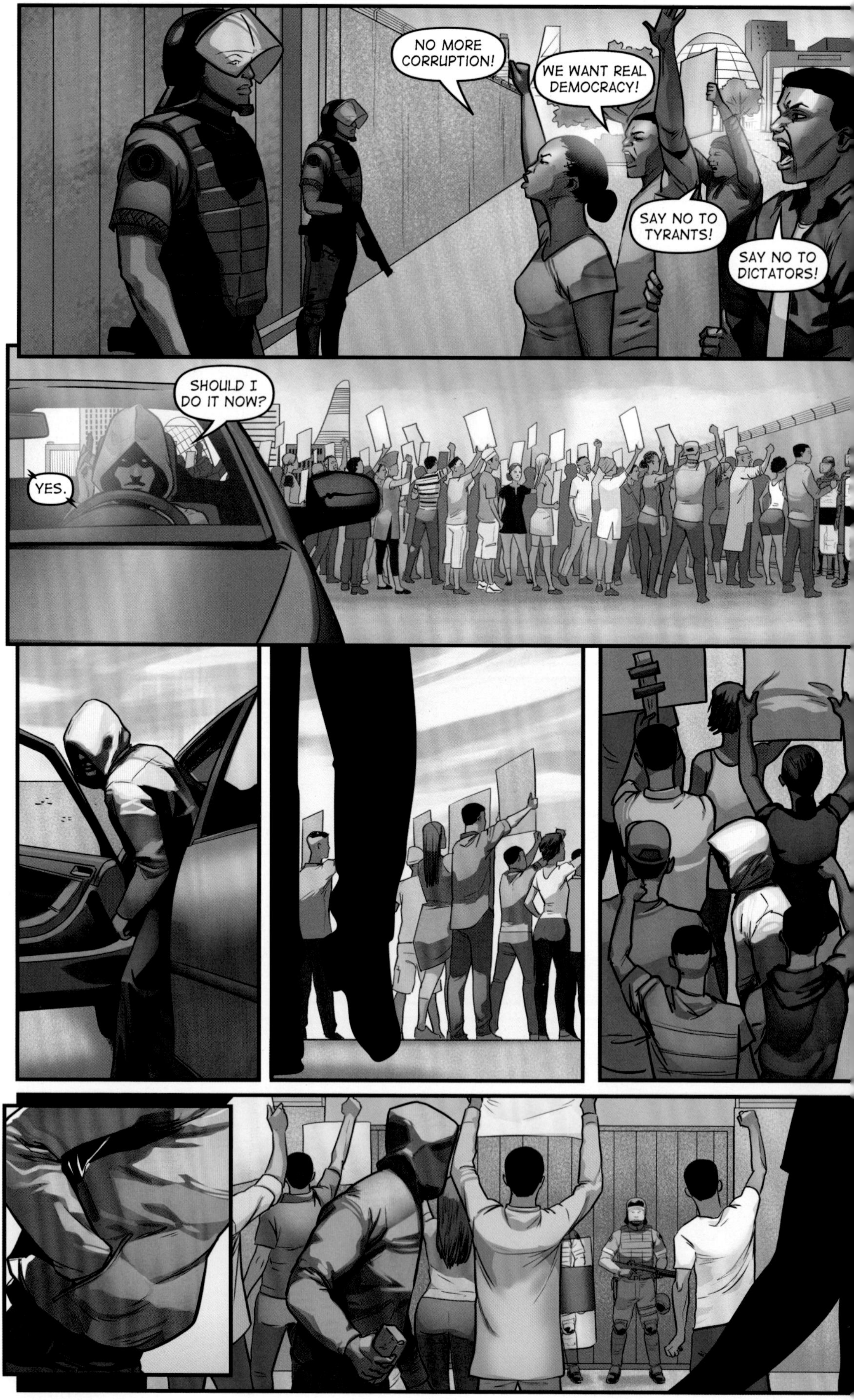

NO MORE CORRUPTION!
WE WANT REAL DEMOCRACY!
SAY NO TO TYRANTS!
SAY NO TO DICTATORS!
SHOULD I DO IT NOW?
YES.

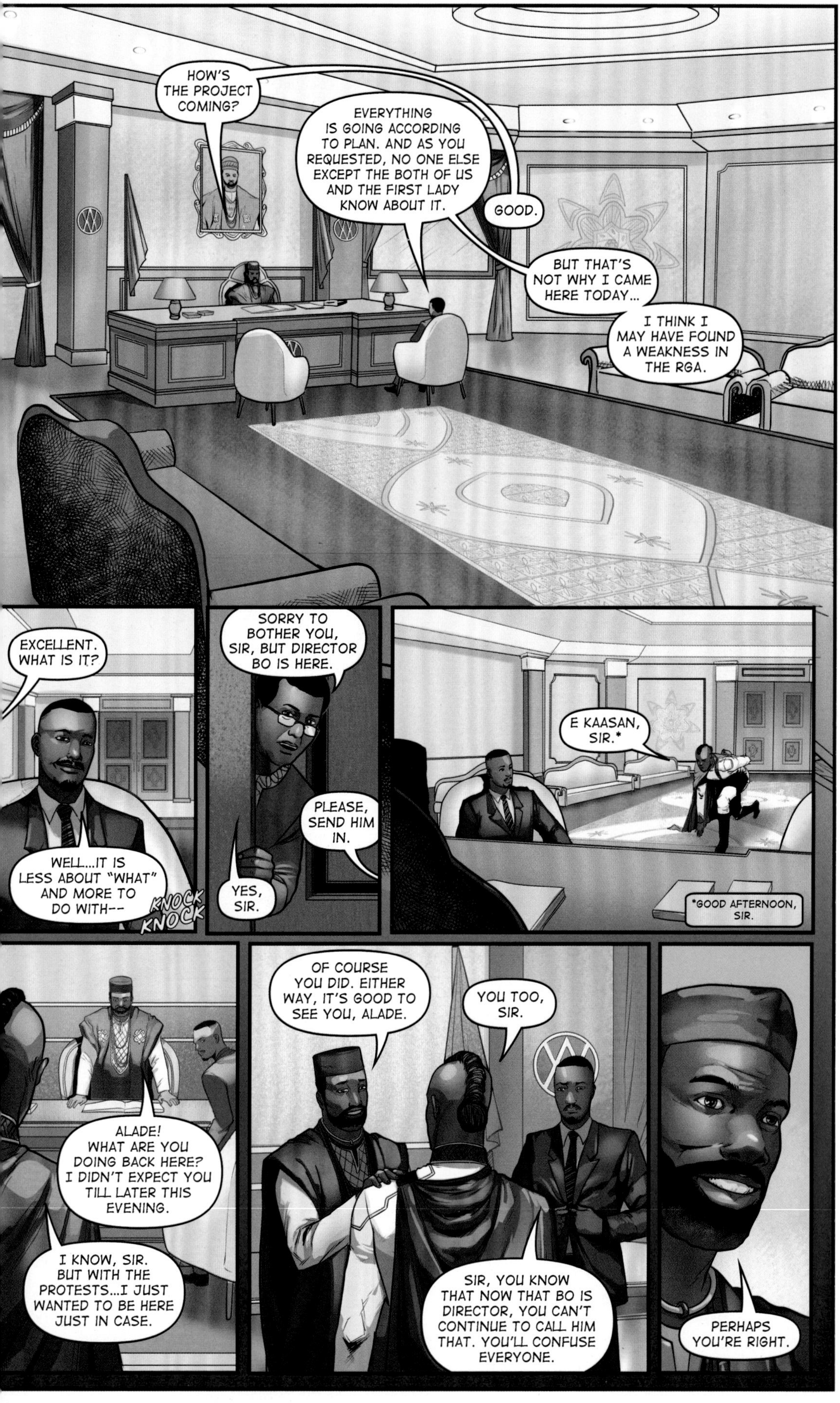

HOW'S THE PROJECT COMING?
EVERYTHING IS GOING ACCORDING TO PLAN. AND AS YOU REQUESTED, NO ONE ELSE EXCEPT THE BOTH OF US AND THE FIRST LADY KNOW ABOUT IT.
GOOD.
BUT THAT'S NOT WHY I CAME HERE TODAY...
I THINK I MAY HAVE FOUND A WEAKNESS IN THE RGA.
EXCELLENT. WHAT IS IT?
WELL...IT IS LESS ABOUT "WHAT" AND MORE TO DO WITH--
KNOCK KNOCK
SORRY TO BOTHER YOU, SIR, BUT DIRECTOR BO IS HERE.
PLEASE, SEND HIM IN.
YES, SIR.
E KAASAN, SIR.*
*GOOD AFTERNOON, SIR.
ALADE! WHAT ARE YOU DOING BACK HERE? I DIDN'T EXPECT YOU TILL LATER THIS EVENING.
I KNOW, SIR. BUT WITH THE PROTESTS...I JUST WANTED TO BE HERE JUST IN CASE.
OF COURSE YOU DID. EITHER WAY, IT'S GOOD TO SEE YOU, ALADE.
YOU TOO, SIR.
SIR, YOU KNOW THAT NOW THAT BO IS DIRECTOR, YOU CAN'T CONTINUE TO CALL HIM THAT. YOU'LL CONFUSE EVERYONE.
PERHAPS YOU'RE RIGHT.

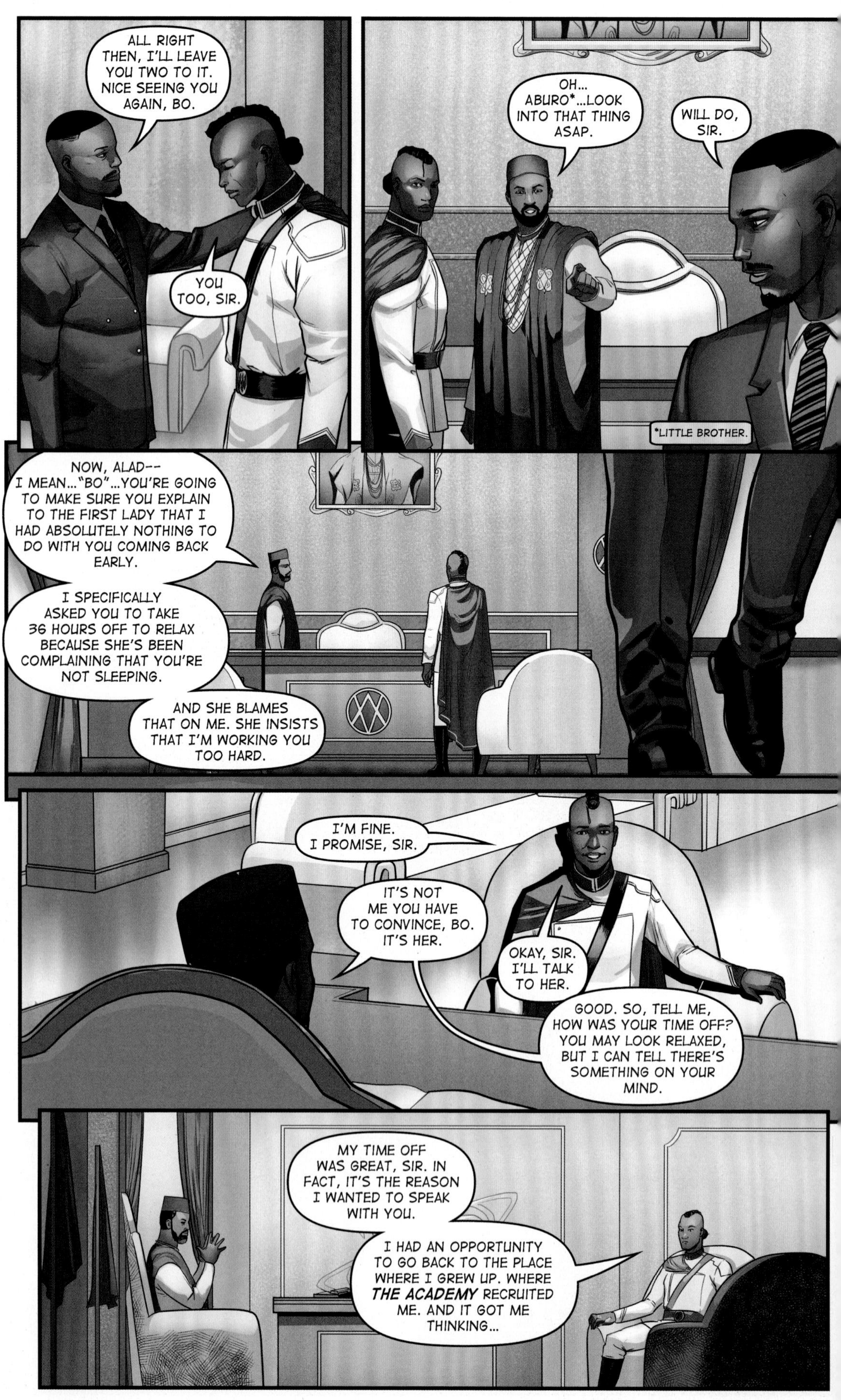
ALL RIGHT THEN, I'LL LEAVE YOU TWO TO IT. NICE SEEING YOU AGAIN, BO.
YOU TOO, SIR.
OH... ABURO*...LOOK INTO THAT THING ASAP.
WILL DO, SIR.
*LITTLE BROTHER.
NOW, ALAD-- I MEAN..."BO"...YOU'RE GOING TO MAKE SURE YOU EXPLAIN TO THE FIRST LADY THAT I HAD ABSOLUTELY NOTHING TO DO WITH YOU COMING BACK EARLY.
I SPECIFICALLY ASKED YOU TO TAKE 36 HOURS OFF TO RELAX BECAUSE SHE'S BEEN COMPLAINING THAT YOU'RE NOT SLEEPING.
AND SHE BLAMES THAT ON ME. SHE INSISTS THAT I'M WORKING YOU TOO HARD.
I'M FINE. I PROMISE, SIR.
IT'S NOT ME YOU HAVE TO CONVINCE, BO. IT'S HER.
OKAY, SIR. I'LL TALK TO HER.
GOOD. SO, TELL ME, HOW WAS YOUR TIME OFF? YOU MAY LOOK RELAXED, BUT I CAN TELL THERE'S SOMETHING ON YOUR MIND.
MY TIME OFF WAS GREAT, SIR. IN FACT, IT'S THE REASON I WANTED TO SPEAK WITH YOU.
I HAD AN OPPORTUNITY TO GO BACK TO THE PLACE WHERE I GREW UP. WHERE *THE ACADEMY* RECRUITED ME. AND IT GOT ME THINKING...

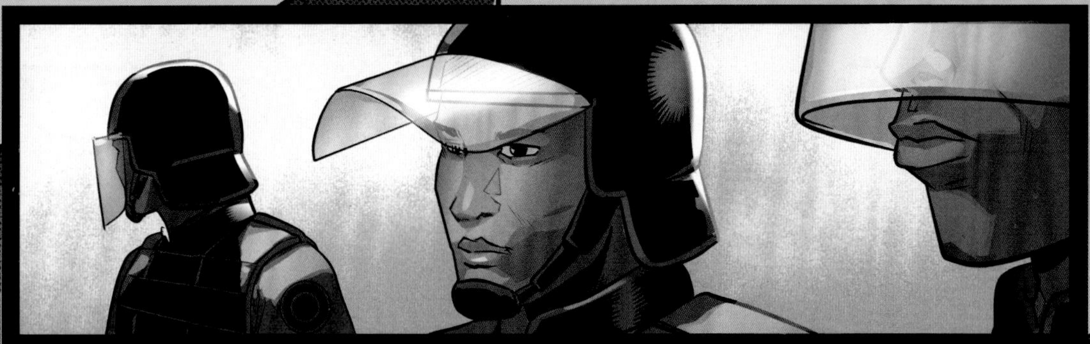

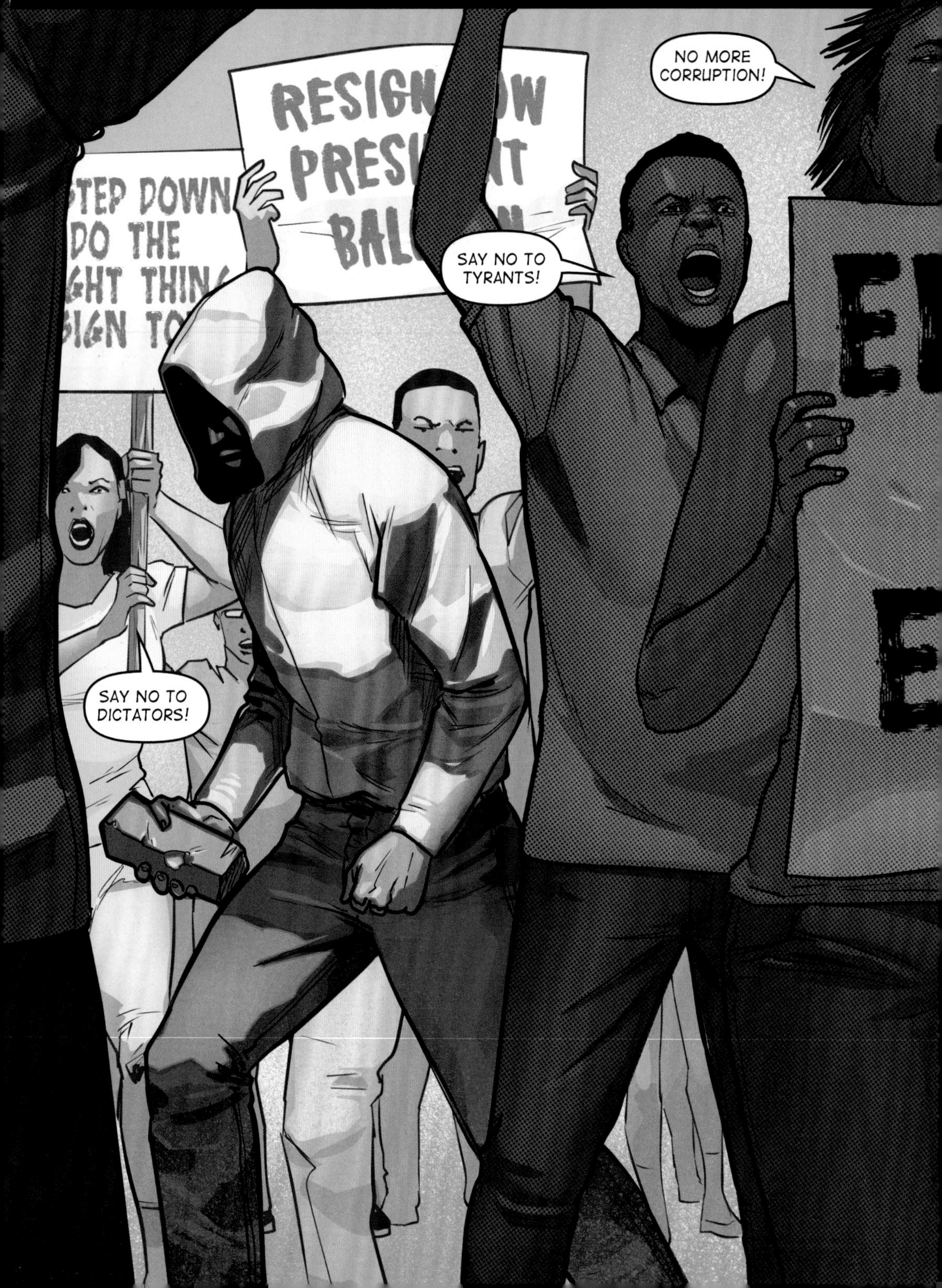
NO MORE CORRUPTION!
SAY NO TO TYRANTS!
SAY NO TO DICTATORS!

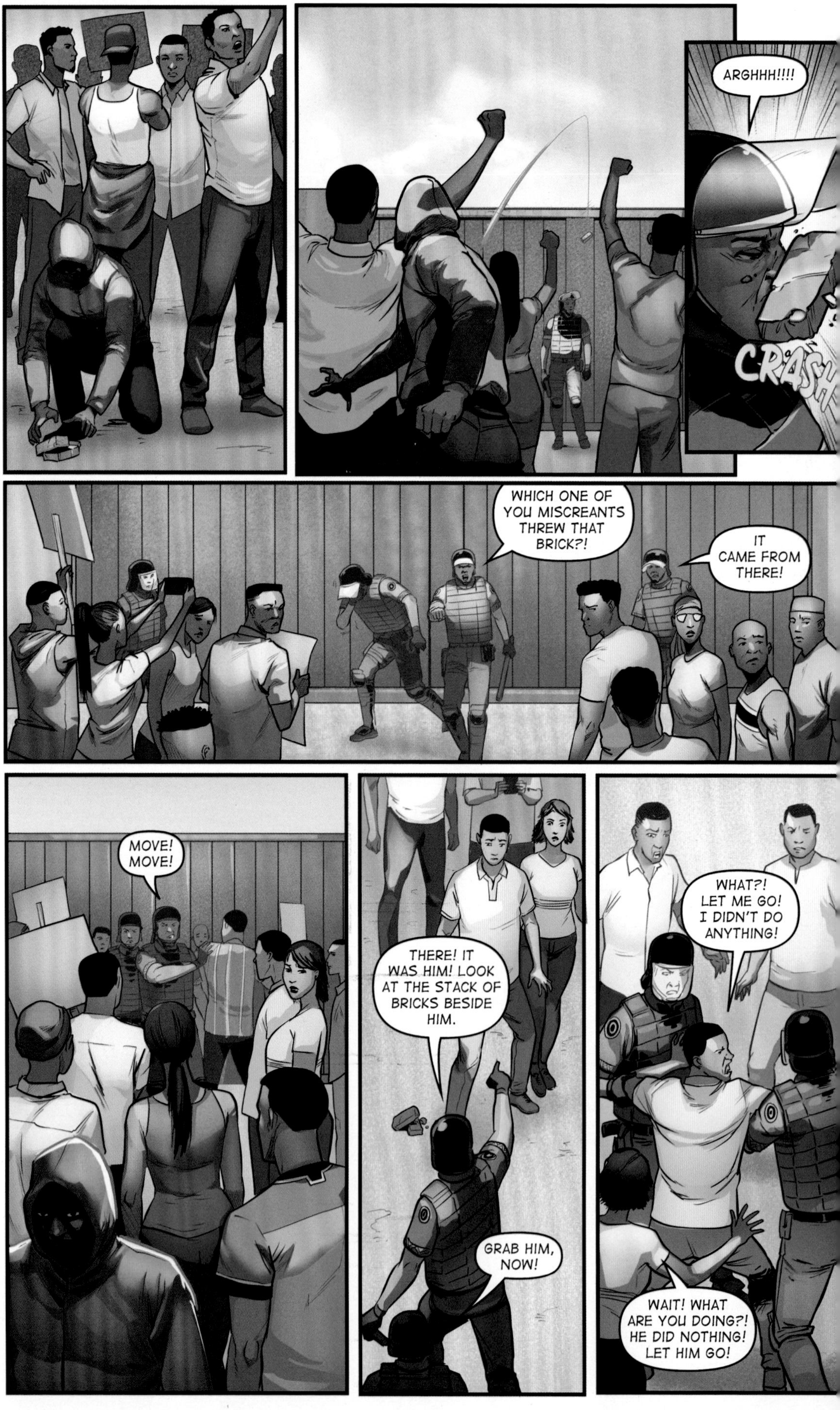
ARGHHH!!!!
CRASH
WHICH ONE OF YOU MISCREANTS THREW THAT BRICK?!
IT CAME FROM THERE!
MOVE! MOVE!
THERE! IT WAS HIM! LOOK AT THE STACK OF BRICKS BESIDE HIM.
GRAB HIM, NOW!
WHAT?! LET ME GO! I DIDN'T DO ANYTHING!
WAIT! WHAT ARE YOU DOING?! HE DID NOTHING! LET HIM GO!

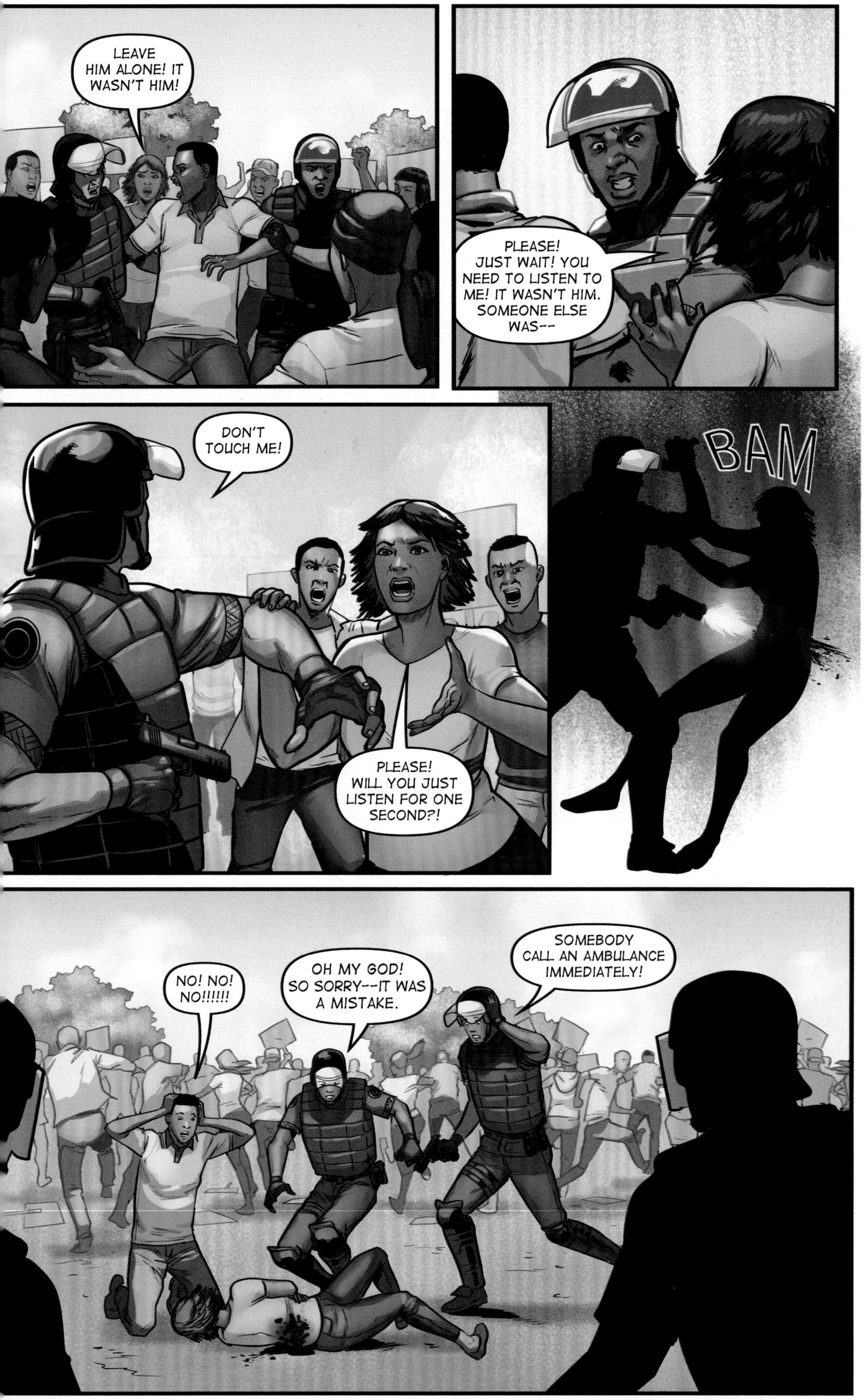
LEAVE HIM ALONE! IT WASN'T HIM!
PLEASE! JUST WAIT! YOU NEED TO LISTEN TO ME! IT WASN'T HIM. SOMEONE ELSE WAS--
DON'T TOUCH ME!
PLEASE! WILL YOU JUST LISTEN FOR ONE SECOND?!
BAM
NO! NO! NO!!!!!!
OH MY GOD! SO SORRY--IT WAS A MISTAKE.
SOMEBODY CALL AN AMBULANCE IMMEDIATELY!

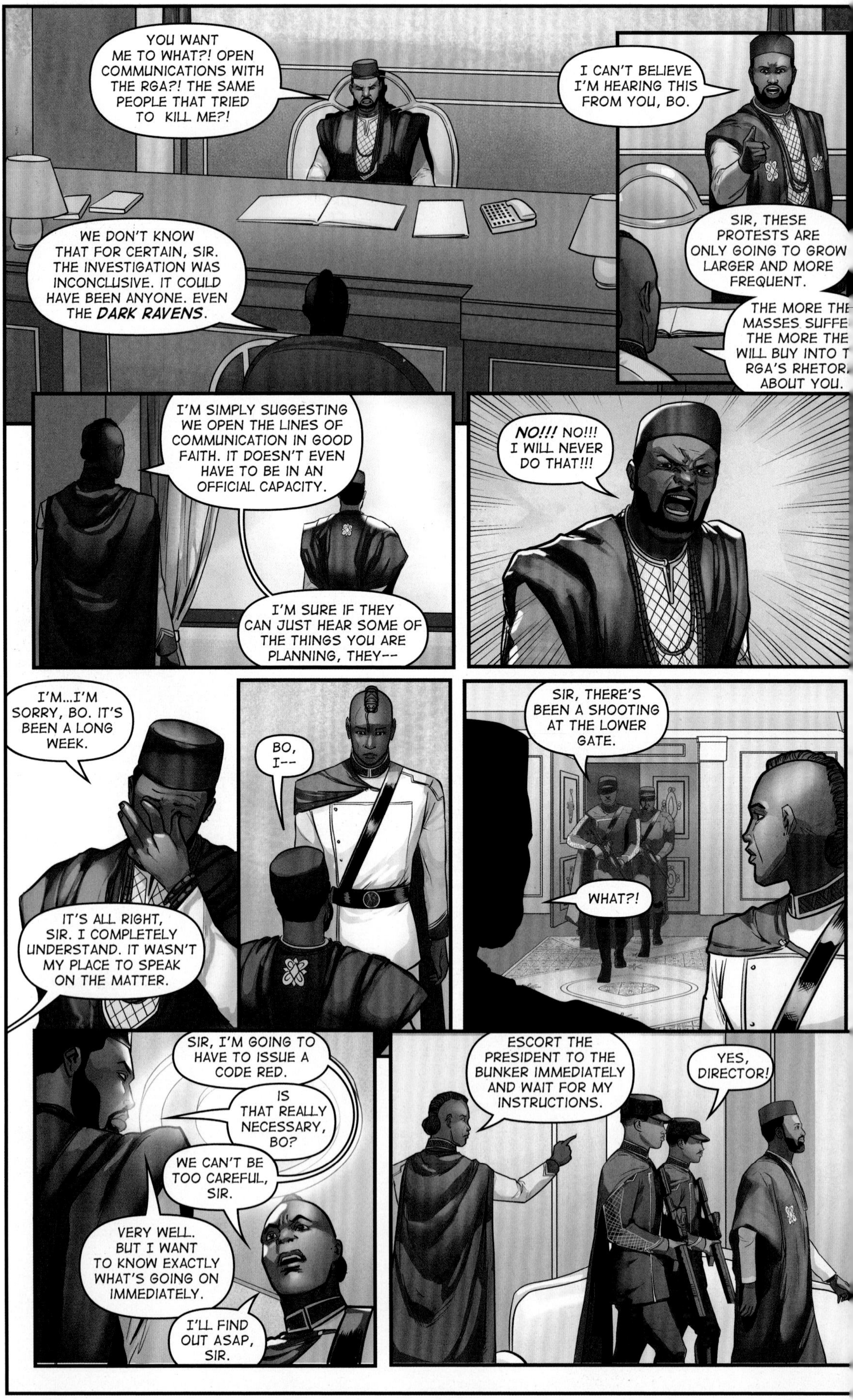
YOU WANT ME TO WHAT?! OPEN COMMUNICATIONS WITH THE RGA?! THE SAME PEOPLE THAT TRIED TO KILL ME?!
WE DON'T KNOW THAT FOR CERTAIN, SIR. THE INVESTIGATION WAS INCONCLUSIVE. IT COULD HAVE BEEN ANYONE. EVEN THE *DARK RAVENS*.
I CAN'T BELIEVE I'M HEARING THIS FROM YOU, BO.
SIR, THESE PROTESTS ARE ONLY GOING TO GROW LARGER AND MORE FREQUENT.
I'M SIMPLY SUGGESTING WE OPEN THE LINES OF COMMUNICATION IN GOOD FAITH. IT DOESN'T EVEN HAVE TO BE IN AN OFFICIAL CAPACITY.
I'M SURE IF THEY CAN JUST HEAR SOME OF THE THINGS YOU ARE PLANNING, THEY--
NO!!! NO!!! I WILL NEVER DO THAT!!!
I'M...I'M SORRY, BO. IT'S BEEN A LONG WEEK.
IT'S ALL RIGHT, SIR. I COMPLETELY UNDERSTAND. IT WASN'T MY PLACE TO SPEAK ON THE MATTER.
BO, I--
SIR, THERE'S BEEN A SHOOTING AT THE LOWER GATE.
WHAT?!
SIR, I'M GOING TO HAVE TO ISSUE A CODE RED.
IS THAT REALLY NECESSARY, BO?
WE CAN'T BE TOO CAREFUL, SIR.
VERY WELL. BUT I WANT TO KNOW EXACTLY WHAT'S GOING ON IMMEDIATELY.
I'LL FIND OUT ASAP, SIR.
ESCORT THE PRESIDENT TO THE BUNKER IMMEDIATELY AND WAIT FOR MY INSTRUCTIONS.
YES, DIRECTOR!

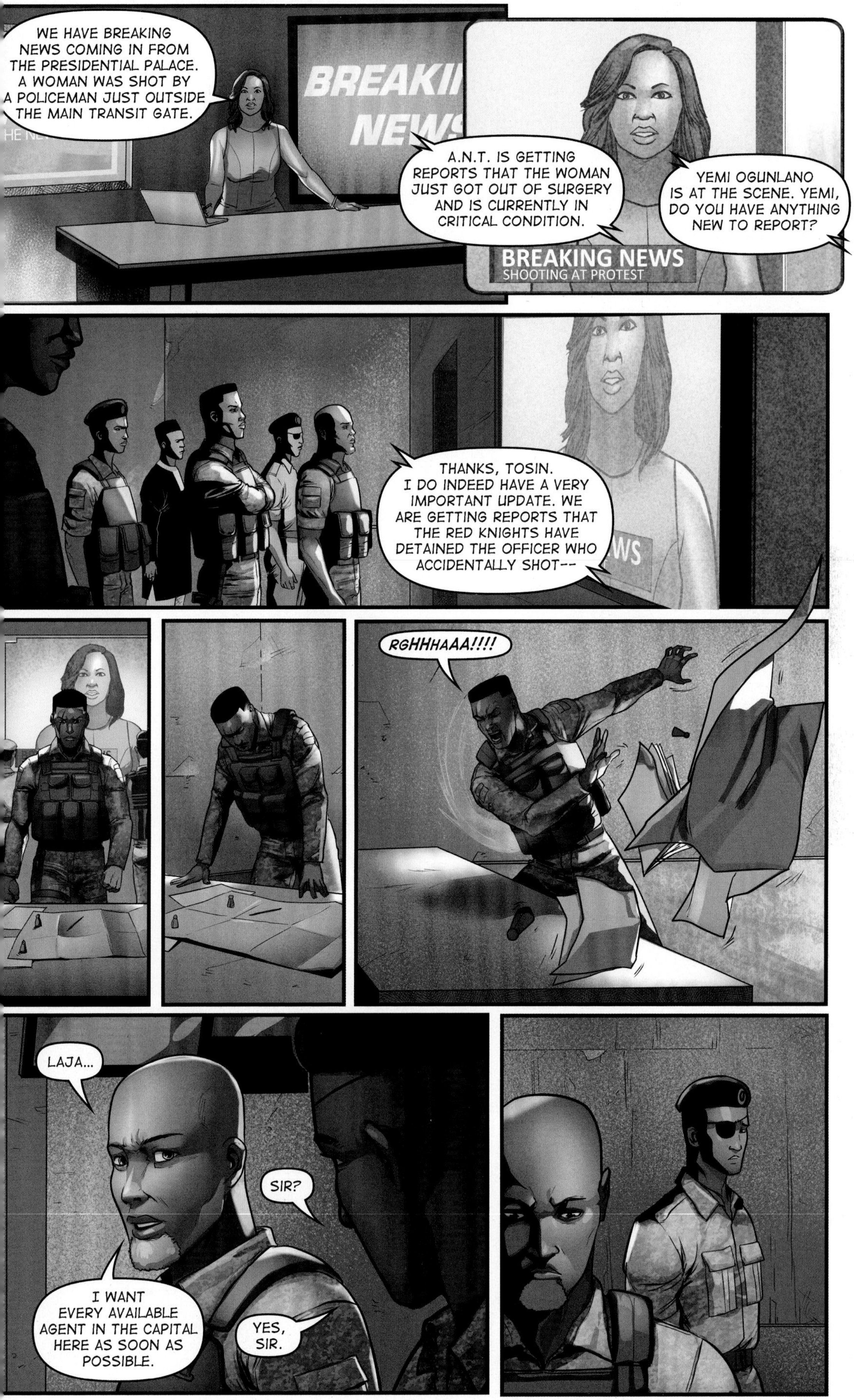
WE HAVE BREAKING NEWS COMING IN FROM THE PRESIDENTIAL PALACE. A WOMAN WAS SHOT BY A POLICEMAN JUST OUTSIDE THE MAIN TRANSIT GATE.
BREAKI NEWS
A.N.T. IS GETTING REPORTS THAT THE WOMAN JUST GOT OUT OF SURGERY AND IS CURRENTLY IN CRITICAL CONDITION.
YEMI OGUNLANO IS AT THE SCENE. YEMI, DO YOU HAVE ANYTHING NEW TO REPORT?
BREAKING NEWS
SHOOTING AT PROTEST
THANKS, TOSIN. I DO INDEED HAVE A VERY IMPORTANT UPDATE. WE ARE GETTING REPORTS THAT THE RED KNIGHTS HAVE DETAINED THE OFFICER WHO ACCIDENTALLY SHOT--
RGHHHAAA!!!!
LAJA...
SIR?
I WANT EVERY AVAILABLE AGENT IN THE CAPITAL HERE AS SOON AS POSSIBLE.
YES, SIR.

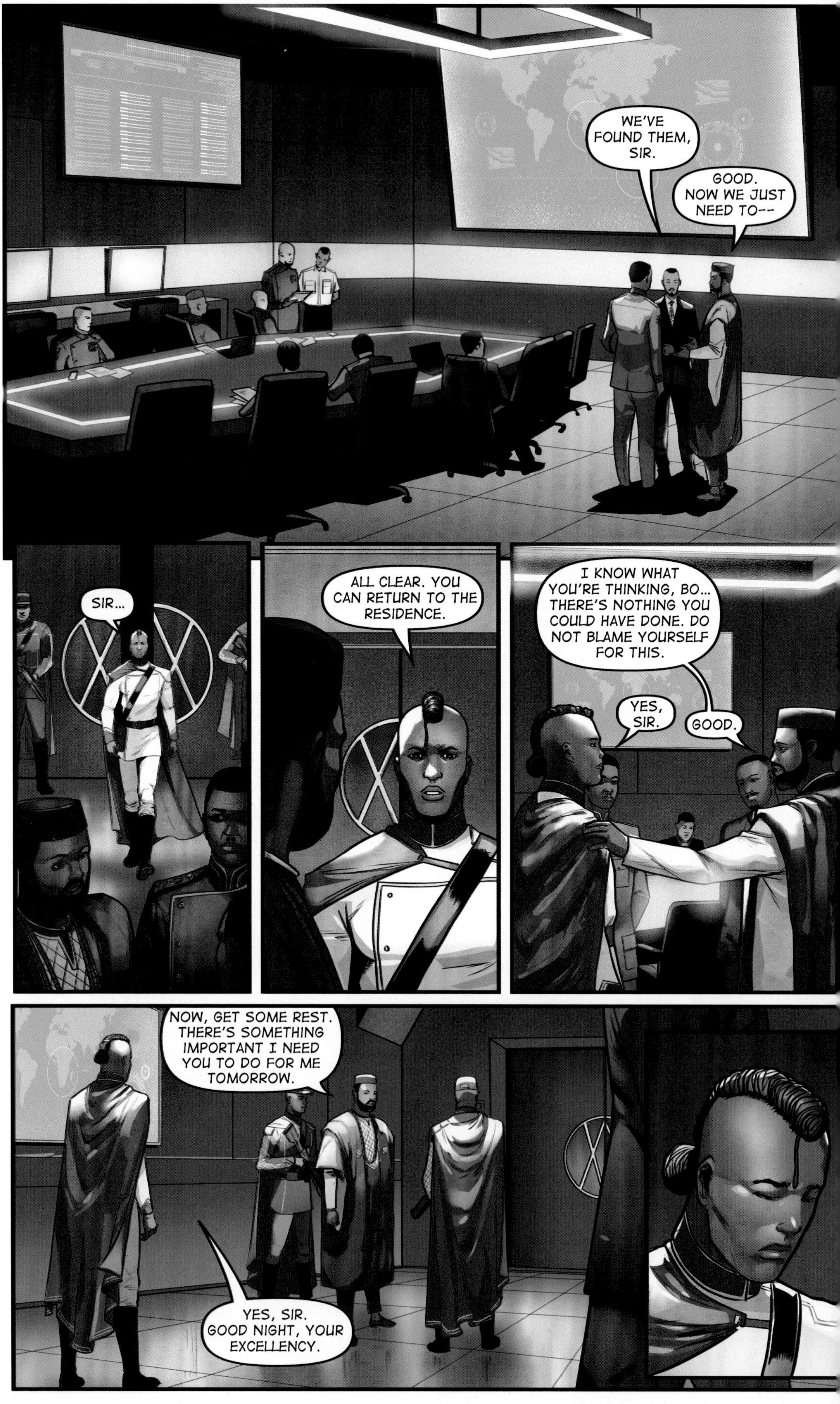
WE'VE FOUND THEM, SIR.
GOOD. NOW WE JUST NEED TO--
SIR...
ALL CLEAR. YOU CAN RETURN TO THE RESIDENCE.
I KNOW WHAT YOU'RE THINKING, BO... THERE'S NOTHING YOU COULD HAVE DONE. DO NOT BLAME YOURSELF FOR THIS.
YES, SIR.
GOOD.
NOW, GET SOME REST. THERE'S SOMETHING IMPORTANT I NEED YOU TO DO FOR ME TOMORROW.
YES, SIR. GOOD NIGHT, YOUR EXCELLENCY.

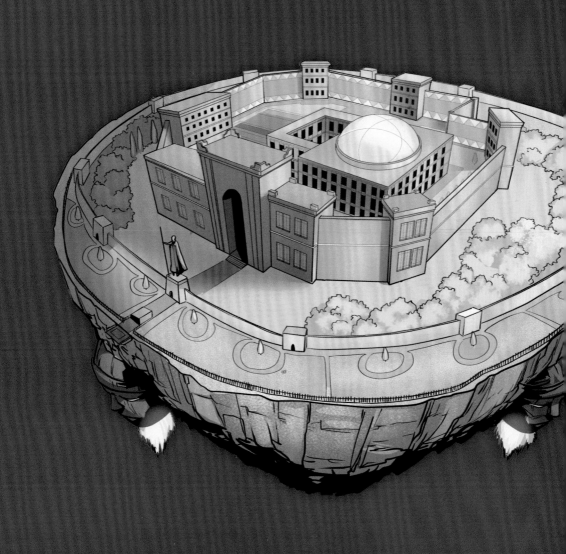

CHAPTER THREE

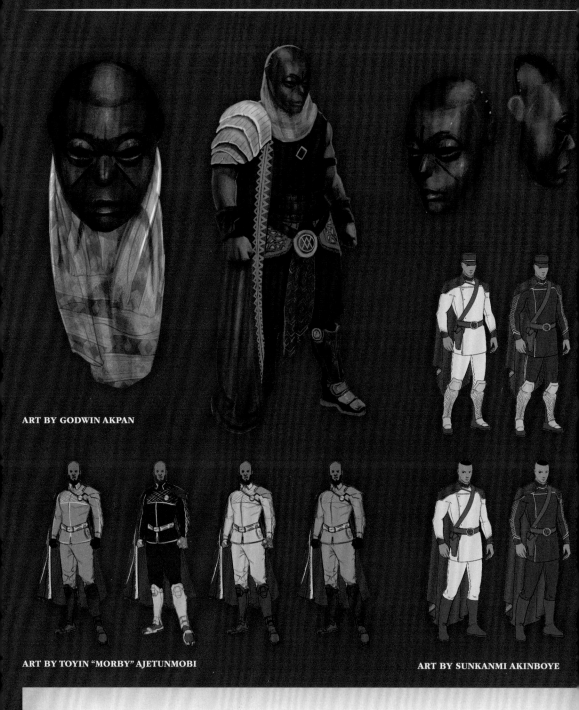

ART BY GODWIN AKPAN

ART BY TOYIN "MORBY" AJETUNMOBI

ART BY SUNKANMI AKINBOYE

Again, if you've followed the YouNeek YouNiverse closely in the previous series, you know that the Red Knights are the most elite warriors of the Red Raven army who served as the Royal Guard for King Bass (a.k.a. the Legendary WindMaker). So, when working on this book, knowing that this is the Republic of Atala now 500+ years removed from the Kingdom of Atala, I thought it would be cool to have the Red Knights of today be protectors of the sitting president.

It was a fun exercise updating their uniforms to the present day (Twenty-first Century) while paying homage to the past.

FUN FACT: The patterns on the cape pay homage to certain patterns you can find on Yoruba ceremonial attire (e.g. Agbada).

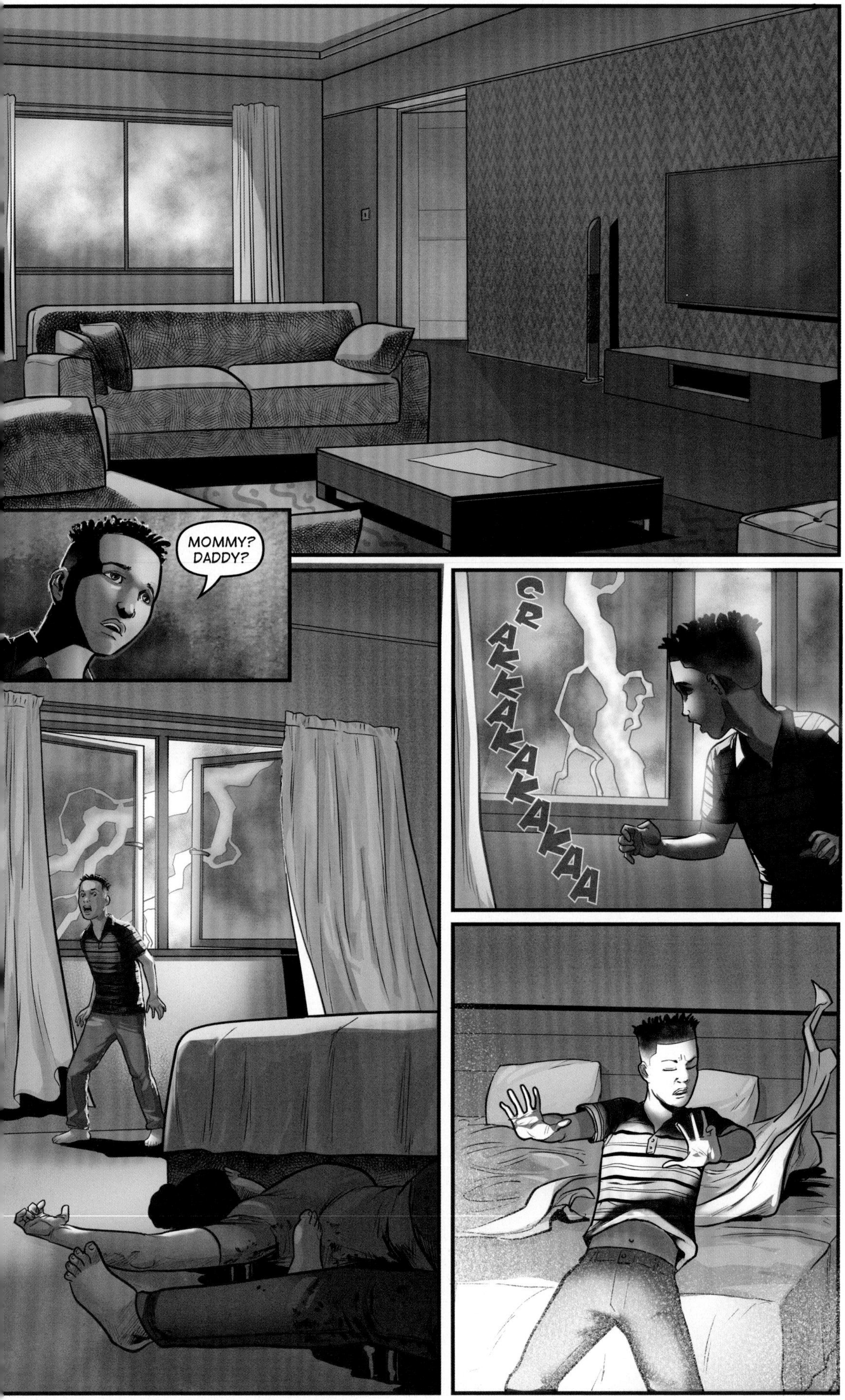
MOMMY?
DADDY?
CRAKAKAKAKAA

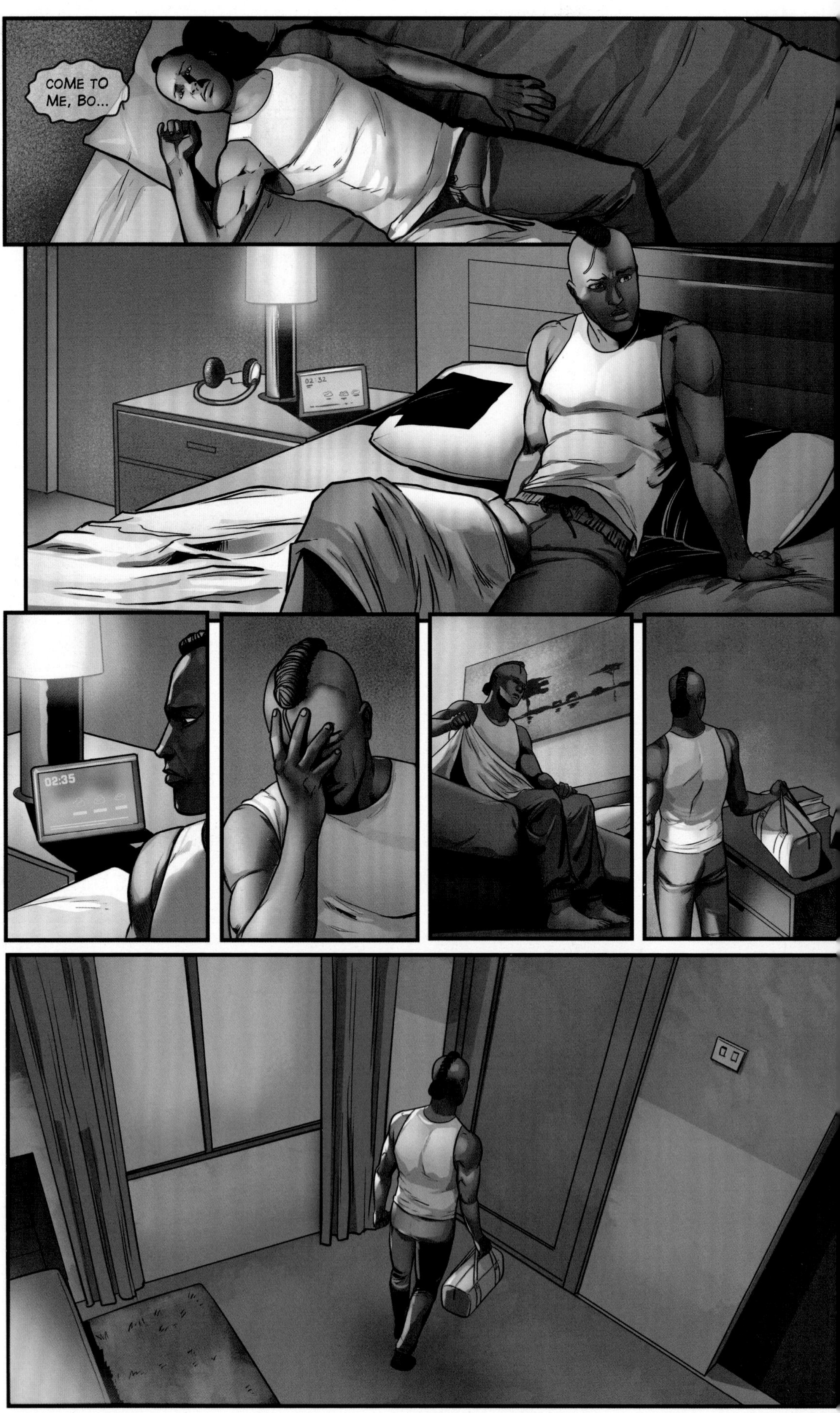
COME TO ME, BO...
02:35

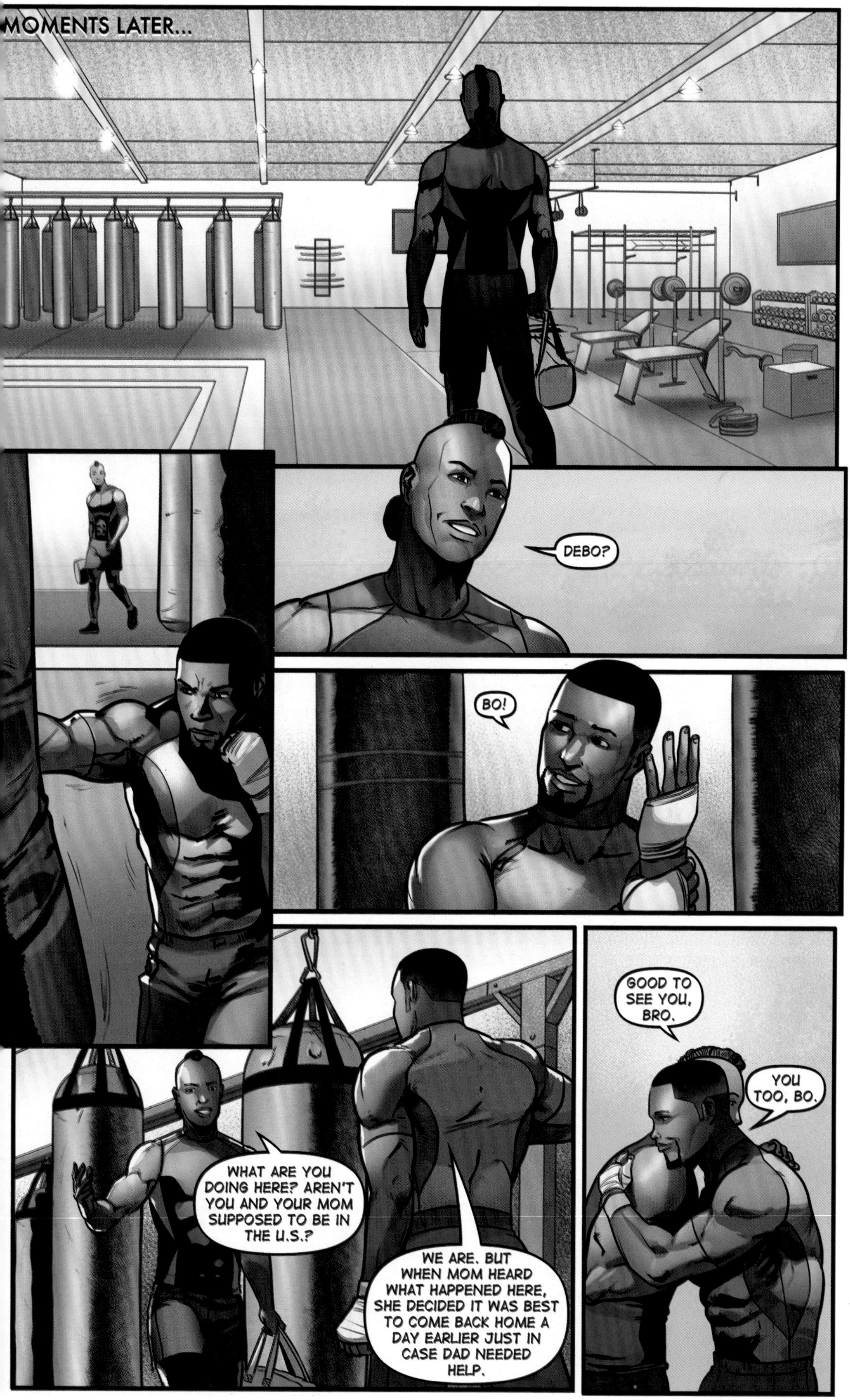
MOMENTS LATER...
DEBO?
BO!
WHAT ARE YOU DOING HERE? AREN'T YOU AND YOUR MOM SUPPOSED TO BE IN THE U.S.?
WE ARE. BUT WHEN MOM HEARD WHAT HAPPENED HERE, SHE DECIDED IT WAS BEST TO COME BACK HOME A DAY EARLIER JUST IN CASE DAD NEEDED HELP.
GOOD TO SEE YOU, BRO.
YOU TOO, BO.

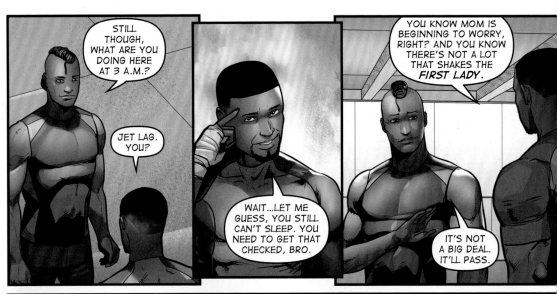

STILL THOUGH, WHAT ARE YOU DOING HERE AT 3 A.M.?

JET LAG. YOU?

WAIT...LET ME GUESS, YOU STILL CAN'T SLEEP. YOU NEED TO GET THAT CHECKED, BRO.

YOU KNOW MOM IS BEGINNING TO WORRY, RIGHT? AND YOU KNOW THERE'S NOT A LOT THAT SHAKES THE *FIRST LADY.*

IT'S NOT A BIG DEAL. IT'LL PASS.

BY THE WAY, CONGRATS ON THE NEW ROLE!

SMART. CHANGING THE TOPIC. AND YES. THANKS. IT'S TOO BAD THAT ALL PEOPLE CAN SEE IS *NEPOTISM* BY THE PRESIDENT.

PEOPLE WILL COME AROUND ONCE THEY SEE WHAT A GREAT JOB YOU'LL DO. YOU'VE WORKED HARD FOR THIS

SURE. NOW...LET'S FIX YOUR SLEEP ISSUES.

HOW?

REMEMBER THOSE INTENSE SPARRING SESSIONS MOM WOULD PUT US THROUGH RIGHT AFTER WEAPONS TRAINING AT THE ACADEMY?

YEAH...

DO YOU REMEMBER WHAT WE ALWAYS DID RIGHT AFTER?

HMPF SLEP

EXACTLY.

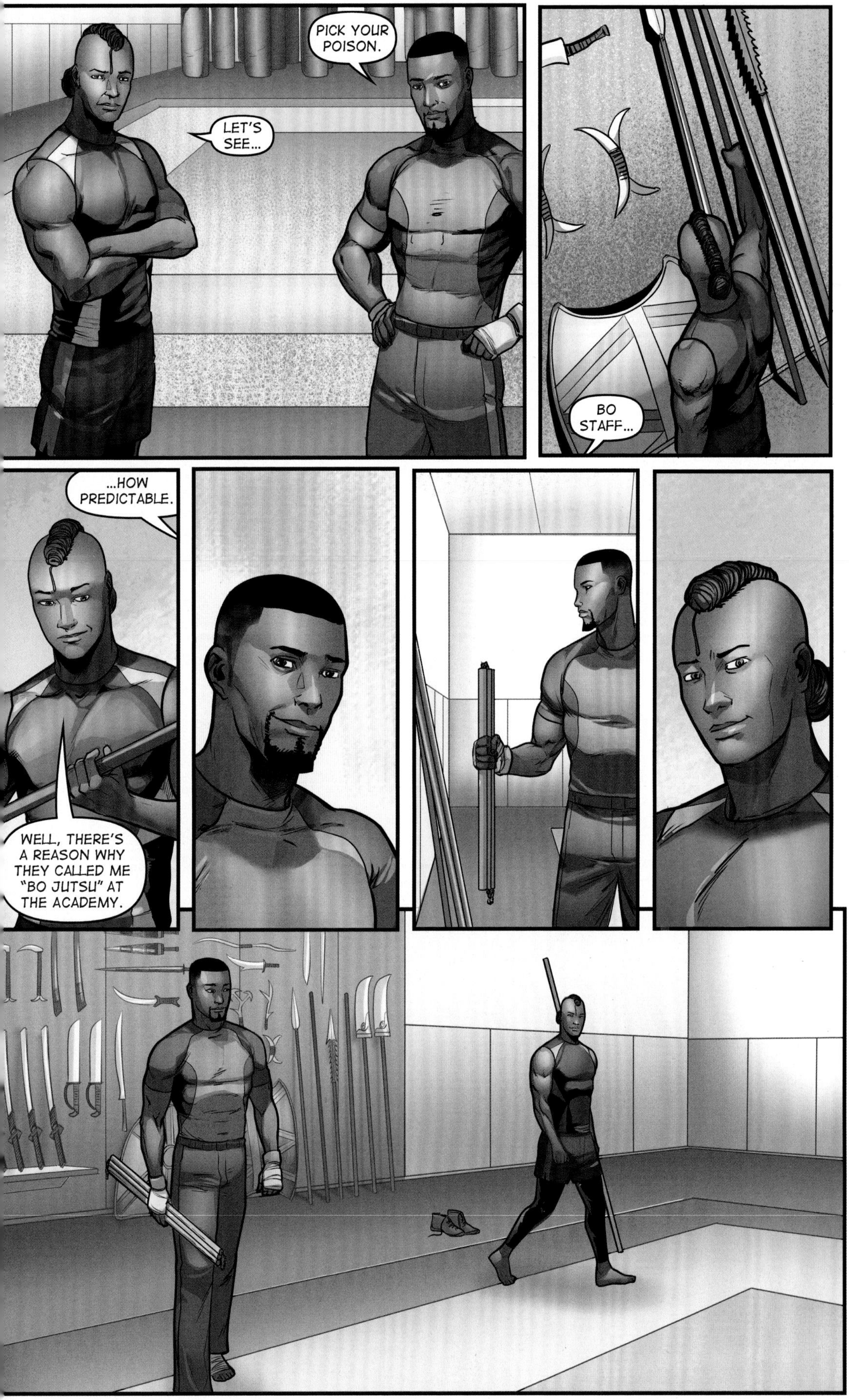
PICK YOUR POISON.
LET'S SEE...
BO STAFF...
...HOW PREDICTABLE.
WELL, THERE'S A REASON WHY THEY CALLED ME "BO JUTSU" AT THE ACADEMY.

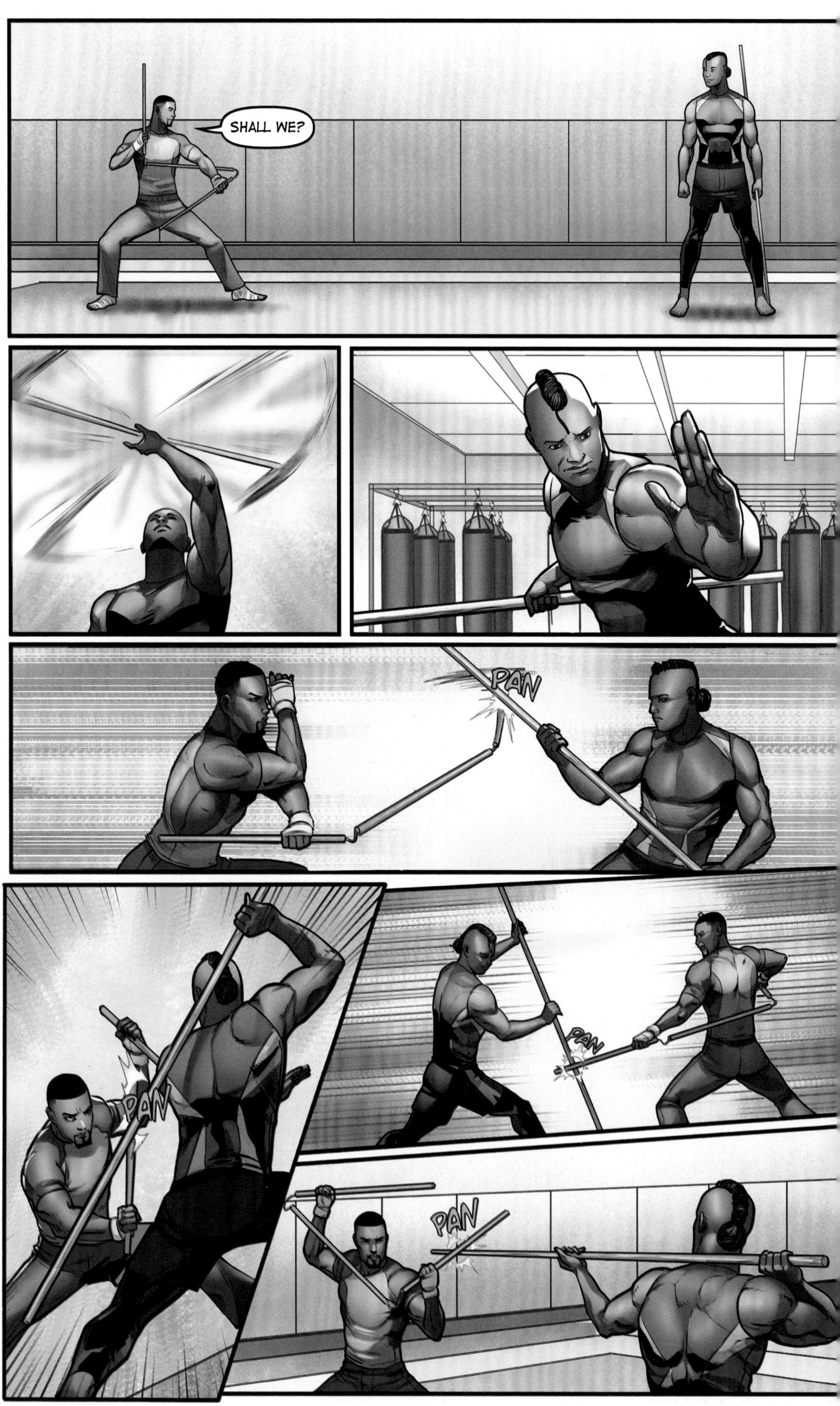
SHALL WE?
PAN
PAN
PAN
PAN

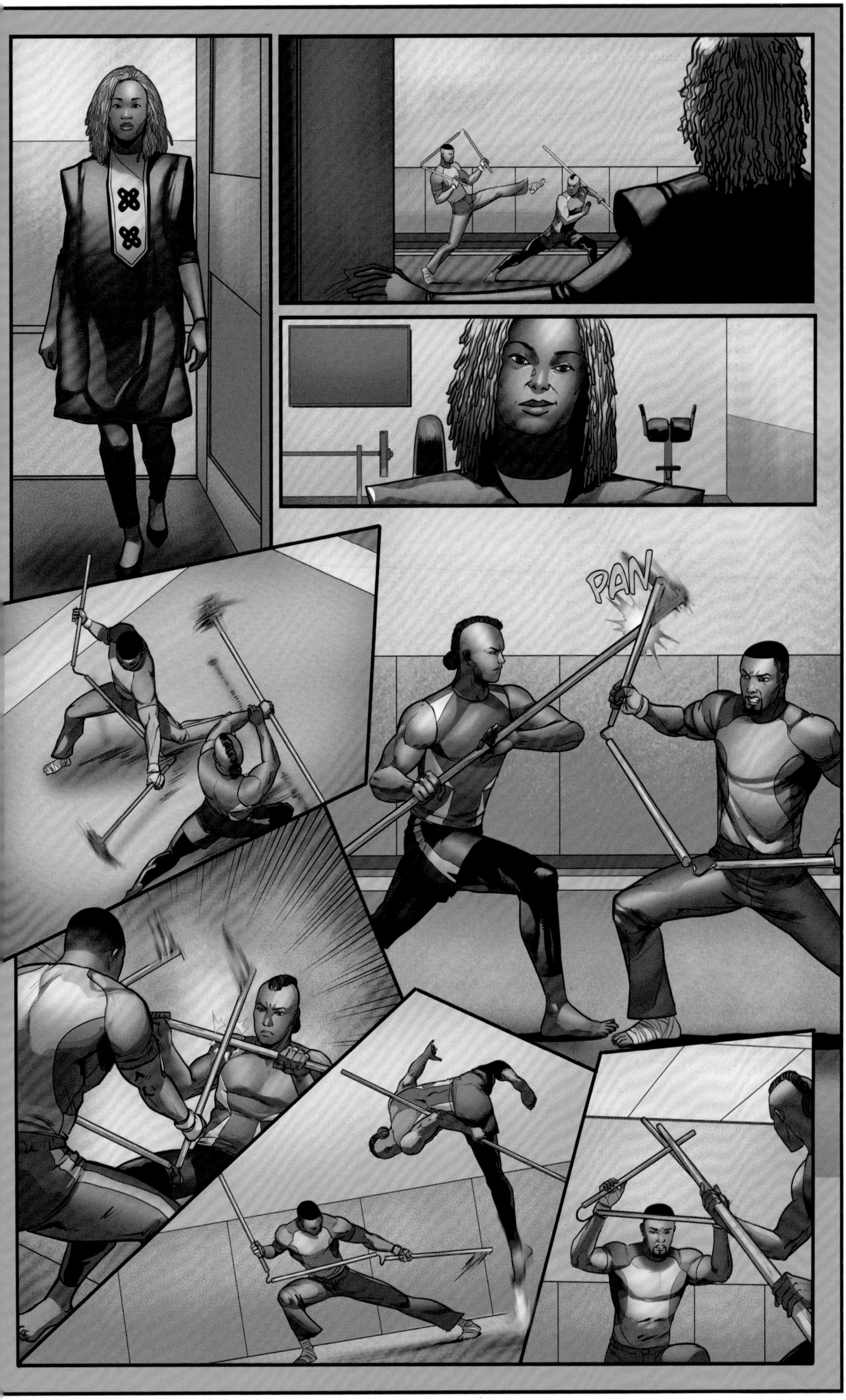
PAN

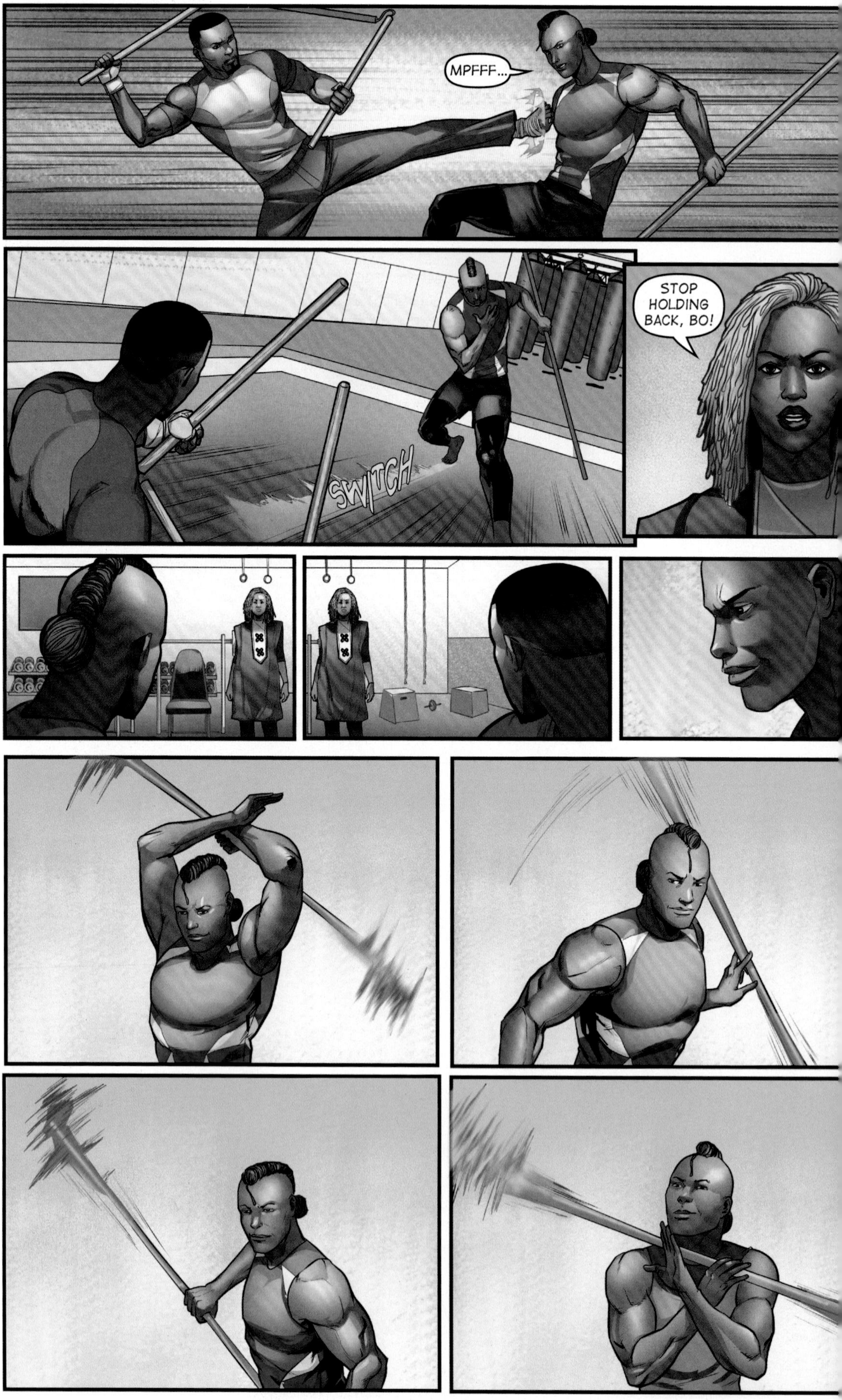
MPFFF...
SWITCH
STOP HOLDING BACK, BO!

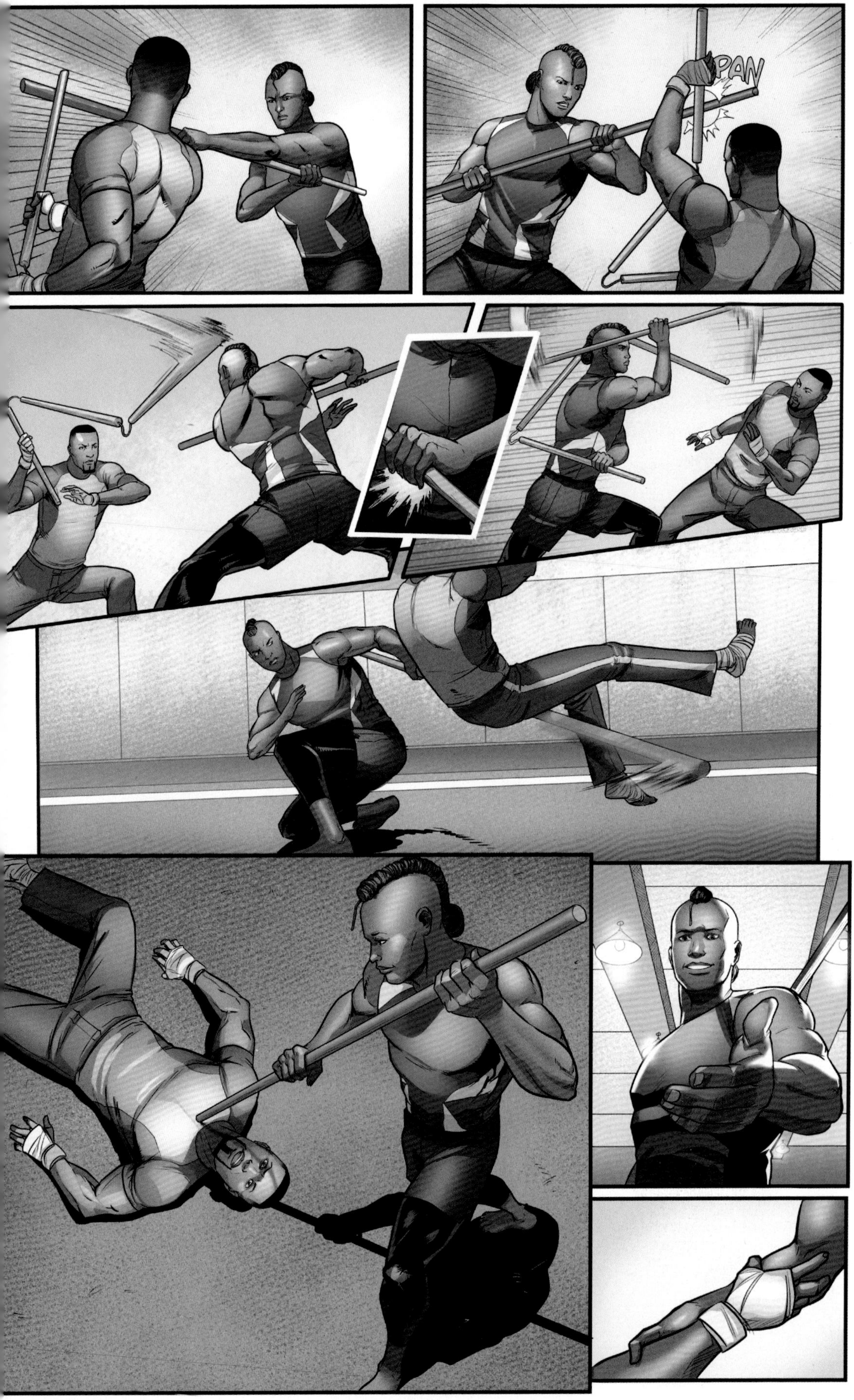
PAN

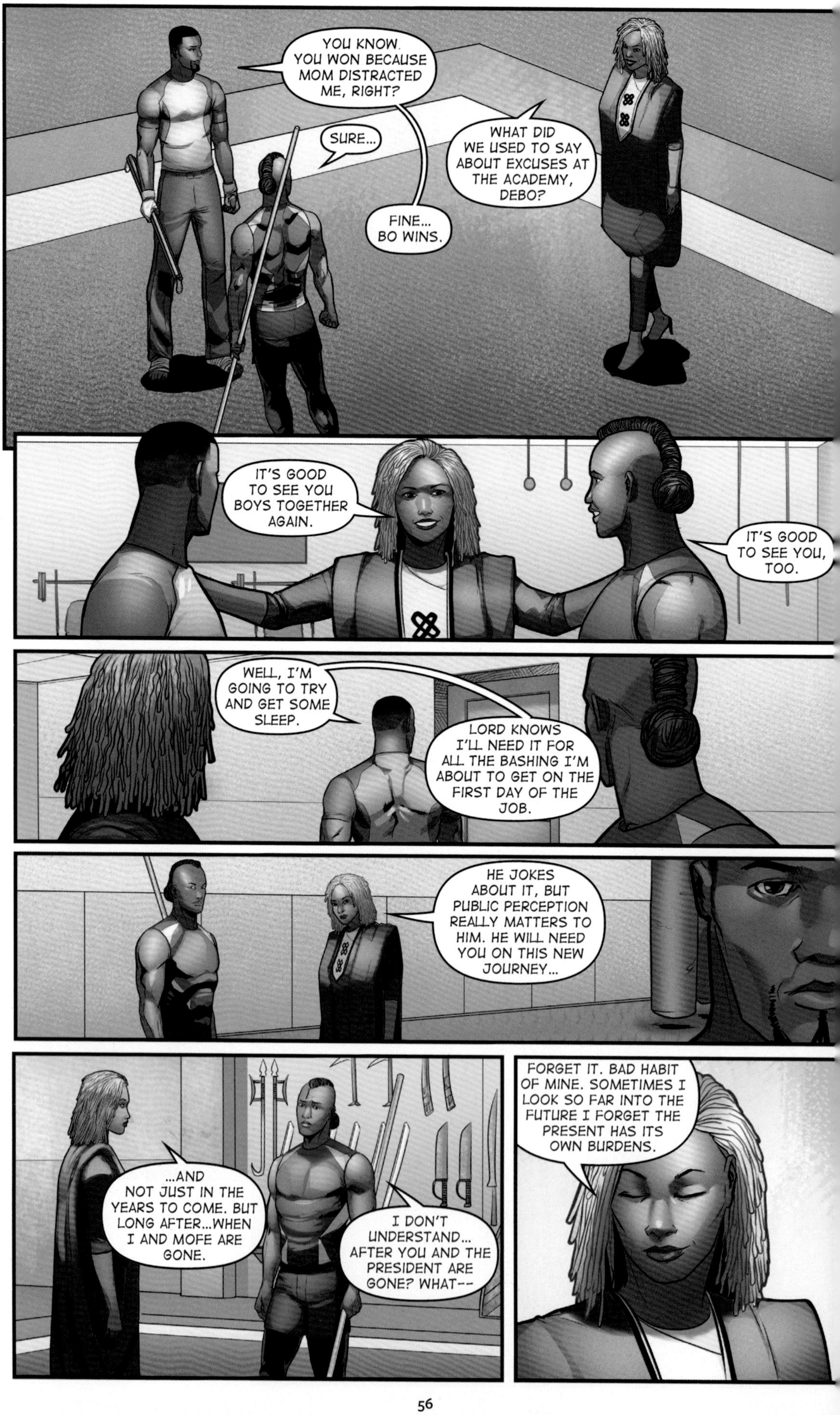
YOU KNOW. YOU WON BECAUSE MOM DISTRACTED ME, RIGHT?
SURE...
FINE... BO WINS.
WHAT DID WE USED TO SAY ABOUT EXCUSES AT THE ACADEMY, DEBO?
IT'S GOOD TO SEE YOU BOYS TOGETHER AGAIN.
IT'S GOOD TO SEE YOU, TOO.
WELL, I'M GOING TO TRY AND GET SOME SLEEP.
LORD KNOWS I'LL NEED IT FOR ALL THE BASHING I'M ABOUT TO GET ON THE FIRST DAY OF THE JOB.
HE JOKES ABOUT IT, BUT PUBLIC PERCEPTION REALLY MATTERS TO HIM. HE WILL NEED YOU ON THIS NEW JOURNEY...
...AND NOT JUST IN THE YEARS TO COME. BUT LONG AFTER...WHEN I AND MOFE ARE GONE.
I DON'T UNDERSTAND... AFTER YOU AND THE PRESIDENT ARE GONE? WHAT--
FORGET IT. BAD HABIT OF MINE. SOMETIMES I LOOK SO FAR INTO THE FUTURE I FORGET THE PRESENT HAS ITS OWN BURDENS.

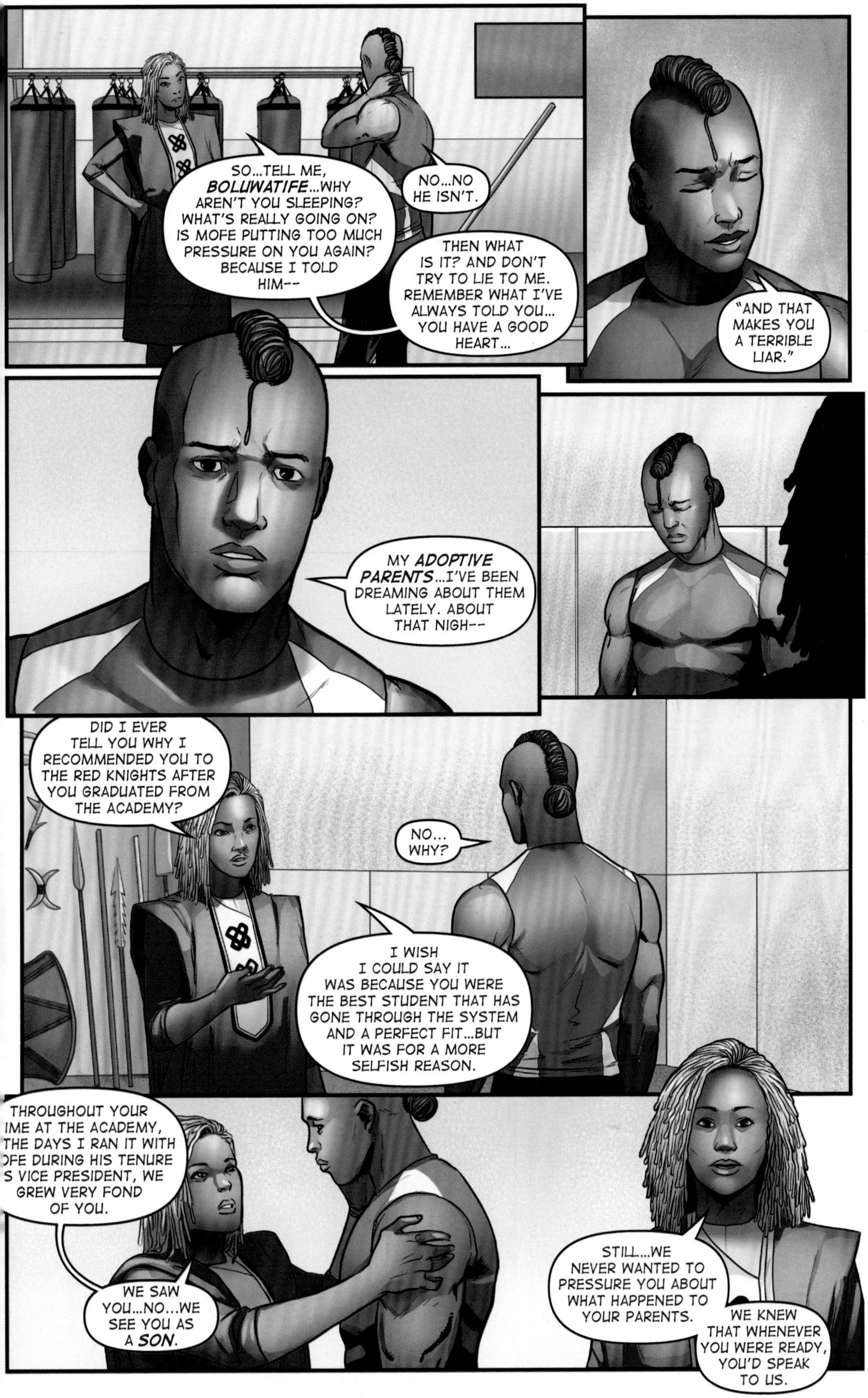
SO...TELL ME, BOLUWATIFE...WHY AREN'T YOU SLEEPING? WHAT'S REALLY GOING ON? IS MOFE PUTTING TOO MUCH PRESSURE ON YOU AGAIN? BECAUSE I TOLD HIM--
NO...NO HE ISN'T.
THEN WHAT IS IT? AND DON'T TRY TO LIE TO ME. REMEMBER WHAT I'VE ALWAYS TOLD YOU... YOU HAVE A GOOD HEART...
"AND THAT MAKES YOU A TERRIBLE LIAR."
MY ADOPTIVE PARENTS...I'VE BEEN DREAMING ABOUT THEM LATELY. ABOUT THAT NIGH--
DID I EVER TELL YOU WHY I RECOMMENDED YOU TO THE RED KNIGHTS AFTER YOU GRADUATED FROM THE ACADEMY?
NO... WHY?
I WISH I COULD SAY IT WAS BECAUSE YOU WERE THE BEST STUDENT THAT HAS GONE THROUGH THE SYSTEM AND A PERFECT FIT...BUT IT WAS FOR A MORE SELFISH REASON.
THROUGHOUT YOUR IME AT THE ACADEMY, THE DAYS I RAN IT WITH OFE DURING HIS TENURE S VICE PRESIDENT, WE GREW VERY FOND OF YOU.
WE SAW YOU...NO...WE SEE YOU AS A SON.
STILL...WE NEVER WANTED TO PRESSURE YOU ABOUT WHAT HAPPENED TO YOUR PARENTS.
WE KNEW THAT WHENEVER YOU WERE READY, YOU'D SPEAK TO US.

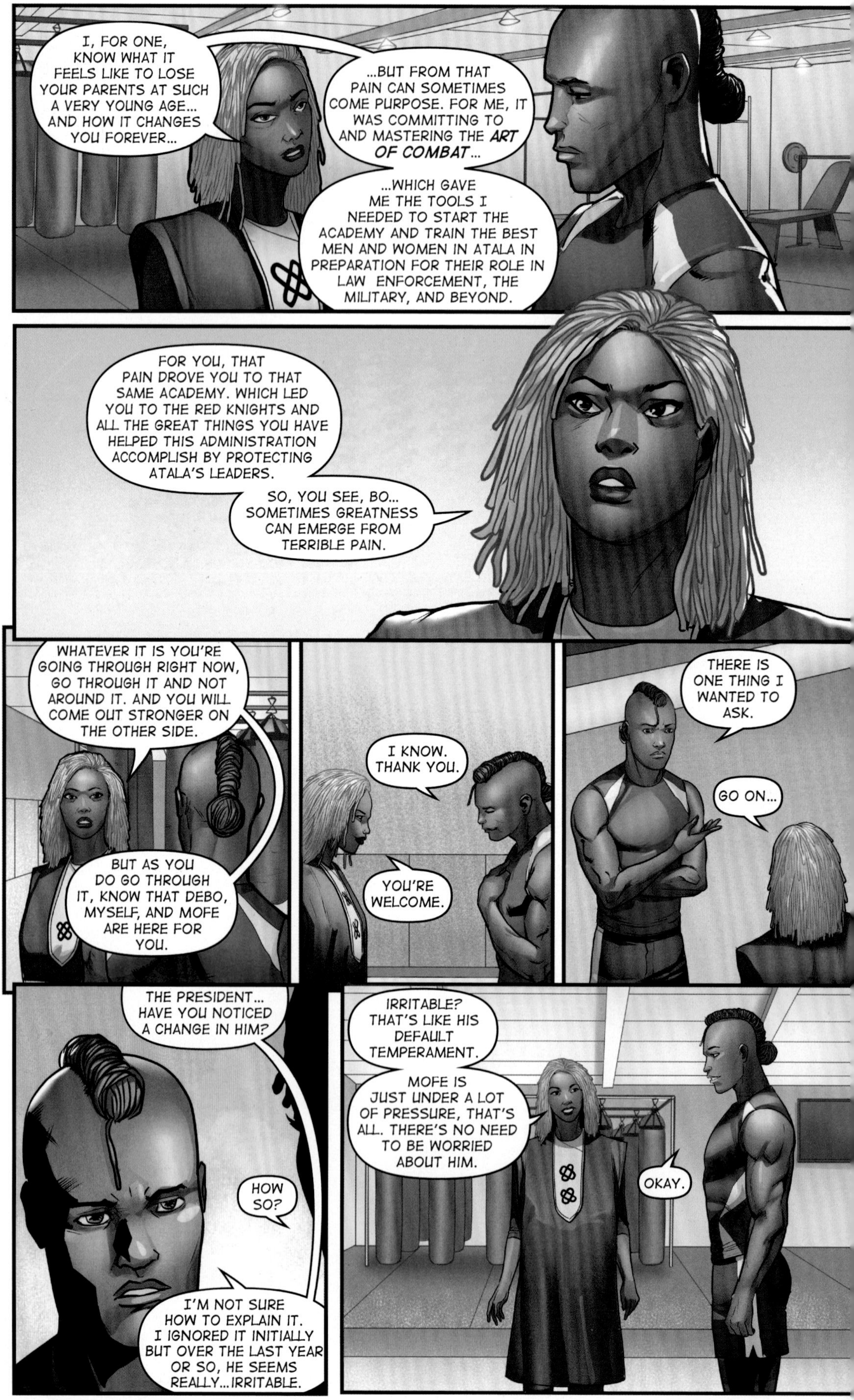
I, FOR ONE, KNOW WHAT IT FEELS LIKE TO LOSE YOUR PARENTS AT SUCH A VERY YOUNG AGE... AND HOW IT CHANGES YOU FOREVER...
...BUT FROM THAT PAIN CAN SOMETIMES COME PURPOSE. FOR ME, IT WAS COMMITTING TO AND MASTERING THE *ART OF COMBAT*...
...WHICH GAVE ME THE TOOLS I NEEDED TO START THE ACADEMY AND TRAIN THE BEST MEN AND WOMEN IN ATALA IN PREPARATION FOR THEIR ROLE IN LAW ENFORCEMENT, THE MILITARY, AND BEYOND.
FOR YOU, THAT PAIN DROVE YOU TO THAT SAME ACADEMY. WHICH LED YOU TO THE RED KNIGHTS AND ALL THE GREAT THINGS YOU HAVE HELPED THIS ADMINISTRATION ACCOMPLISH BY PROTECTING ATALA'S LEADERS.
SO, YOU SEE, BO... SOMETIMES GREATNESS CAN EMERGE FROM TERRIBLE PAIN.
WHATEVER IT IS YOU'RE GOING THROUGH RIGHT NOW, GO THROUGH IT AND NOT AROUND IT. AND YOU WILL COME OUT STRONGER ON THE OTHER SIDE.
BUT AS YOU DO GO THROUGH IT, KNOW THAT DEBO, MYSELF, AND MOFE ARE HERE FOR YOU.
I KNOW. THANK YOU.
YOU'RE WELCOME.
THERE IS ONE THING I WANTED TO ASK.
GO ON...
THE PRESIDENT... HAVE YOU NOTICED A CHANGE IN HIM?
HOW SO?
I'M NOT SURE HOW TO EXPLAIN IT. I IGNORED IT INITIALLY BUT OVER THE LAST YEAR OR SO, HE SEEMS REALLY...IRRITABLE.
IRRITABLE? THAT'S LIKE HIS DEFAULT TEMPERAMENT.
MOFE IS JUST UNDER A LOT OF PRESSURE, THAT'S ALL. THERE'S NO NEED TO BE WORRIED ABOUT HIM.
OKAY.

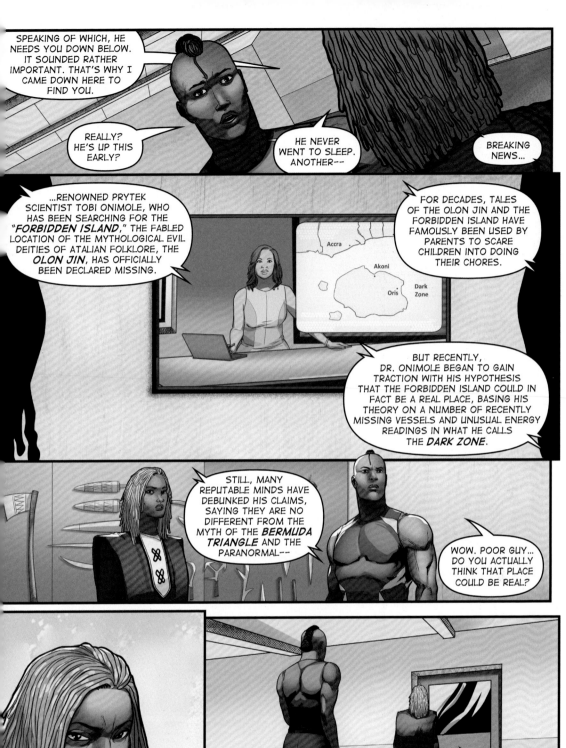

SPEAKING OF WHICH, HE NEEDS YOU DOWN BELOW. IT SOUNDED RATHER IMPORTANT. THAT'S WHY I CAME DOWN HERE TO FIND YOU.

REALLY? HE'S UP THIS EARLY?

HE NEVER WENT TO SLEEP. ANOTHER--

BREAKING NEWS...

...RENOWNED PRYTEK SCIENTIST TOBI ONIMOLE, WHO HAS BEEN SEARCHING FOR THE "*FORBIDDEN ISLAND*," THE FABLED LOCATION OF THE MYTHOLOGICAL EVIL DEITIES OF ATALIAN FOLKLORE, THE *OLON JIN*, HAS OFFICIALLY BEEN DECLARED MISSING.

Accra

Akoni

Oris

Dark Zone

FOR DECADES, TALES OF THE OLON JIN AND THE FORBIDDEN ISLAND HAVE FAMOUSLY BEEN USED BY PARENTS TO SCARE CHILDREN INTO DOING THEIR CHORES.

BUT RECENTLY, DR. ONIMOLE BEGAN TO GAIN TRACTION WITH HIS HYPOTHESIS THAT THE FORBIDDEN ISLAND COULD IN FACT BE A REAL PLACE, BASING HIS THEORY ON A NUMBER OF RECENTLY MISSING VESSELS AND UNUSUAL ENERGY READINGS IN WHAT HE CALLS THE *DARK ZONE*.

STILL, MANY REPUTABLE MINDS HAVE DEBUNKED HIS CLAIMS, SAYING THEY ARE NO DIFFERENT FROM THE MYTH OF THE *BERMUDA TRIANGLE* AND THE PARANORMAL--

WOW. POOR GUY... DO YOU ACTUALLY THINK THAT PLACE COULD BE REAL?

ATALIANS GENERALLY CAN'T SEEM TO DIFFERENTIATE BETWEEN WHAT IS MYTH AND WHAT IS HISTORY SO...WHO KNOWS.

I WILL SAY THAT ONE SHOULD NOT VENTURE INTO PLACES UNKNOWN TO INVESTIGATE THINGS THAT DO NOT CONCERN US MORTALS.

COME NOW. YOU SHOULDN'T KEEP THE PRESIDENT WAITING.

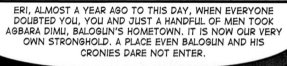

ERI, ALMOST A YEAR AGO TO THIS DAY, WHEN EVERYONE DOUBTED YOU, YOU AND JUST A HANDFUL OF MEN TOOK AGBARA DIMU, BALOGUN'S HOMETOWN. IT IS NOW OUR VERY OWN STRONGHOLD. A PLACE EVEN BALOGUN AND HIS CRONIES DARE NOT ENTER.

SINCE THEN, THE RGA HAS GROWN TEN TIMES IN SIZE. WE GOT TO THIS POINT BECAUSE OF BOLD MOVES, NOT DIPLOMACY. THE PRESIDENT THREW THAT OPTION OUT THE WINDOW WHEN HE DECIDED TO BECOME *A DICTATOR*.

I KNOW YOU THINK YOU KNOW THIS MAN. I GET IT, YOU TWO WERE LIKE BROTHERS IN THE ARMY.

BUT EVEN YOU CANNOT DENY THAT IN THE LAST FOUR YEARS THIS MAN HAS BECOME NOTHING BUT A PSYCHOTIC NIGHTMARE!

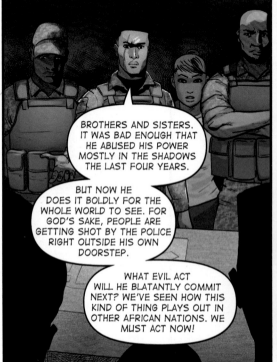

BROTHERS AND SISTERS. IT WAS BAD ENOUGH THAT HE ABUSED HIS POWER MOSTLY IN THE SHADOWS THE LAST FOUR YEARS.

BUT NOW HE DOES IT BOLDLY FOR THE WHOLE WORLD TO SEE. FOR GOD'S SAKE, PEOPLE ARE GETTING SHOT BY THE POLICE RIGHT OUTSIDE HIS OWN DOORSTEP.

WHAT EVIL ACT WILL HE BLATANTLY COMMIT NEXT? WE'VE SEEN HOW THIS KIND OF THING PLAYS OUT IN OTHER AFRICAN NATIONS. WE MUST ACT NOW!

HE HAS A POINT, ERI.

AND I DO NOT DOUBT THAT. IT IS WHAT HE SUGGESTS WE DO NEXT I CANNOT AGREE TO.

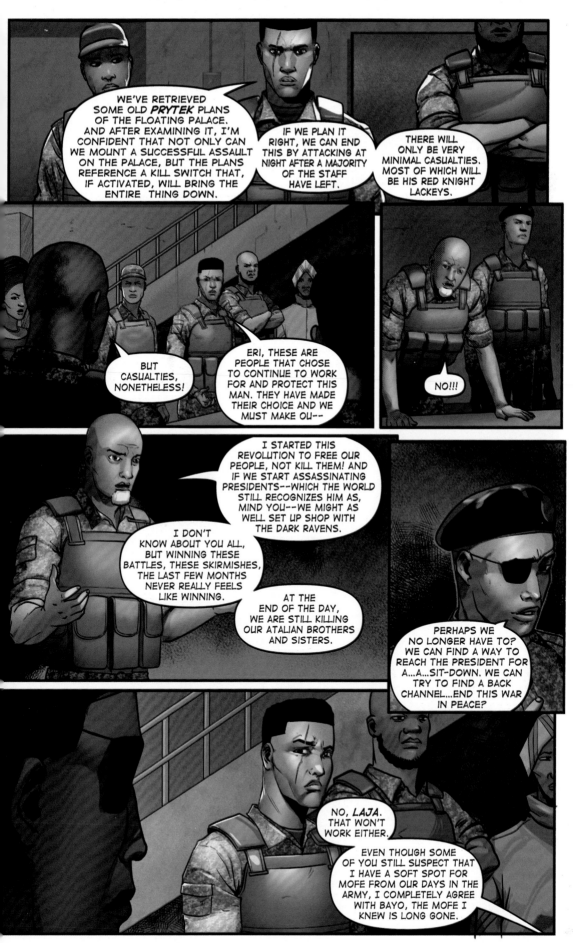

WE'VE RETRIEVED SOME OLD *PRYTEK* PLANS OF THE FLOATING PALACE. AND AFTER EXAMINING IT, I'M CONFIDENT THAT NOT ONLY CAN WE MOUNT A SUCCESSFUL ASSAULT ON THE PALACE, BUT THE PLANS REFERENCE A KILL SWITCH THAT, IF ACTIVATED, WILL BRING THE ENTIRE THING DOWN.

IF WE PLAN IT RIGHT, WE CAN END THIS BY ATTACKING AT NIGHT AFTER A MAJORITY OF THE STAFF HAVE LEFT.

THERE WILL ONLY BE VERY MINIMAL CASUALTIES. MOST OF WHICH WILL BE HIS RED KNIGHT LACKEYS.

BUT CASUALTIES, NONETHELESS!

ERI, THESE ARE PEOPLE THAT CHOSE TO CONTINUE TO WORK FOR AND PROTECT THIS MAN. THEY HAVE MADE THEIR CHOICE AND WE MUST MAKE OU--

NO!!!

I STARTED THIS REVOLUTION TO FREE OUR PEOPLE, NOT KILL THEM! AND IF WE START ASSASSINATING PRESIDENTS--WHICH THE WORLD STILL RECOGNIZES HIM AS, MIND YOU--WE MIGHT AS WELL SET UP SHOP WITH THE DARK RAVENS.

I DON'T KNOW ABOUT YOU ALL, BUT WINNING THESE BATTLES, THESE SKIRMISHES, THE LAST FEW MONTHS NEVER REALLY FEELS LIKE WINNING.

AT THE END OF THE DAY, WE ARE STILL KILLING OUR ATALIAN BROTHERS AND SISTERS.

PERHAPS WE NO LONGER HAVE TO? WE CAN FIND A WAY TO REACH THE PRESIDENT FOR A...A...SIT-DOWN. WE CAN TRY TO FIND A BACK CHANNEL....END THIS WAR IN PEACE?

NO, *LAJA*. THAT WON'T WORK EITHER.

EVEN THOUGH SOME OF YOU STILL SUSPECT THAT I HAVE A SOFT SPOT FOR MOFE FROM OUR DAYS IN THE ARMY, I COMPLETELY AGREE WITH BAYO, THE MOFE I KNEW IS LONG GONE.

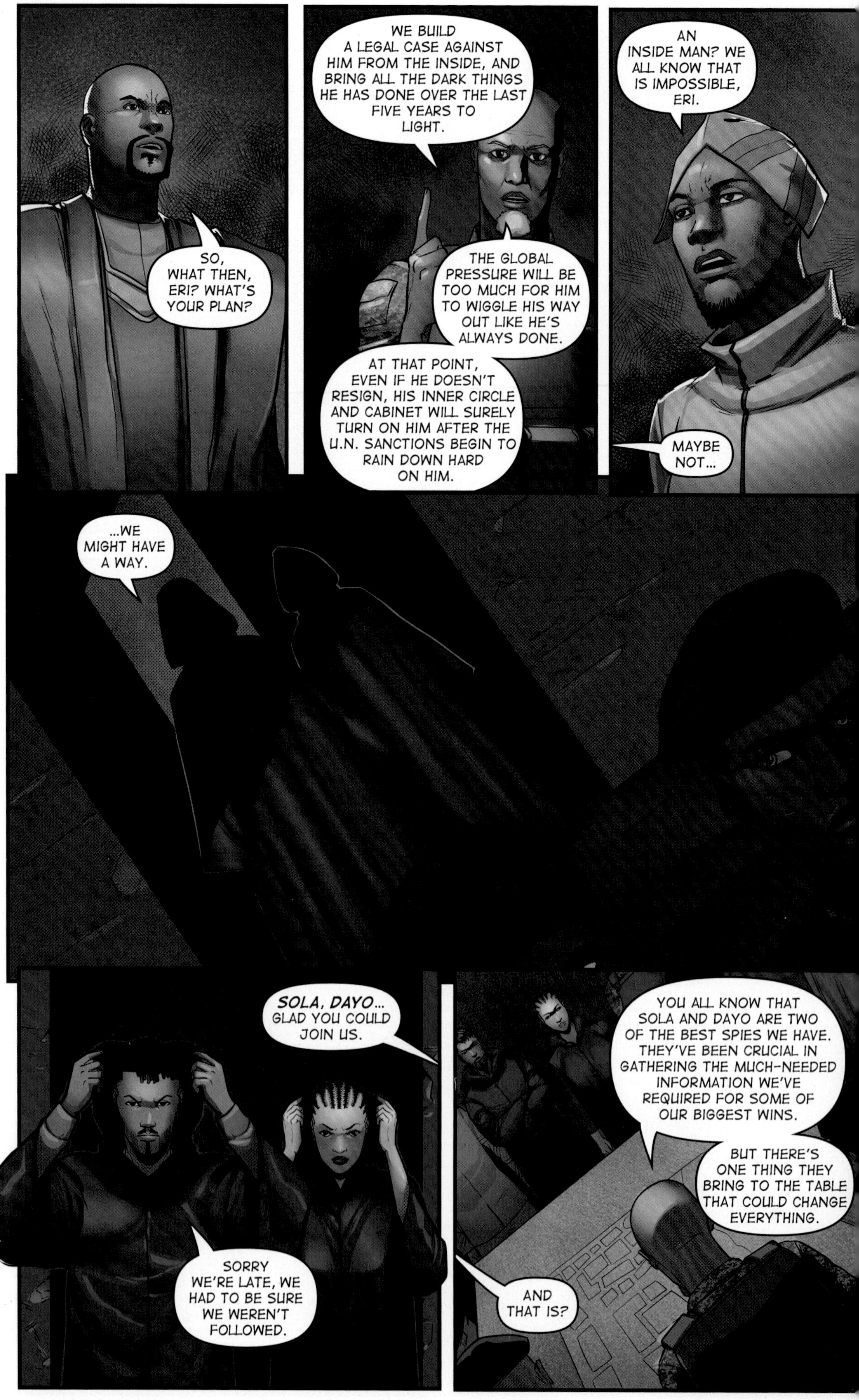
SO, WHAT THEN, ERI? WHAT'S YOUR PLAN?
WE BUILD A LEGAL CASE AGAINST HIM FROM THE INSIDE, AND BRING ALL THE DARK THINGS HE HAS DONE OVER THE LAST FIVE YEARS TO LIGHT.
THE GLOBAL PRESSURE WILL BE TOO MUCH FOR HIM TO WIGGLE HIS WAY OUT LIKE HE'S ALWAYS DONE.
AT THAT POINT, EVEN IF HE DOESN'T RESIGN, HIS INNER CIRCLE AND CABINET WILL SURELY TURN ON HIM AFTER THE U.N. SANCTIONS BEGIN TO RAIN DOWN HARD ON HIM.
AN INSIDE MAN? WE ALL KNOW THAT IS IMPOSSIBLE, ERI.
MAYBE NOT...
...WE MIGHT HAVE A WAY.
SOLA, DAYO... GLAD YOU COULD JOIN US.
SORRY WE'RE LATE, WE HAD TO BE SURE WE WEREN'T FOLLOWED.
YOU ALL KNOW THAT SOLA AND DAYO ARE TWO OF THE BEST SPIES WE HAVE. THEY'VE BEEN CRUCIAL IN GATHERING THE MUCH-NEEDED INFORMATION WE'VE REQUIRED FOR SOME OF OUR BIGGEST WINS.
BUT THERE'S ONE THING THEY BRING TO THE TABLE THAT COULD CHANGE EVERYTHING.
AND THAT IS?

A RELATIONSHIP WITH BO ABIOLA.

THE DIRECTOR OF THE RED KNIGHTS?

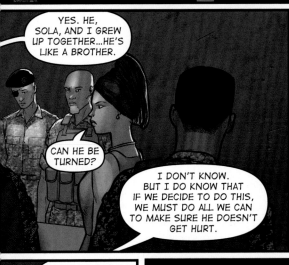

YES. HE, SOLA, AND I GREW UP TOGETHER...HE'S LIKE A BROTHER.

CAN HE BE TURNED?

I DON'T KNOW. BUT I DO KNOW THAT IF WE DECIDE TO DO THIS, WE MUST DO ALL WE CAN TO MAKE SURE HE DOESN'T GET HURT.

ARE YOU OKAY, LAJA?

BAYO! AH...YES...

WE WILL.

I WAS JUST...I WAS JUST TRYING TO TAKE IT ALL IN.

I NEED SOME AIR.

THE PROBLEM IS BO IS LOYAL TO A FAULT. IT'S JUST WHO HE IS.

I FEAR THAT HE'LL CONTINUE TO BE COMPLETELY BLIND TO ALL THE TERRIBLE THINGS BALOGUN DOES. I DON'T SEE HOW WE CAN TURN HIM.

SWSSHHH

PERHAPS THIS CAN HELP...

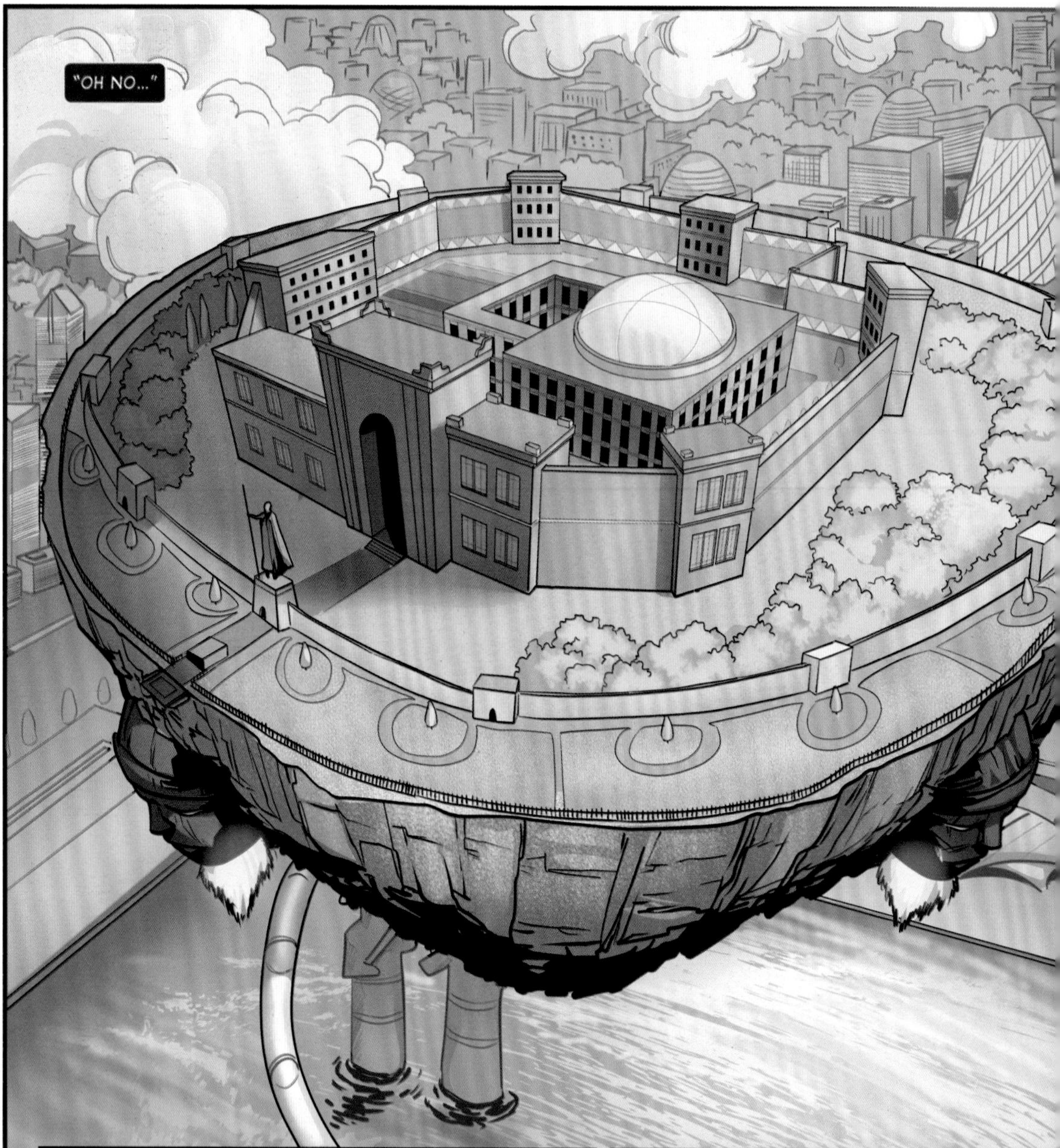
"OH NO..."

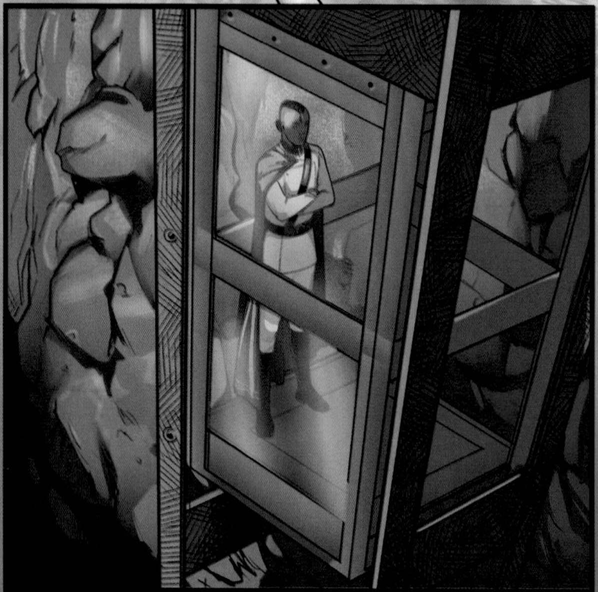

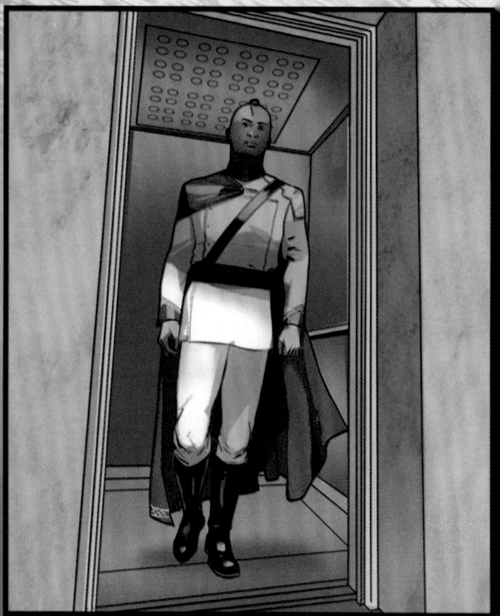

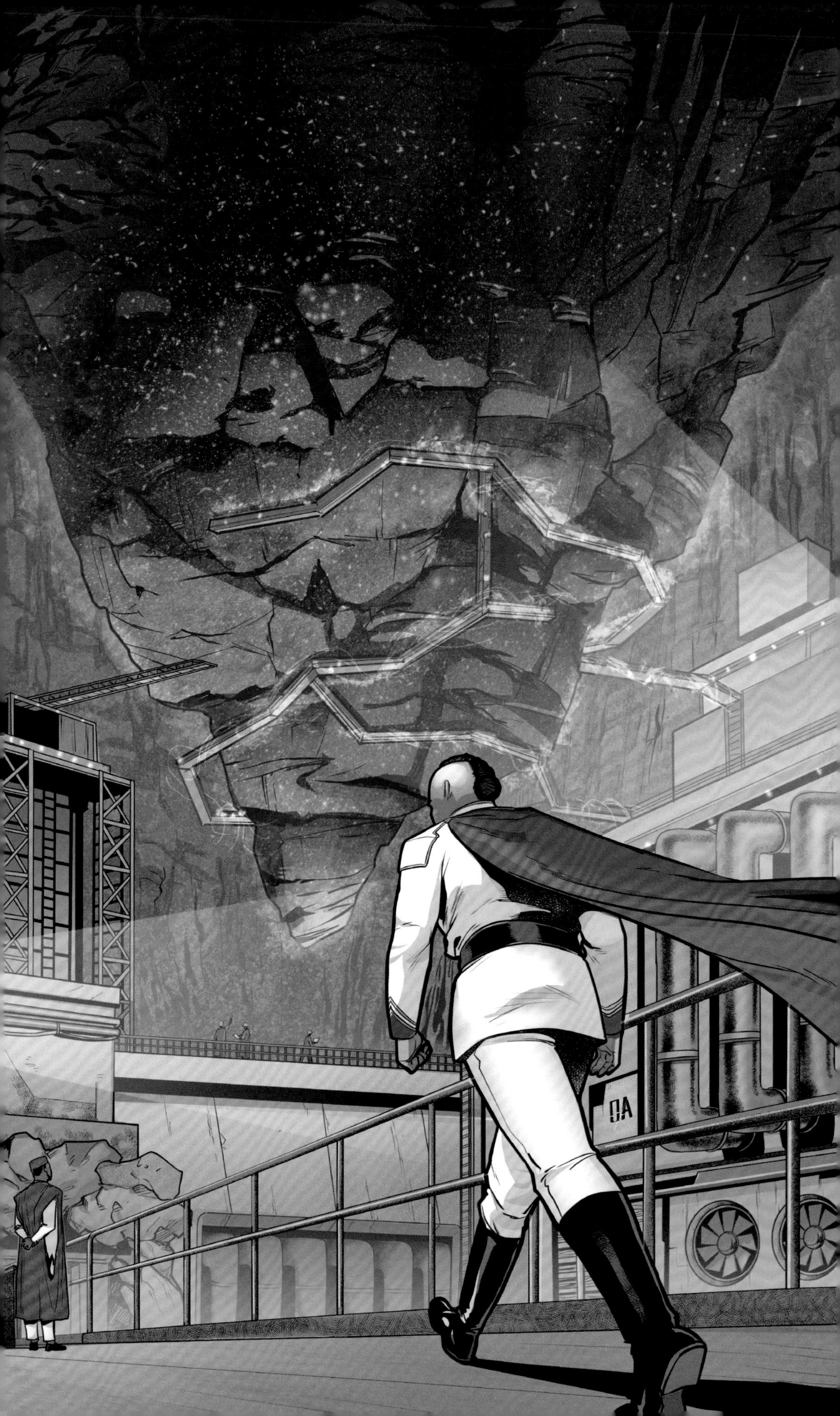
OA

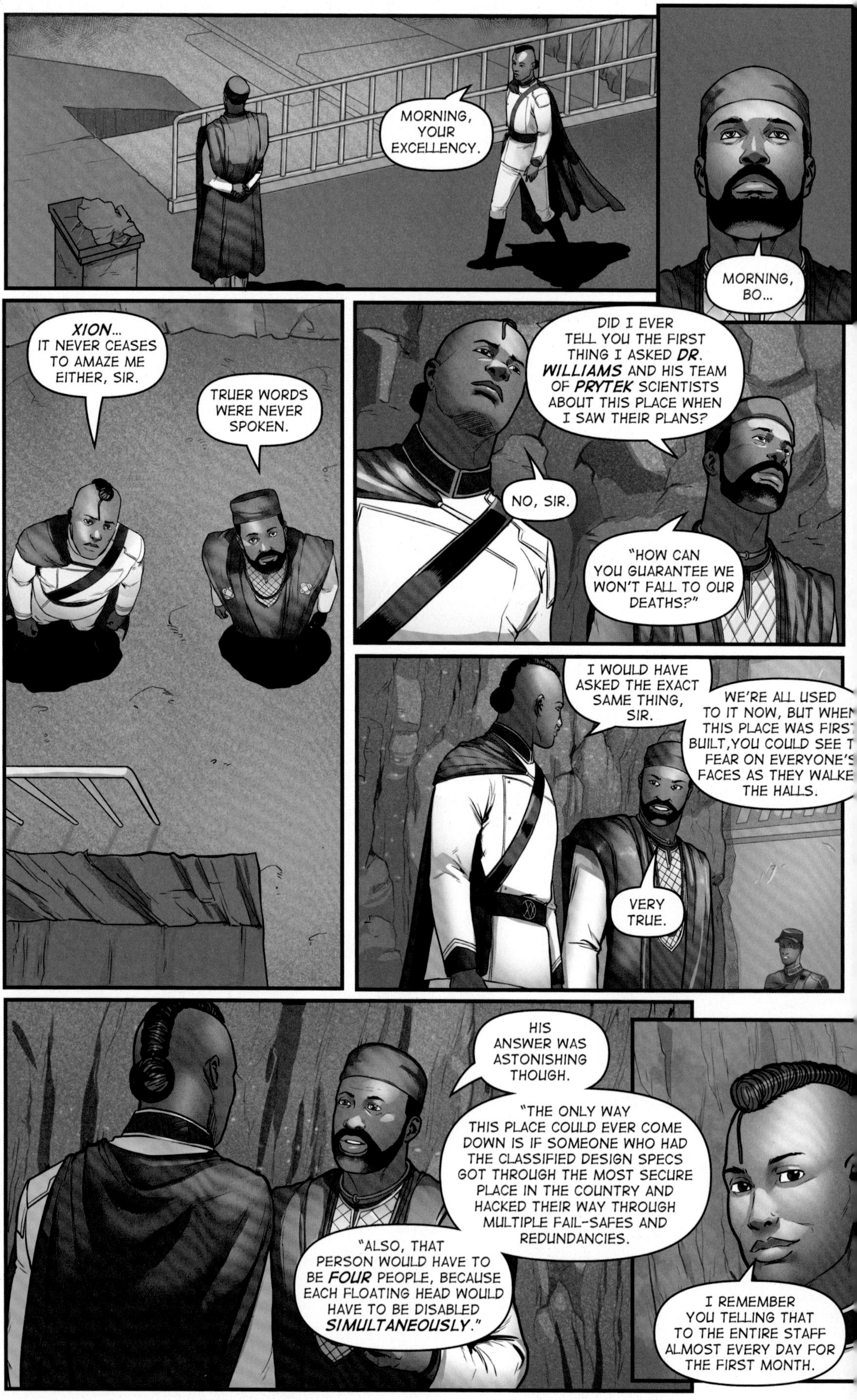
MORNING, YOUR EXCELLENCY.
MORNING, BO...
XION... IT NEVER CEASES TO AMAZE ME EITHER, SIR.
TRUER WORDS WERE NEVER SPOKEN.
DID I EVER TELL YOU THE FIRST THING I ASKED DR. WILLIAMS AND HIS TEAM OF PRYTEK SCIENTISTS ABOUT THIS PLACE WHEN I SAW THEIR PLANS?
NO, SIR.
"HOW CAN YOU GUARANTEE WE WON'T FALL TO OUR DEATHS?"
I WOULD HAVE ASKED THE EXACT SAME THING, SIR.
VERY TRUE.
HIS ANSWER WAS ASTONISHING THOUGH.
"THE ONLY WAY THIS PLACE COULD EVER COME DOWN IS IF SOMEONE WHO HAD THE CLASSIFIED DESIGN SPECS GOT THROUGH THE MOST SECURE PLACE IN THE COUNTRY AND HACKED THEIR WAY THROUGH MULTIPLE FAIL-SAFES AND REDUNDANCIES.
"ALSO, THAT PERSON WOULD HAVE TO BE FOUR PEOPLE, BECAUSE EACH FLOATING HEAD WOULD HAVE TO BE DISABLED SIMULTANEOUSLY."
I REMEMBER YOU TELLING THAT TO THE ENTIRE STAFF ALMOST EVERY DAY FOR THE FIRST MONTH.

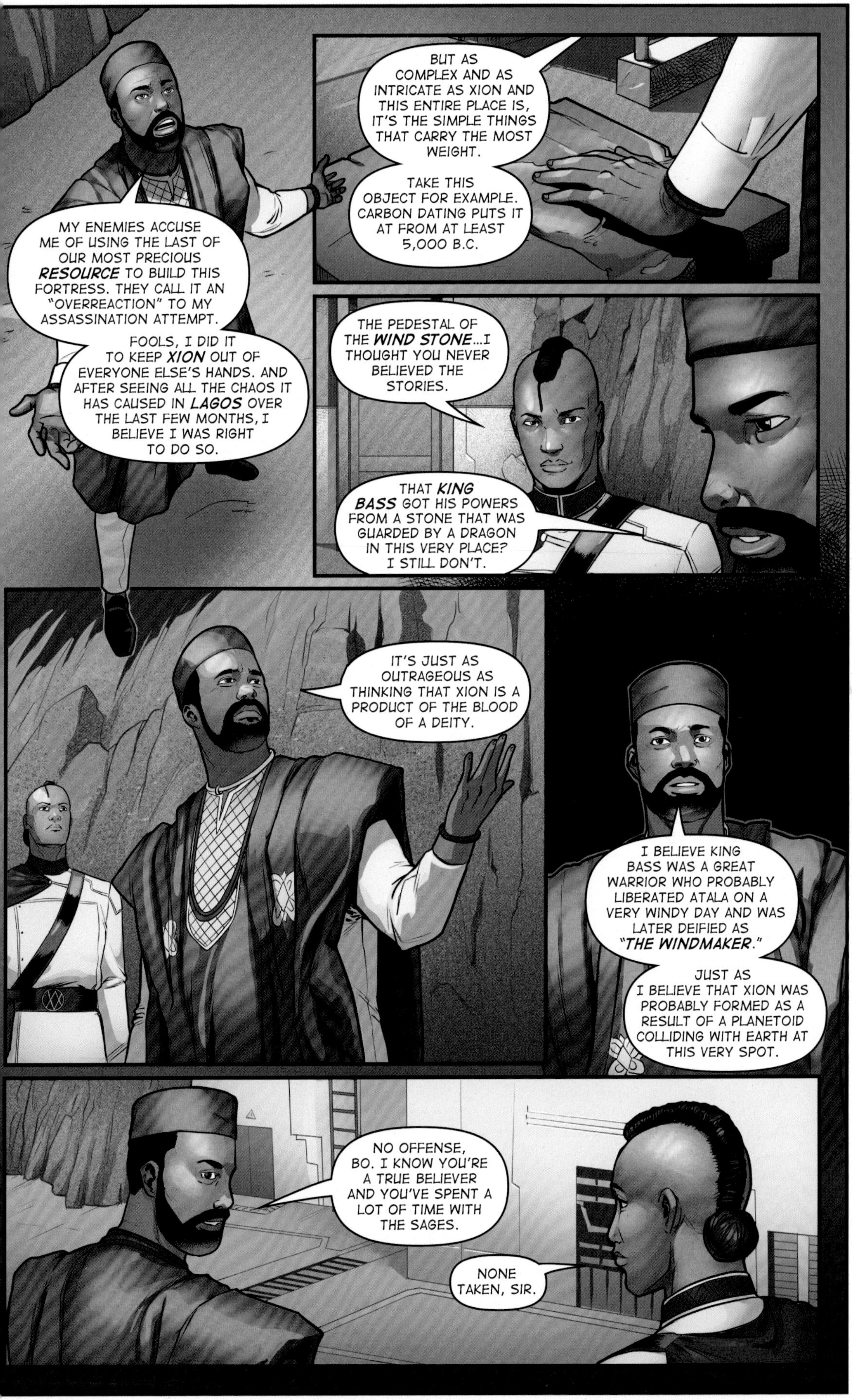
MY ENEMIES ACCUSE ME OF USING THE LAST OF OUR MOST PRECIOUS **RESOURCE** TO BUILD THIS FORTRESS. THEY CALL IT AN "OVERREACTION" TO MY ASSASSINATION ATTEMPT.
FOOLS, I DID IT TO KEEP **XION** OUT OF EVERYONE ELSE'S HANDS. AND AFTER SEEING ALL THE CHAOS IT HAS CAUSED IN **LAGOS** OVER THE LAST FEW MONTHS, I BELIEVE I WAS RIGHT TO DO SO.
BUT AS COMPLEX AND AS INTRICATE AS XION AND THIS ENTIRE PLACE IS, IT'S THE SIMPLE THINGS THAT CARRY THE MOST WEIGHT.
TAKE THIS OBJECT FOR EXAMPLE. CARBON DATING PUTS IT AT FROM AT LEAST 5,000 B.C.
THE PEDESTAL OF THE **WIND STONE**...I THOUGHT YOU NEVER BELIEVED THE STORIES.
THAT **KING BASS** GOT HIS POWERS FROM A STONE THAT WAS GUARDED BY A DRAGON IN THIS VERY PLACE? I STILL DON'T.
IT'S JUST AS OUTRAGEOUS AS THINKING THAT XION IS A PRODUCT OF THE BLOOD OF A DEITY.
I BELIEVE KING BASS WAS A GREAT WARRIOR WHO PROBABLY LIBERATED ATALA ON A VERY WINDY DAY AND WAS LATER DEIFIED AS "**THE WINDMAKER**."
JUST AS I BELIEVE THAT XION WAS PROBABLY FORMED AS A RESULT OF A PLANETOID COLLIDING WITH EARTH AT THIS VERY SPOT.
NO OFFENSE, BO. I KNOW YOU'RE A TRUE BELIEVER AND YOU'VE SPENT A LOT OF TIME WITH THE SAGES.
NONE TAKEN, SIR.

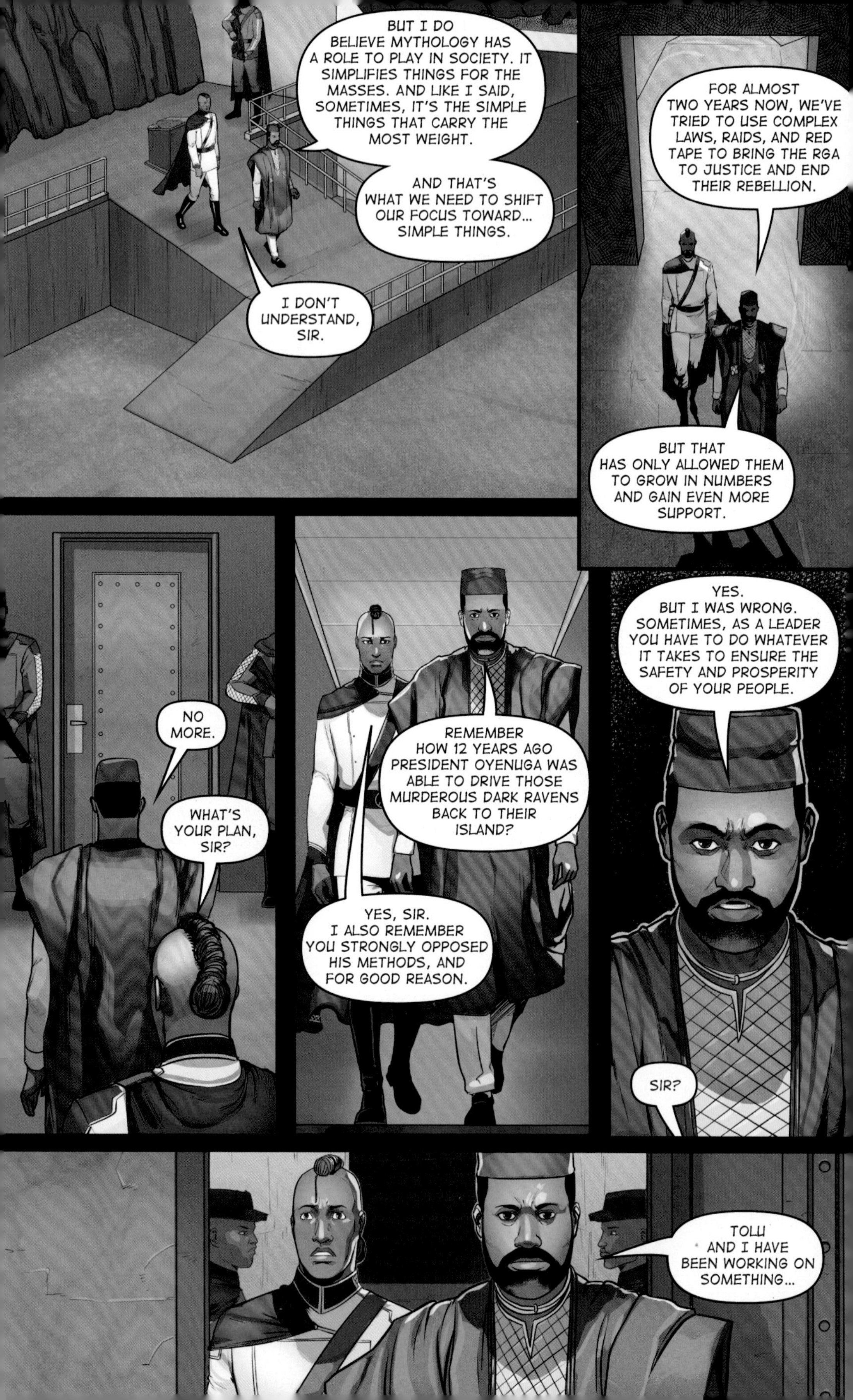
BUT I DO BELIEVE MYTHOLOGY HAS A ROLE TO PLAY IN SOCIETY. IT SIMPLIFIES THINGS FOR THE MASSES. AND LIKE I SAID, SOMETIMES, IT'S THE SIMPLE THINGS THAT CARRY THE MOST WEIGHT.
AND THAT'S WHAT WE NEED TO SHIFT OUR FOCUS TOWARD... SIMPLE THINGS.
I DON'T UNDERSTAND, SIR.
FOR ALMOST TWO YEARS NOW, WE'VE TRIED TO USE COMPLEX LAWS, RAIDS, AND RED TAPE TO BRING THE RGA TO JUSTICE AND END THEIR REBELLION.
BUT THAT HAS ONLY ALLOWED THEM TO GROW IN NUMBERS AND GAIN EVEN MORE SUPPORT.
NO MORE.
WHAT'S YOUR PLAN, SIR?
REMEMBER HOW 12 YEARS AGO PRESIDENT OYENUGA WAS ABLE TO DRIVE THOSE MURDEROUS DARK RAVENS BACK TO THEIR ISLAND?
YES, SIR. I ALSO REMEMBER YOU STRONGLY OPPOSED HIS METHODS, AND FOR GOOD REASON.
YES. BUT I WAS WRONG. SOMETIMES, AS A LEADER YOU HAVE TO DO WHATEVER IT TAKES TO ENSURE THE SAFETY AND PROSPERITY OF YOUR PEOPLE.
SIR?
TOLU AND I HAVE BEEN WORKING ON SOMETHING...

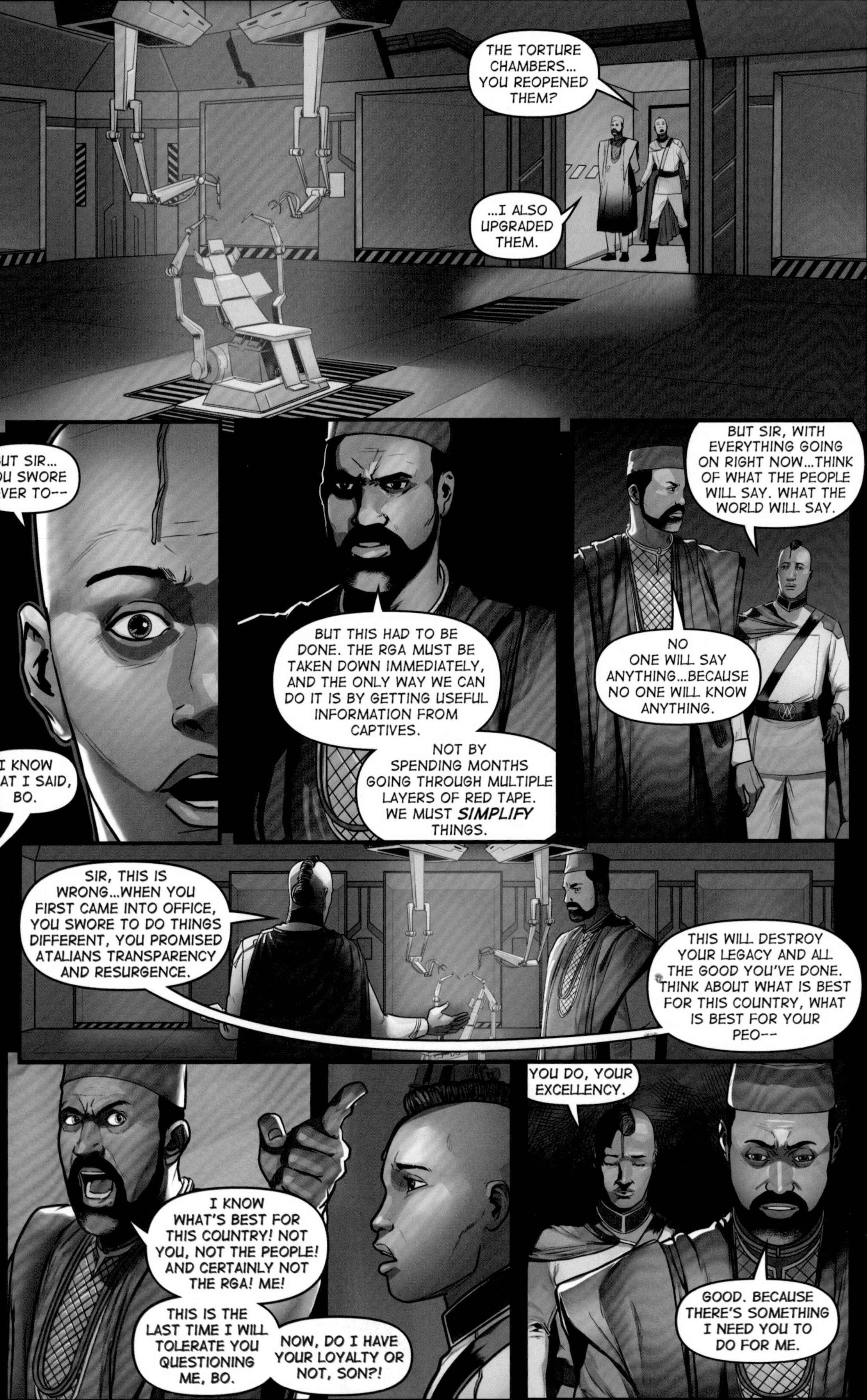
THE TORTURE CHAMBERS... YOU REOPENED THEM?
...I ALSO UPGRADED THEM.
UT SIR... OU SWORE VER TO--
BUT THIS HAD TO BE DONE. THE RGA MUST BE TAKEN DOWN IMMEDIATELY, AND THE ONLY WAY WE CAN DO IT IS BY GETTING USEFUL INFORMATION FROM CAPTIVES.
I KNOW AT I SAID, BO.
NOT BY SPENDING MONTHS GOING THROUGH MULTIPLE LAYERS OF RED TAPE. WE MUST *SIMPLIFY* THINGS.
BUT SIR, WITH EVERYTHING GOING ON RIGHT NOW...THINK OF WHAT THE PEOPLE WILL SAY. WHAT THE WORLD WILL SAY.
NO ONE WILL SAY ANYTHING...BECAUSE NO ONE WILL KNOW ANYTHING.
SIR, THIS IS WRONG...WHEN YOU FIRST CAME INTO OFFICE, YOU SWORE TO DO THINGS DIFFERENT, YOU PROMISED ATALIANS TRANSPARENCY AND RESURGENCE.
THIS WILL DESTROY YOUR LEGACY AND ALL THE GOOD YOU'VE DONE. THINK ABOUT WHAT IS BEST FOR THIS COUNTRY, WHAT IS BEST FOR YOUR PEO--
I KNOW WHAT'S BEST FOR THIS COUNTRY! NOT YOU, NOT THE PEOPLE! AND CERTAINLY NOT THE RGA! ME!
THIS IS THE LAST TIME I WILL TOLERATE YOU QUESTIONING ME, BO.
NOW, DO I HAVE YOUR LOYALTY OR NOT, SON?!
YOU DO, YOUR EXCELLENCY.
GOOD. BECAUSE THERE'S SOMETHING I NEED YOU TO DO FOR ME.

CHAPTER FOUR

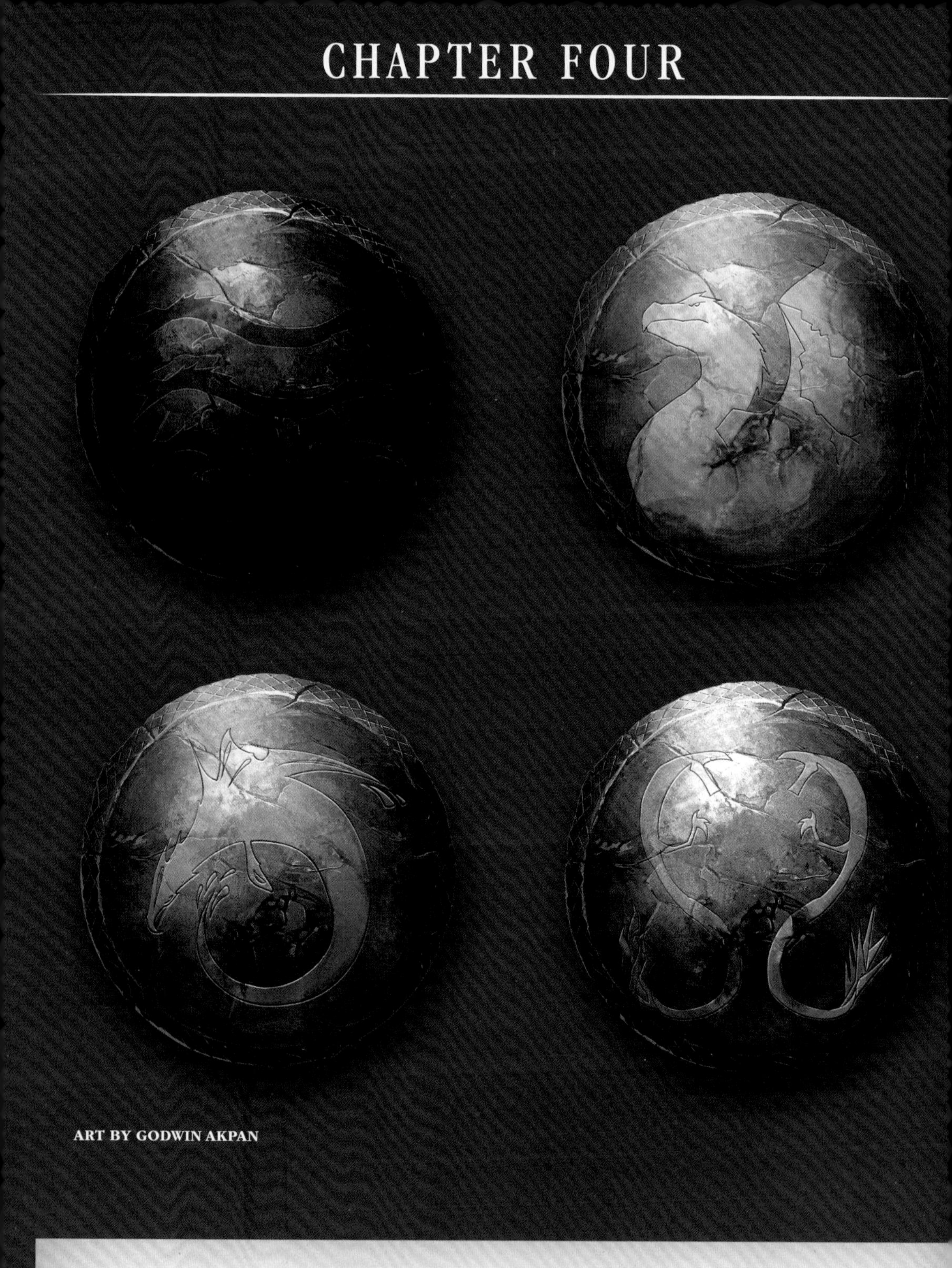

ART BY GODWIN AKPAN

The Dragon Stones play a huge role within the YouNeek YouNiverse. Scattered across the globe thousands of years ago, one way or the other, many of the key heroes in the YouNeek YouNiverse come into contact (sometimes indirectly) with the stones and harness or absorb their powers.

For example, King Bass of Atala found the Wind Stone buried on an island in the Fifteenth Century. As such, he was able to absorb its powers and become, you guessed it, the (legendary) WindMaker. FireFrost (with the Fire & Frost stone) and Hasan Bakwa (with the Shock Stone) are two other characters in the YouNiverse that have also come in contact with the Dragon Stones and harnessed their powers.

FUN FACT: The power from the Stones can sometimes be passed down to children.

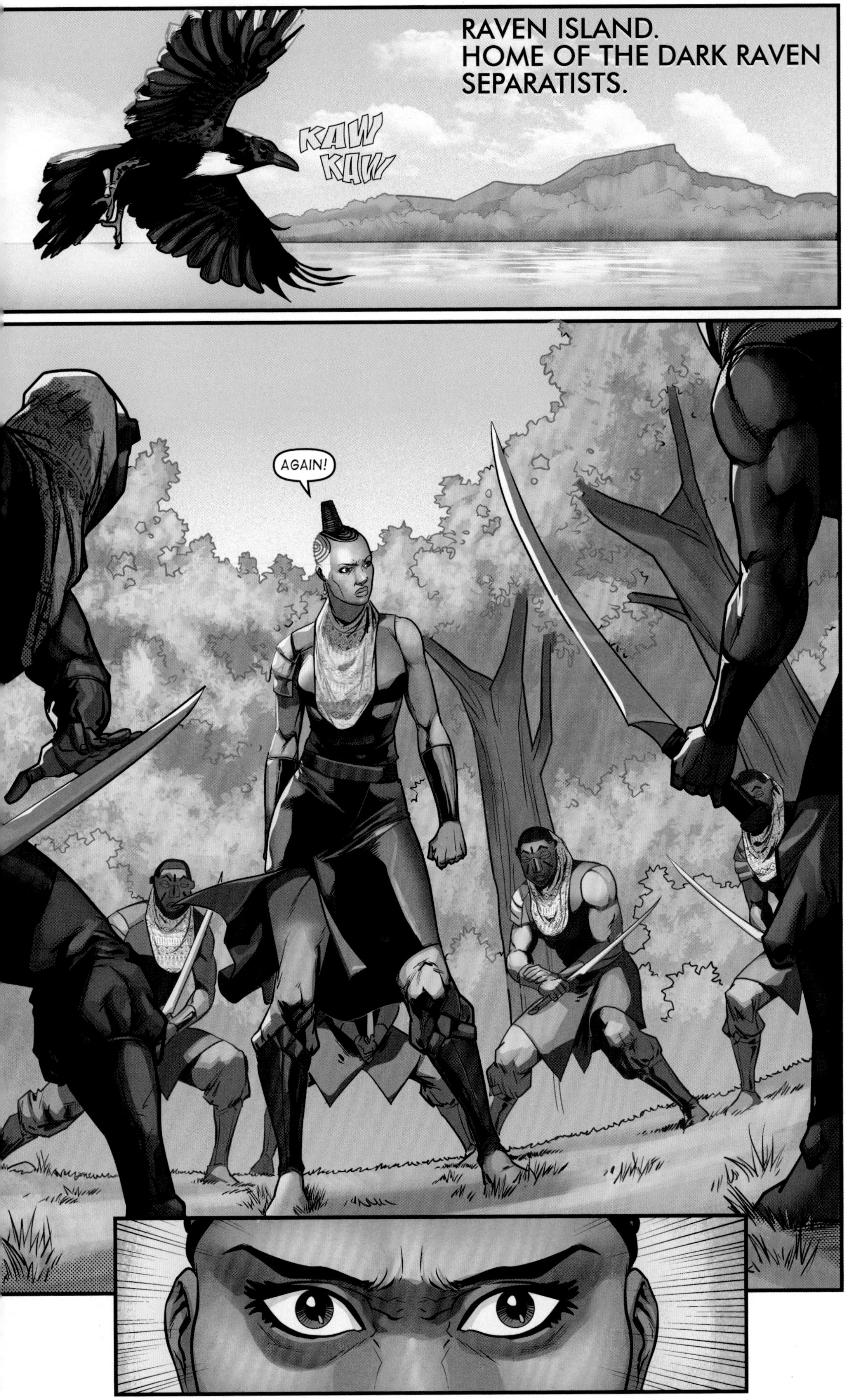

RAVEN ISLAND.
HOME OF THE DARK RAVEN SEPARATISTS.
KAW KAW
AGAIN!

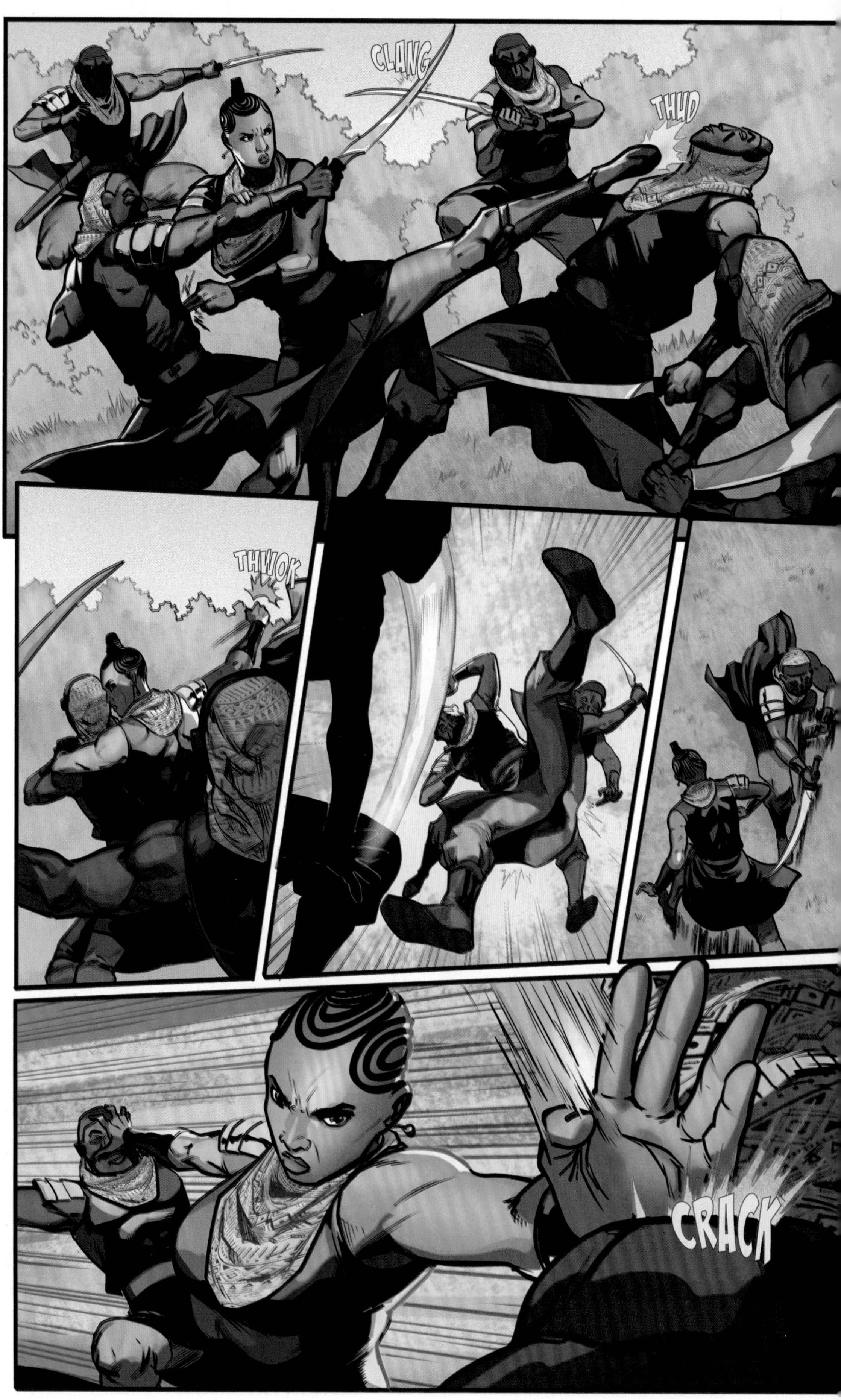
CLANG
THUD
THWOK
CRACK

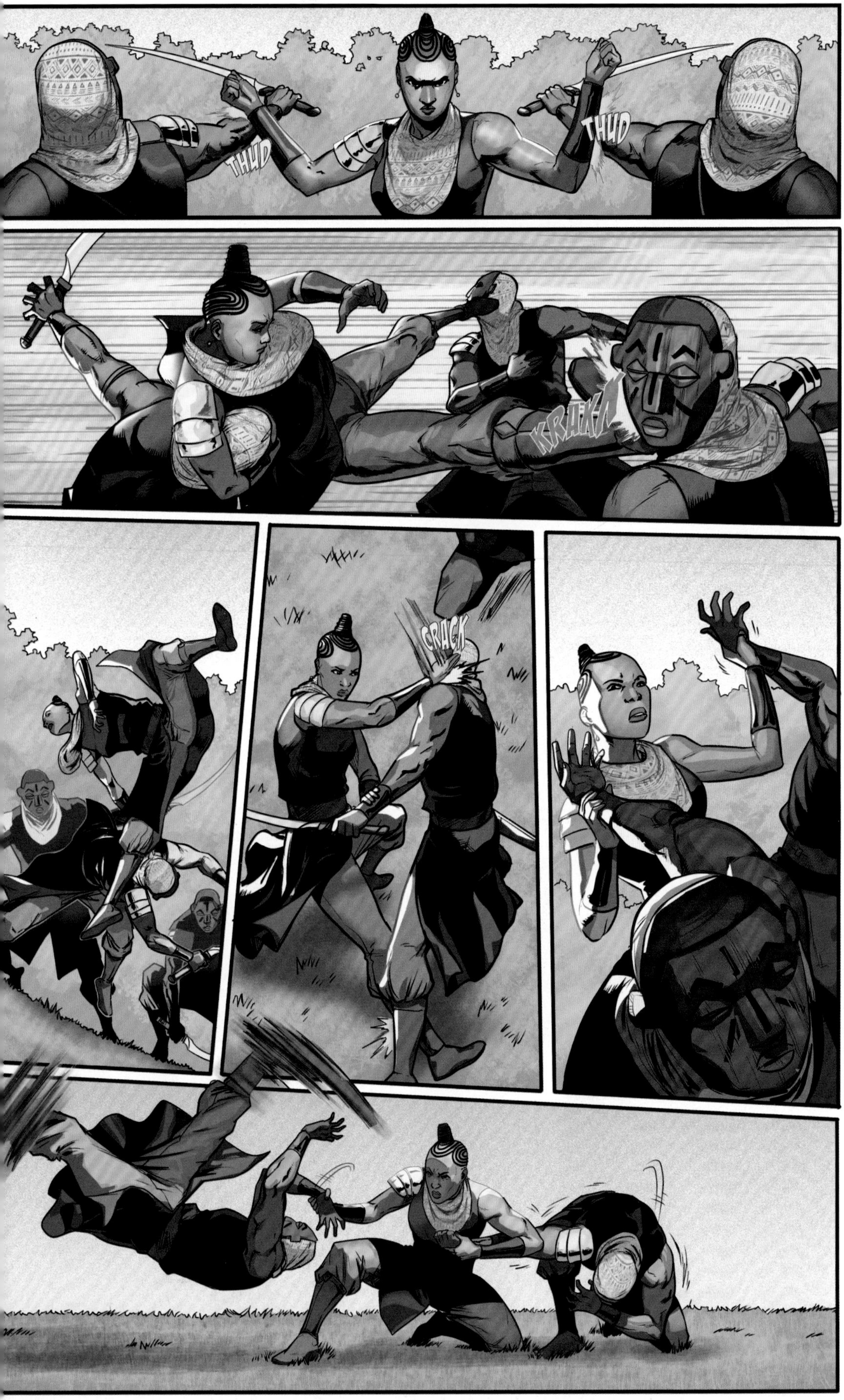
THUD
THUD
KRAK
CRACK

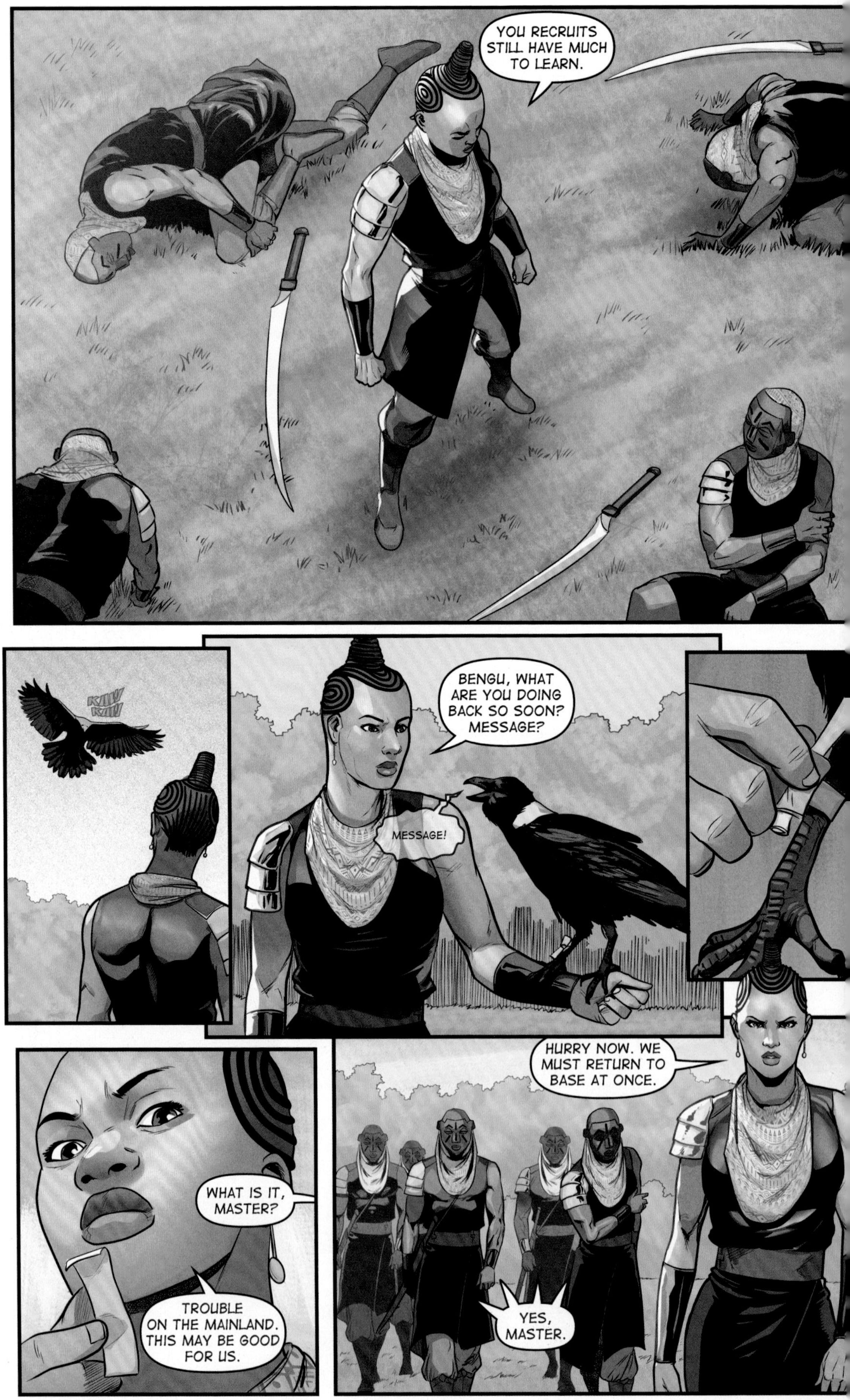
YOU RECRUITS STILL HAVE MUCH TO LEARN.
KAW KAW
BENGU, WHAT ARE YOU DOING BACK SO SOON? MESSAGE?
MESSAGE!
WHAT IS IT, MASTER?
TROUBLE ON THE MAINLAND. THIS MAY BE GOOD FOR US.
HURRY NOW. WE MUST RETURN TO BASE AT ONCE.
YES, MASTER.

IF WE CAN PUT TOGETHER *EVIDENCE* OF THE LENGTHY LIST OF THE CORRUPT ACTIVITIES WE ALL KNOW BALOGUN HAS BEEN INVOLVED IN, WE CAN PUT HIS *DICTATORSHIP* TO AN END WITHOUT ANY MORE BLOODSHED.

EVEN IF HIS CABINET DOESN'T TURN ON HIM, WHICH I SERIOUSLY DOUBT, *E.C.O.W.A.S.** HAS ALREADY STARTED MOUNTING PRESSURE ON HIM FOR OVERSTAYING HIS SECOND TERM.

HIS ATTEMPT TO MANIPULATE THE CONSTITUTION FOR A THIRD TERM, DESPITE HIS "SECURITY" CLAIMS, HASN'T HELPED EITHER.

*ECONOMIC COMMUNITY OF WEST AFRICAN STATES. A REGIONAL POLITICAL AND ECONOMIC UNION OF COUNTRIES LOCATED IN WEST AFRICA.

THE KEYWORD IS "IF," ERI. WE STILL DON'T NOW IF WE CAN TURN BO. THIS IS THE DIRECTOR OF THE RED KNIGHTS WE ARE TALKING ABOUT.

PLUS, ALL E.C.O.W.A.S. HAS DONE THE LAST TWO YEARS HAS BEEN "TALKS." WE ALL KNOW THAT NEVER LEADS TO ANYTHING.

I HAVE FAITH THAT THEY WILL ESCALATE THINGS ONCE WE EXPOSE BALOGUN. JUST LIKE I HAVE FAITH BO, AS LOYAL AS HE IS, WILL SEE REASON AFTER HE SEES WHAT I'VE FOUND.

I URGE YOU ALL TO TRUST ME ON THIS.

THIS IS HOW WE END THIS. THIS IS HOW WE WIN. THIS IS HOW WE END TYRANNY AND ENSURE DEMOCRACY FOR ATALA FOR AGES TO CO--

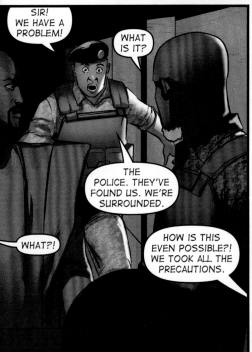

SIR! WE HAVE A PROBLEM!

WHAT IS IT?

THE POLICE. THEY'VE FOUND US. WE'RE SURROUNDED.

WHAT?!

HOW IS THIS EVEN POSSIBLE?! WE TOOK ALL THE PRECAUTIONS.

HAS ANYONE SEEN *LAJA*?

THIS DOESN'T MAKE ANY SENSE. DID SOMEONE SELL US OUT?

I HAVE...BUT YOU WON'T LIKE WHERE.

THAT ONE-EYED-- HE BETRAYED US!

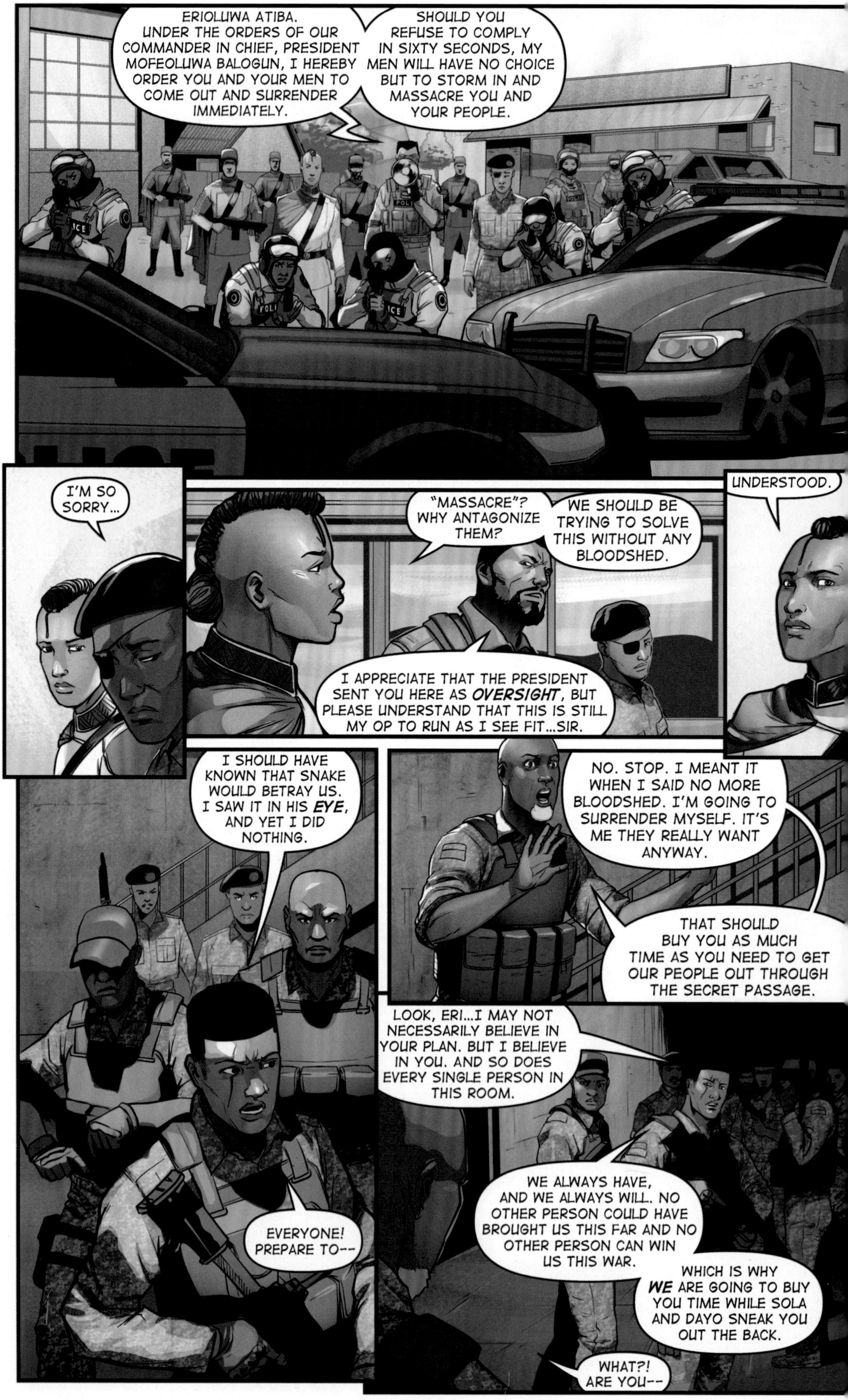
ERIOLUWA ATIBA. UNDER THE ORDERS OF OUR COMMANDER IN CHIEF, PRESIDENT MOFEOLUWA BALOGUN, I HEREBY ORDER YOU AND YOUR MEN TO COME OUT AND SURRENDER IMMEDIATELY.
SHOULD YOU REFUSE TO COMPLY IN SIXTY SECONDS, MY MEN WILL HAVE NO CHOICE BUT TO STORM IN AND MASSACRE YOU AND YOUR PEOPLE.
I'M SO SORRY...
"MASSACRE"? WHY ANTAGONIZE THEM?
WE SHOULD BE TRYING TO SOLVE THIS WITHOUT ANY BLOODSHED.
I APPRECIATE THAT THE PRESIDENT SENT YOU HERE AS *OVERSIGHT*, BUT PLEASE UNDERSTAND THAT THIS IS STILL MY OP TO RUN AS I SEE FIT...SIR.
UNDERSTOOD.
I SHOULD HAVE KNOWN THAT SNAKE WOULD BETRAY US. I SAW IT IN HIS *EYE*, AND YET I DID NOTHING.
EVERYONE! PREPARE TO--
NO. STOP. I MEANT IT WHEN I SAID NO MORE BLOODSHED. I'M GOING TO SURRENDER MYSELF. IT'S ME THEY REALLY WANT ANYWAY.
THAT SHOULD BUY YOU AS MUCH TIME AS YOU NEED TO GET OUR PEOPLE OUT THROUGH THE SECRET PASSAGE.
LOOK, ERI...I MAY NOT NECESSARILY BELIEVE IN YOUR PLAN. BUT I BELIEVE IN YOU. AND SO DOES EVERY SINGLE PERSON IN THIS ROOM.
WE ALWAYS HAVE, AND WE ALWAYS WILL. NO OTHER PERSON COULD HAVE BROUGHT US THIS FAR AND NO OTHER PERSON CAN WIN US THIS WAR.
WHICH IS WHY *WE* ARE GOING TO BUY YOU TIME WHILE SOLA AND DAYO SNEAK YOU OUT THE BACK.
WHAT?! ARE YOU--

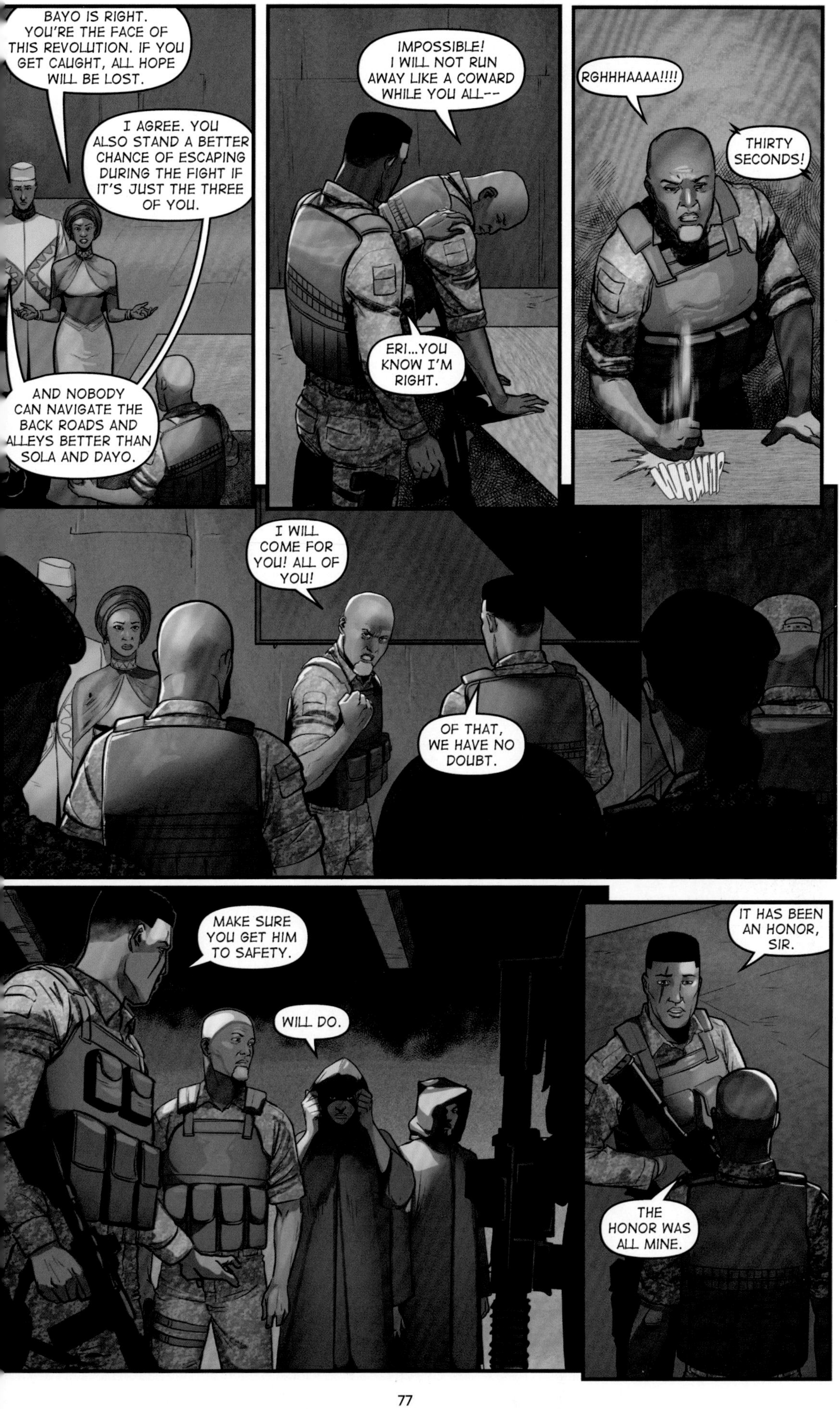
BAYO IS RIGHT. YOU'RE THE FACE OF THIS REVOLUTION. IF YOU GET CAUGHT, ALL HOPE WILL BE LOST.
I AGREE. YOU ALSO STAND A BETTER CHANCE OF ESCAPING DURING THE FIGHT IF IT'S JUST THE THREE OF YOU.
AND NOBODY CAN NAVIGATE THE BACK ROADS AND ALLEYS BETTER THAN SOLA AND DAYO.
IMPOSSIBLE! I WILL NOT RUN AWAY LIKE A COWARD WHILE YOU ALL--
ERI...YOU KNOW I'M RIGHT.
RGHHHAAAA!!!!
THIRTY SECONDS!
WHUMP
I WILL COME FOR YOU! ALL OF YOU!
OF THAT, WE HAVE NO DOUBT.
MAKE SURE YOU GET HIM TO SAFETY.
WILL DO.
IT HAS BEEN AN HONOR, SIR.
THE HONOR WAS ALL MINE.

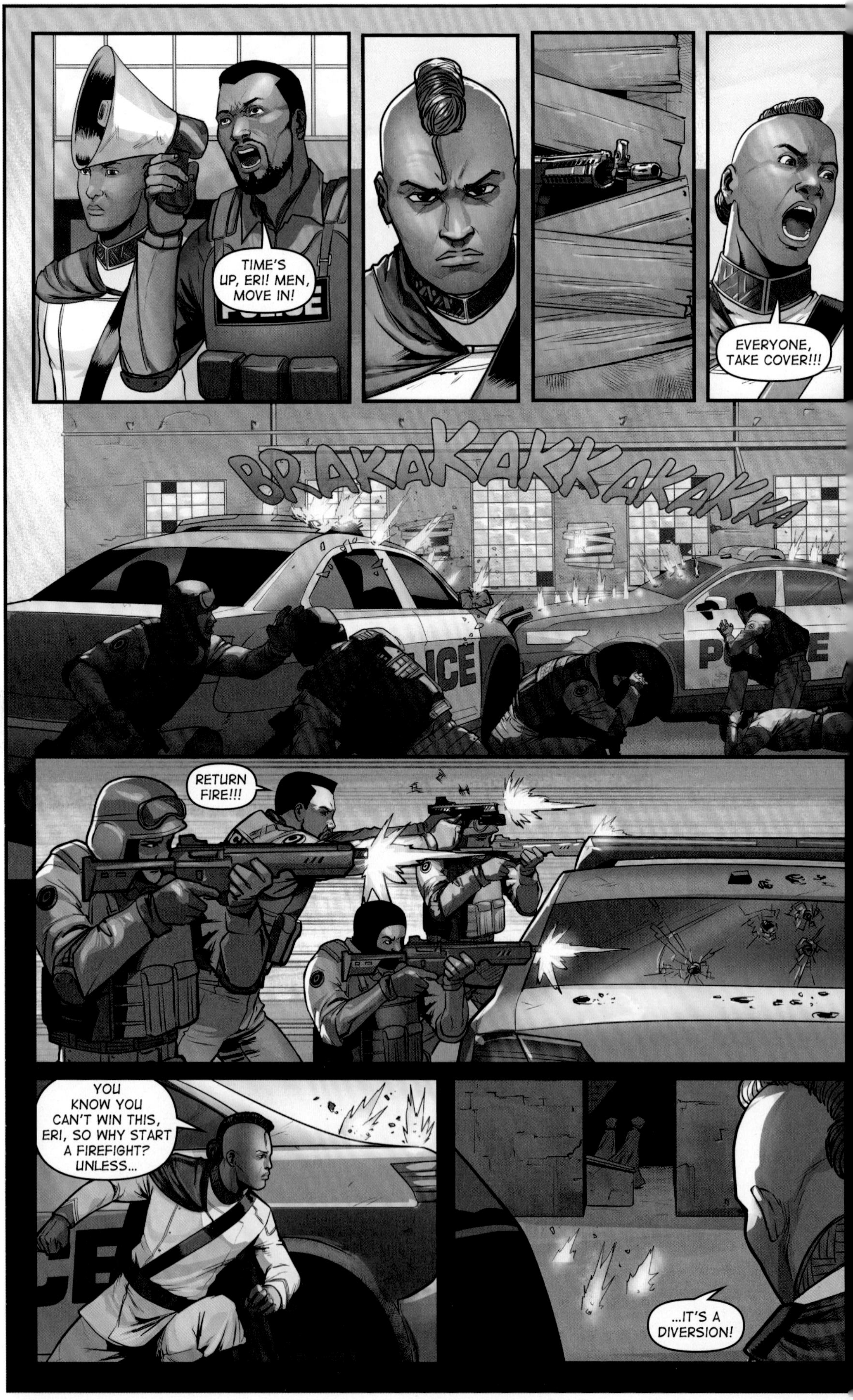
TIME'S UP, ERI! MEN, MOVE IN!
EVERYONE, TAKE COVER!!!
BRAKAKAKKAKAKKA
RETURN FIRE!!!
YOU KNOW YOU CAN'T WIN THIS, ERI, SO WHY START A FIREFIGHT? UNLESS...
...IT'S A DIVERSION!

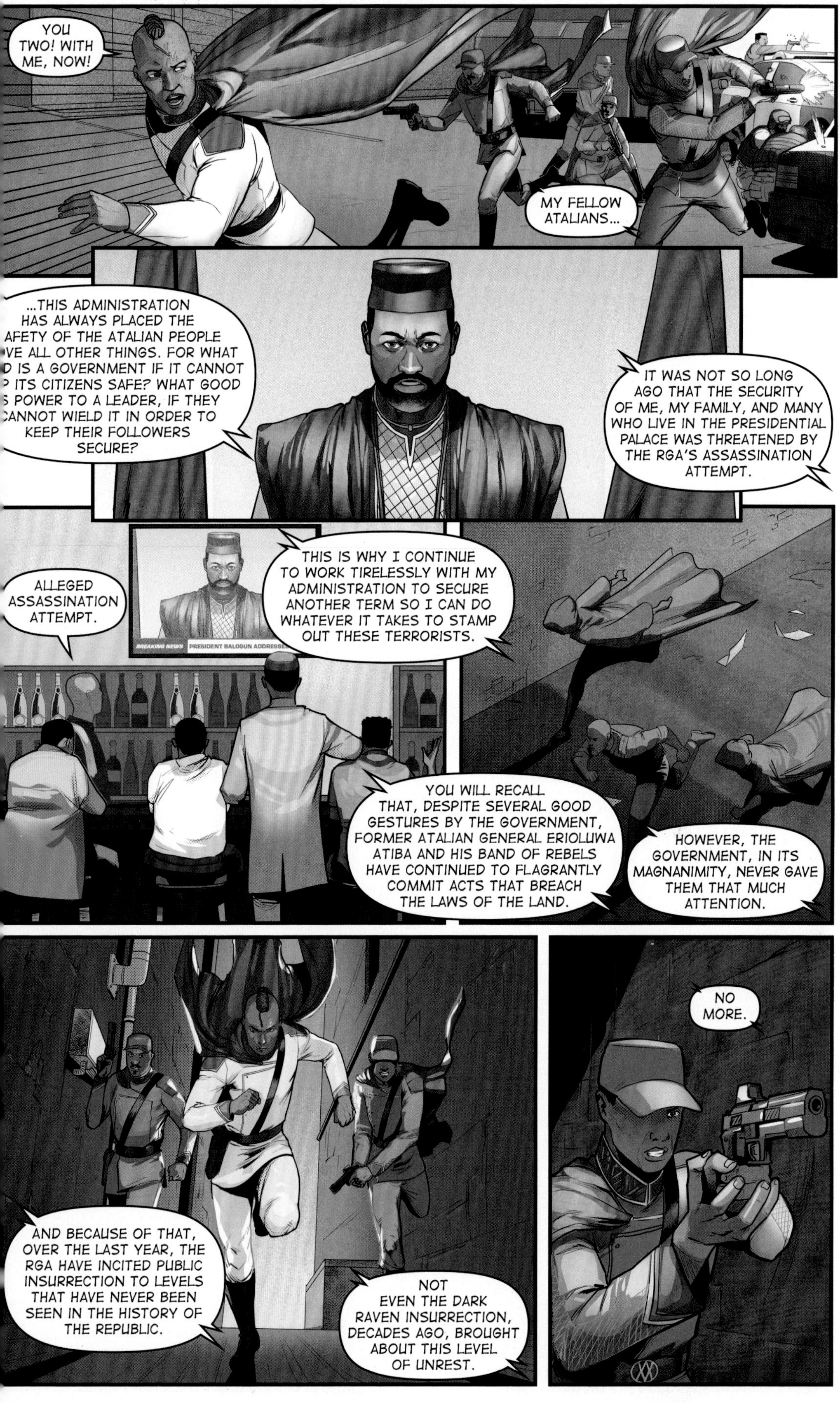
YOU TWO! WITH ME, NOW!
MY FELLOW ATALIANS...
...THIS ADMINISTRATION HAS ALWAYS PLACED THE AFETY OF THE ATALIAN PEOPLE VE ALL OTHER THINGS. FOR WHAT D IS A GOVERNMENT IF IT CANNOT P ITS CITIZENS SAFE? WHAT GOOD S POWER TO A LEADER, IF THEY CANNOT WIELD IT IN ORDER TO KEEP THEIR FOLLOWERS SECURE?
IT WAS NOT SO LONG AGO THAT THE SECURITY OF ME, MY FAMILY, AND MANY WHO LIVE IN THE PRESIDENTIAL PALACE WAS THREATENED BY THE RGA'S ASSASSINATION ATTEMPT.
BREAKING NEWS PRESIDENT BALOGUN ADDRESSE
ALLEGED ASSASSINATION ATTEMPT.
THIS IS WHY I CONTINUE TO WORK TIRELESSLY WITH MY ADMINISTRATION TO SECURE ANOTHER TERM SO I CAN DO WHATEVER IT TAKES TO STAMP OUT THESE TERRORISTS.
YOU WILL RECALL THAT, DESPITE SEVERAL GOOD GESTURES BY THE GOVERNMENT, FORMER ATALIAN GENERAL ERIOLUWA ATIBA AND HIS BAND OF REBELS HAVE CONTINUED TO FLAGRANTLY COMMIT ACTS THAT BREACH THE LAWS OF THE LAND.
HOWEVER, THE GOVERNMENT, IN ITS MAGNANIMITY, NEVER GAVE THEM THAT MUCH ATTENTION.
AND BECAUSE OF THAT, OVER THE LAST YEAR, THE RGA HAVE INCITED PUBLIC INSURRECTION TO LEVELS THAT HAVE NEVER BEEN SEEN IN THE HISTORY OF THE REPUBLIC.
NOT EVEN THE DARK RAVEN INSURRECTION, DECADES AGO, BROUGHT ABOUT THIS LEVEL OF UNREST.
NO MORE.

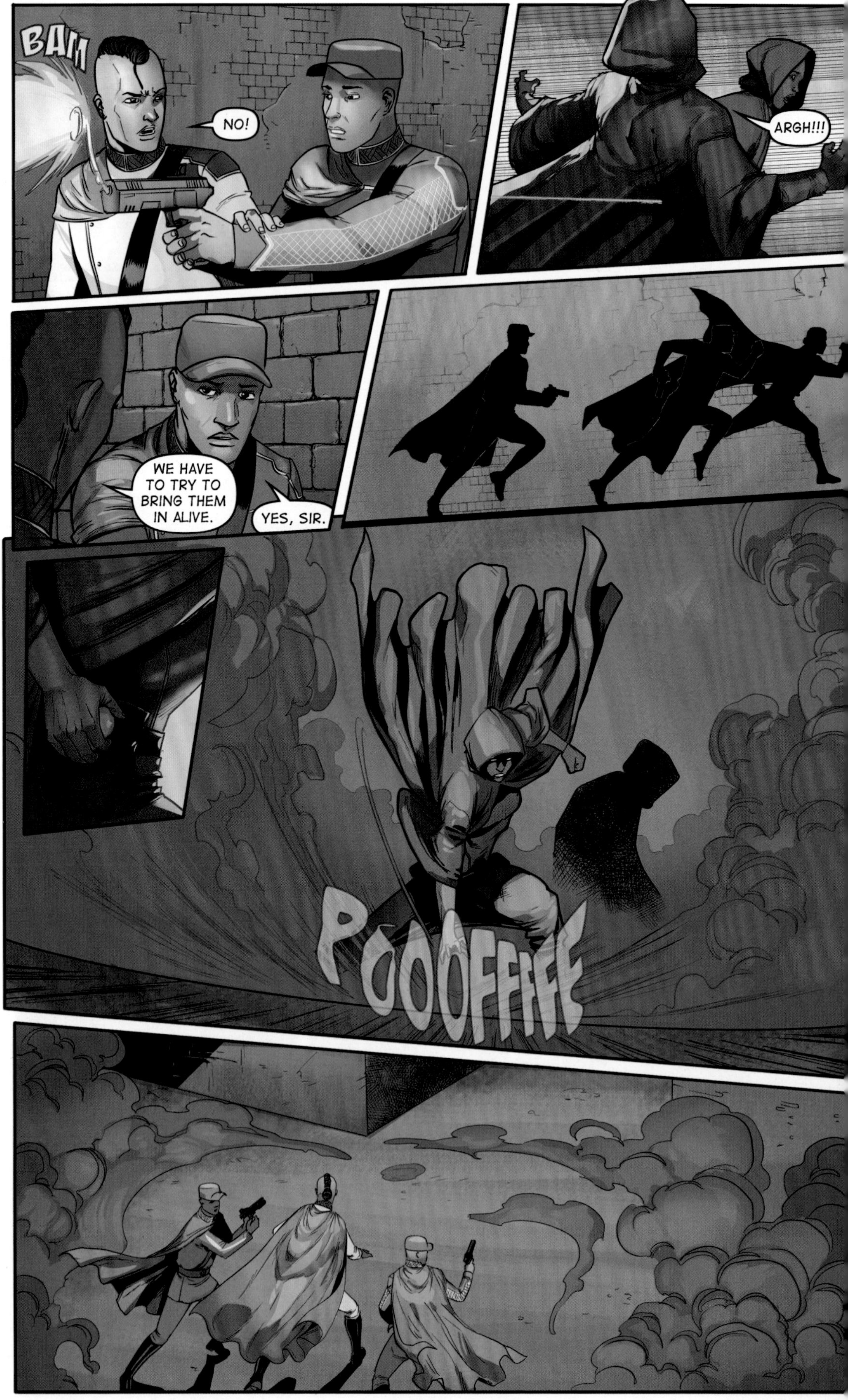
BAM
NO!
ARGH!!!
WE HAVE TO TRY TO BRING THEM IN ALIVE.
YES, SIR.
POOOFFFFF

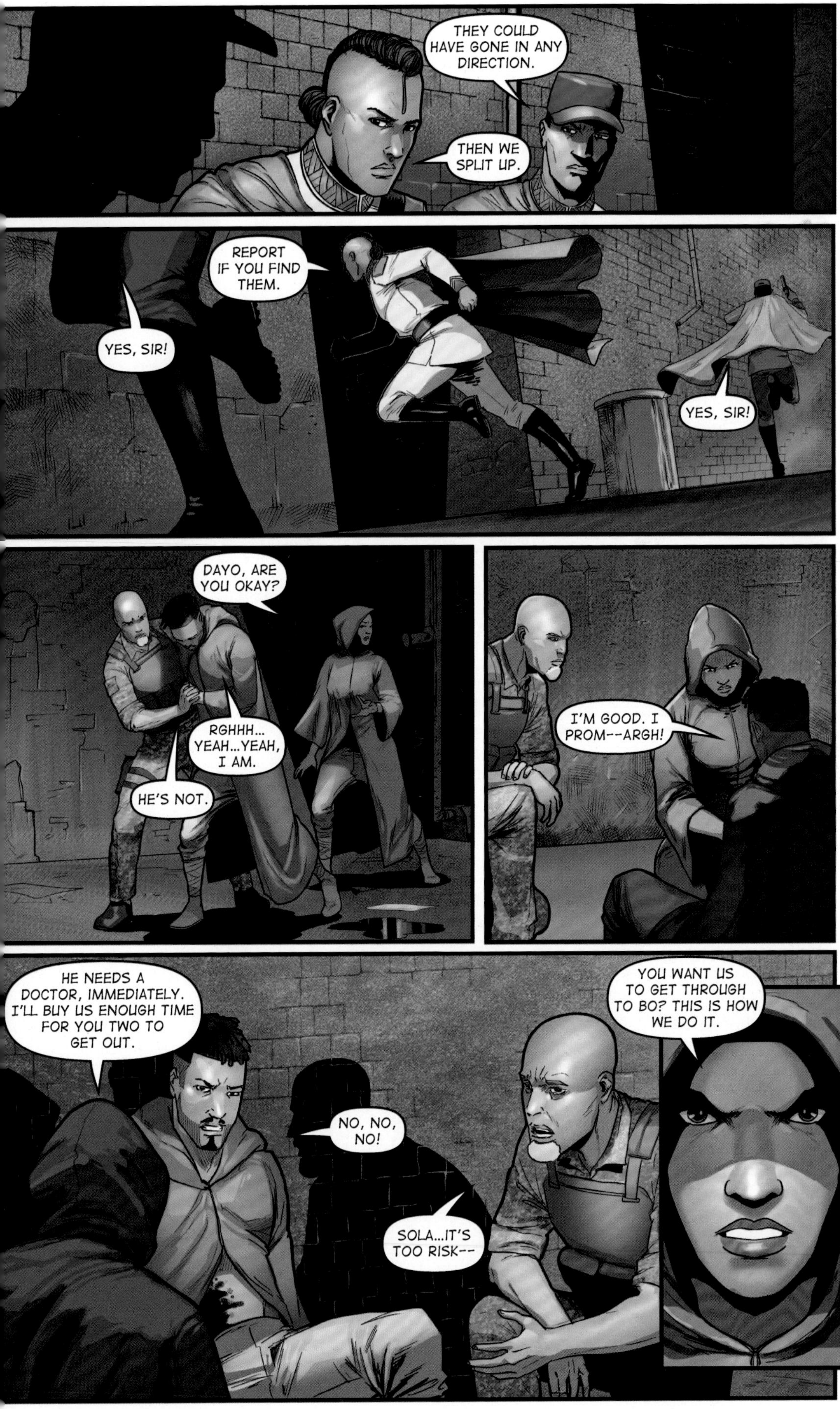
THEY COULD HAVE GONE IN ANY DIRECTION.
THEN WE SPLIT UP.
REPORT IF YOU FIND THEM.
YES, SIR!
YES, SIR!
DAYO, ARE YOU OKAY?
RGHHH... YEAH...YEAH, I AM.
HE'S NOT.
I'M GOOD. I PROM--ARGH!
HE NEEDS A DOCTOR, IMMEDIATELY. I'LL BUY US ENOUGH TIME FOR YOU TWO TO GET OUT.
NO, NO, NO!
SOLA...IT'S TOO RISK--
YOU WANT US TO GET THROUGH TO BO? THIS IS HOW WE DO IT.

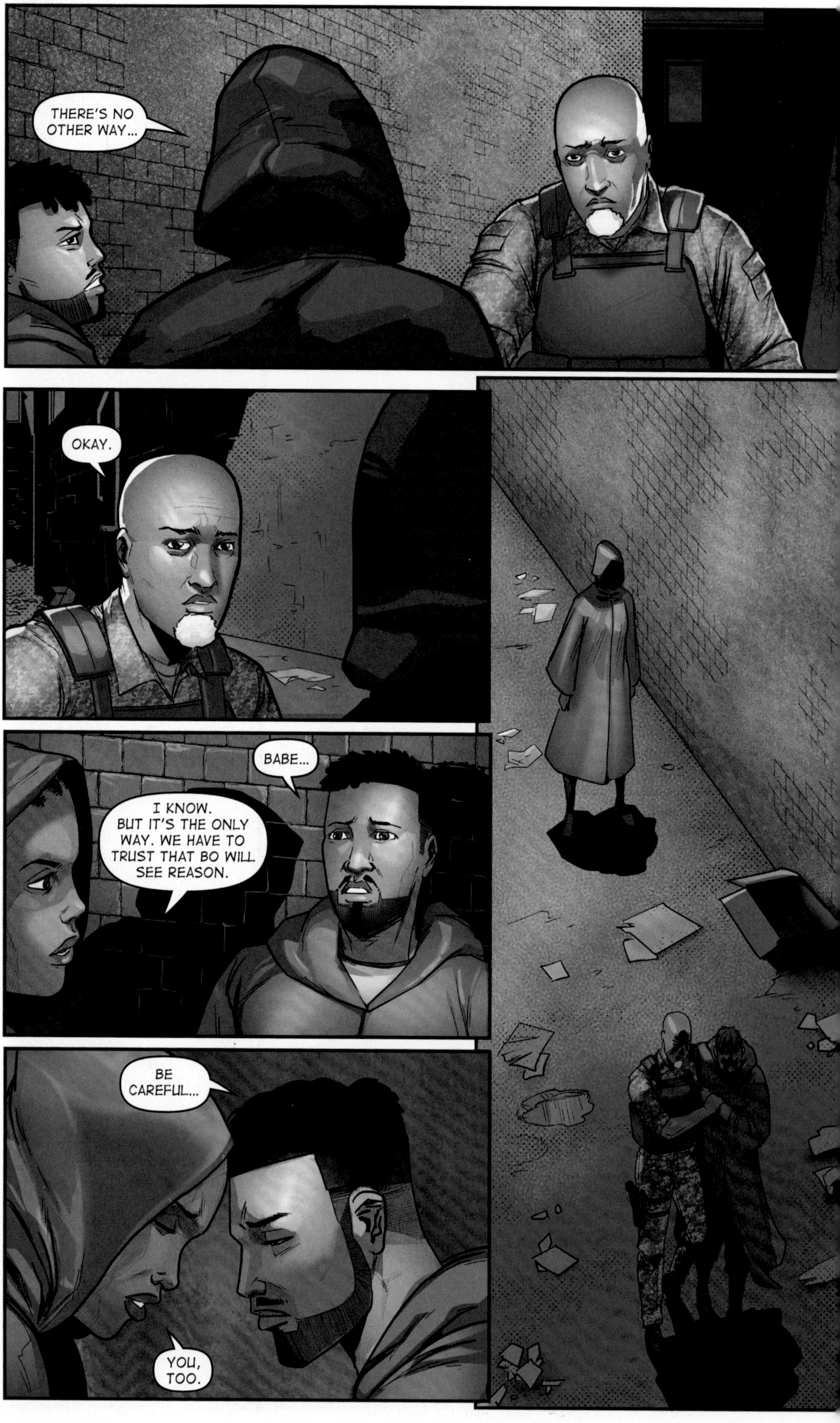

THERE'S NO OTHER WAY...
OKAY.
BABE...
I KNOW. BUT IT'S THE ONLY WAY. WE HAVE TO TRUST THAT BO WILL SEE REASON.
BE CAREFUL...
YOU, TOO.

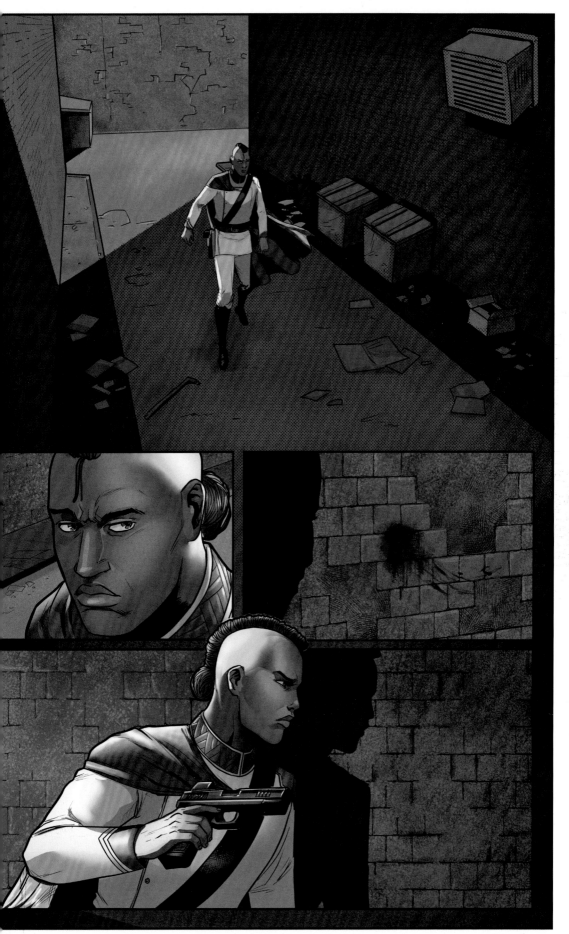

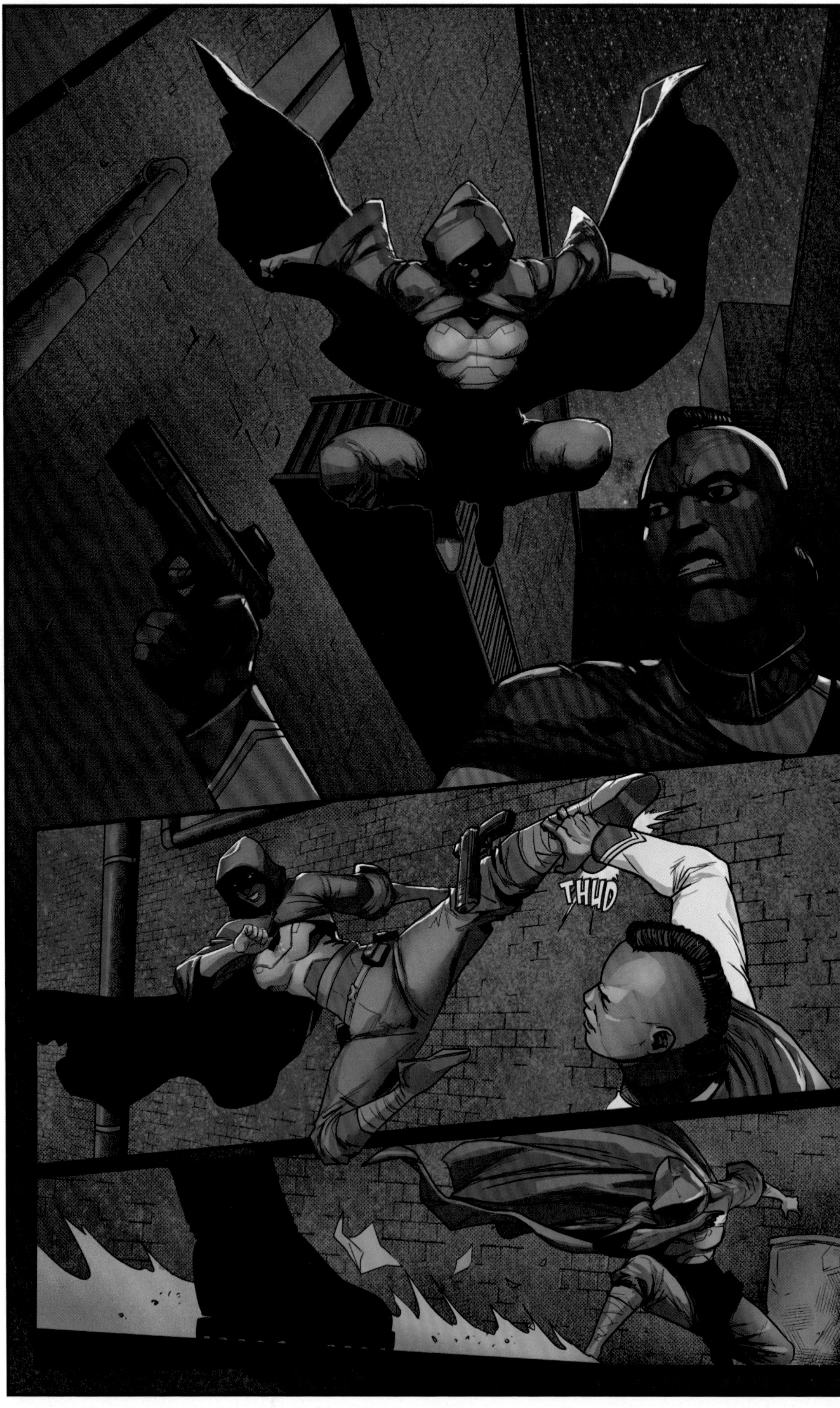
THUD

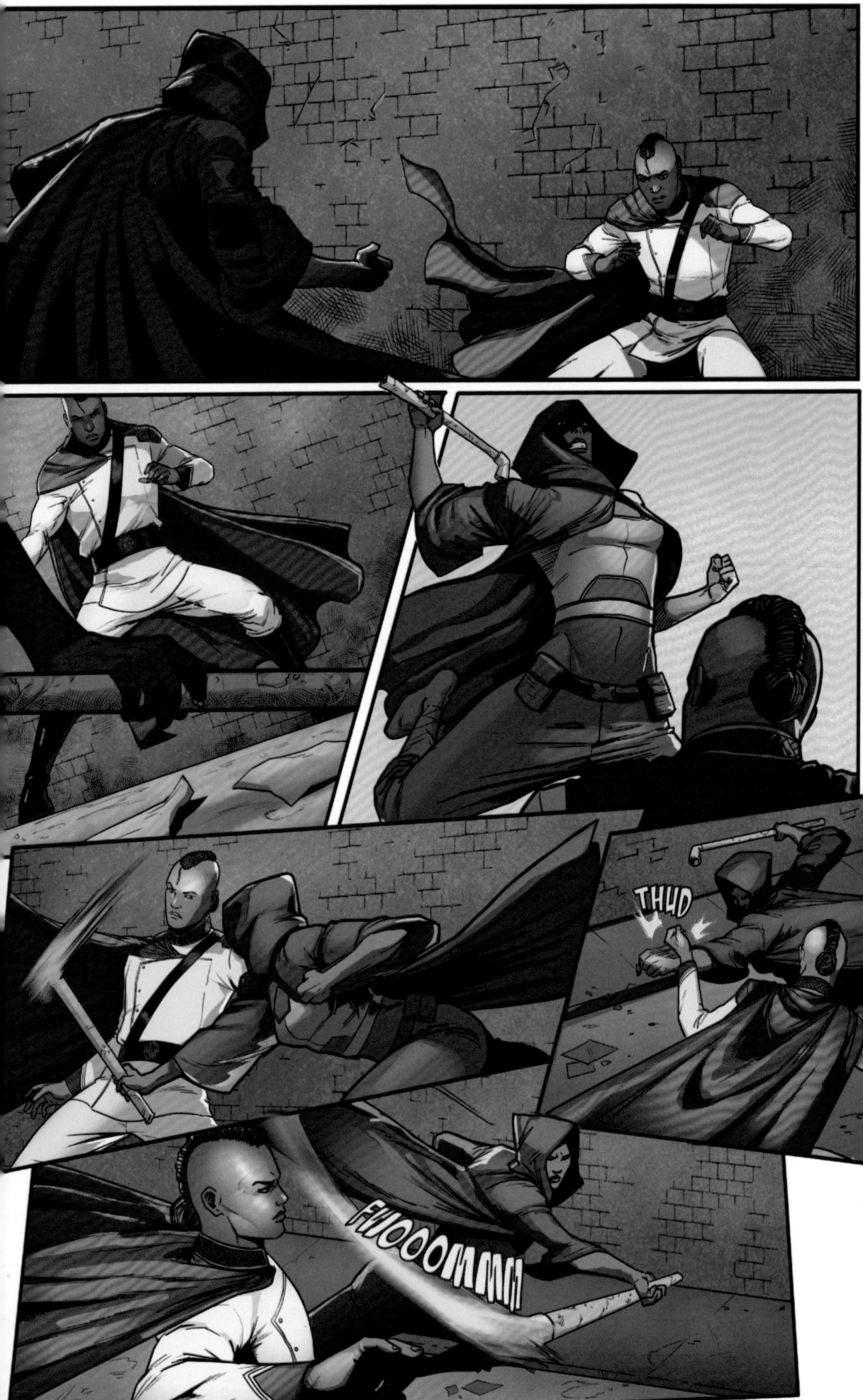
THUD
FWOOOMMM

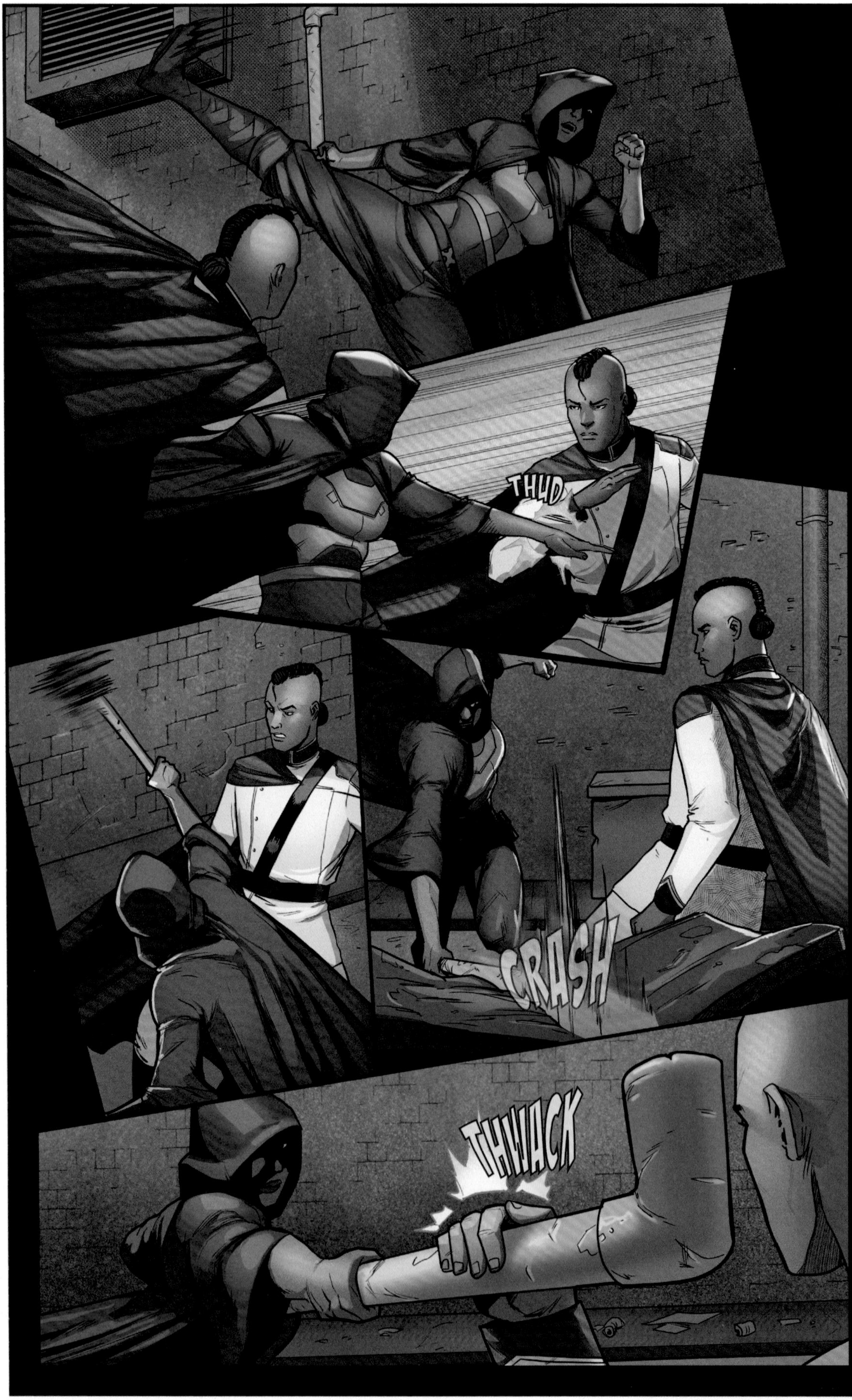
THUD
CRASH
THWACK

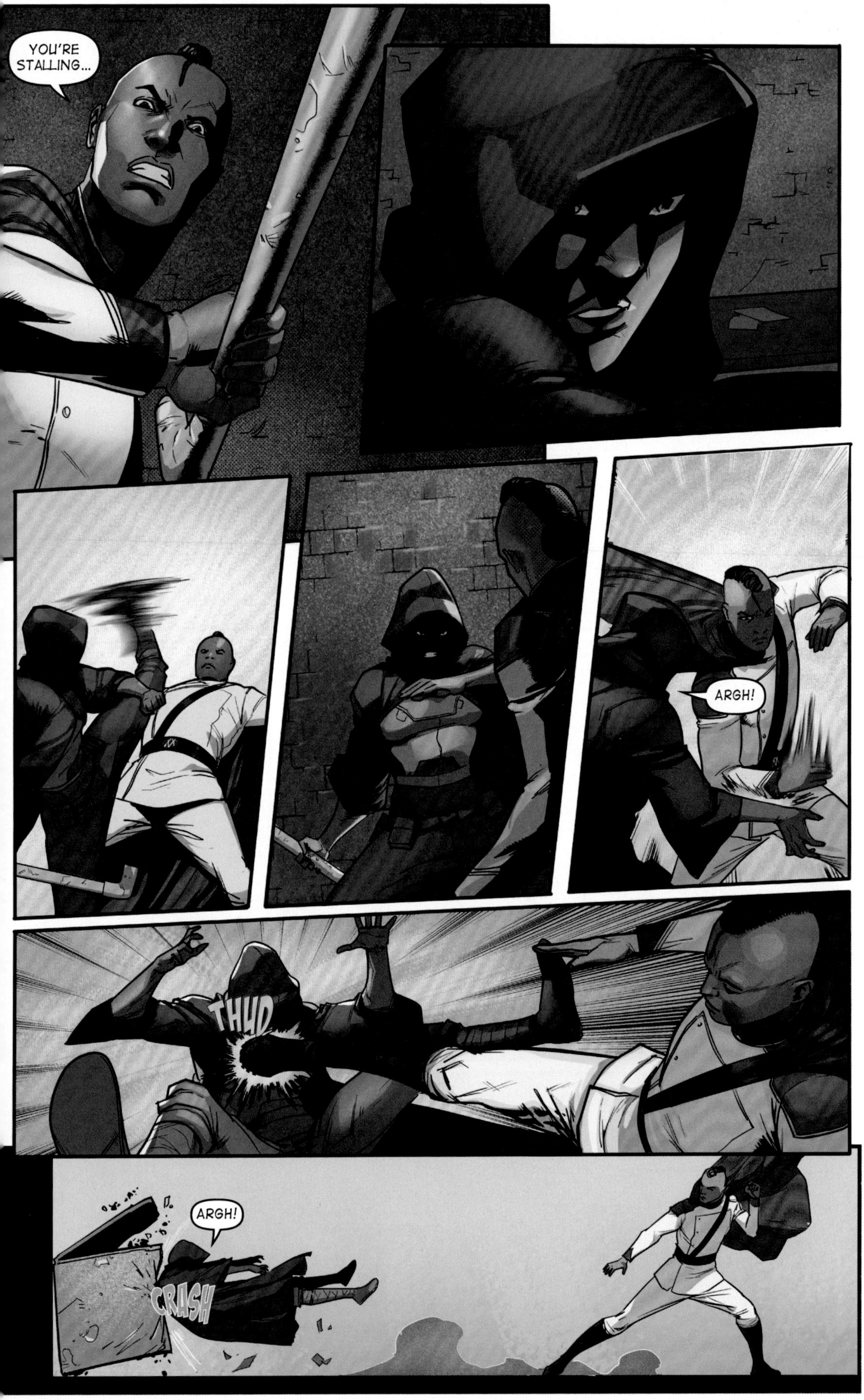
YOU'RE STALLING...
ARGH!
THUD
ARGH!
CRASH

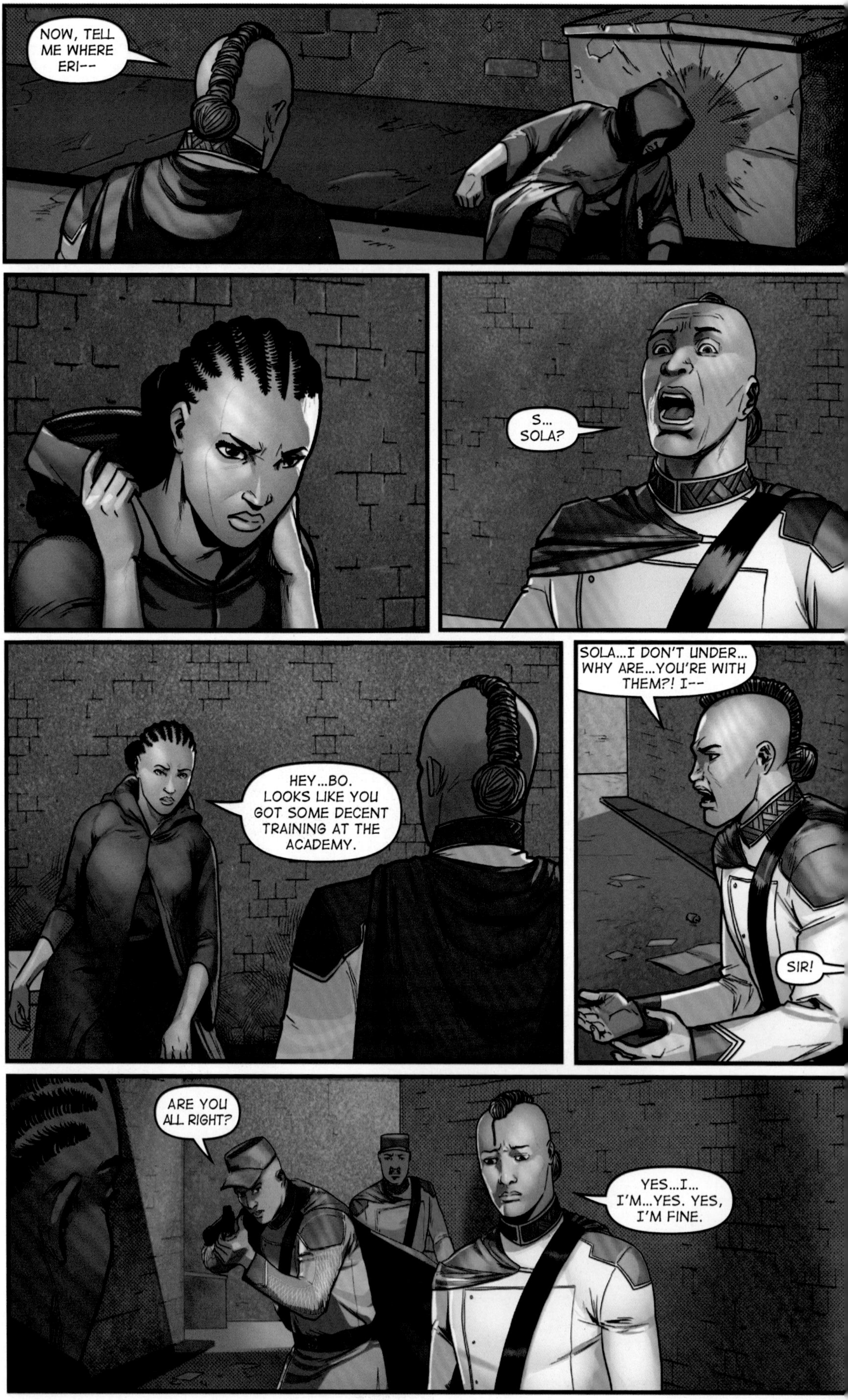
NOW, TELL ME WHERE ERI--
S... SOLA?
HEY...BO. LOOKS LIKE YOU GOT SOME DECENT TRAINING AT THE ACADEMY.
SOLA...I DON'T UNDER... WHY ARE...YOU'RE WITH THEM?! I--
SIR!
ARE YOU ALL RIGHT?
YES...I... I'M...YES. YES, I'M FINE.

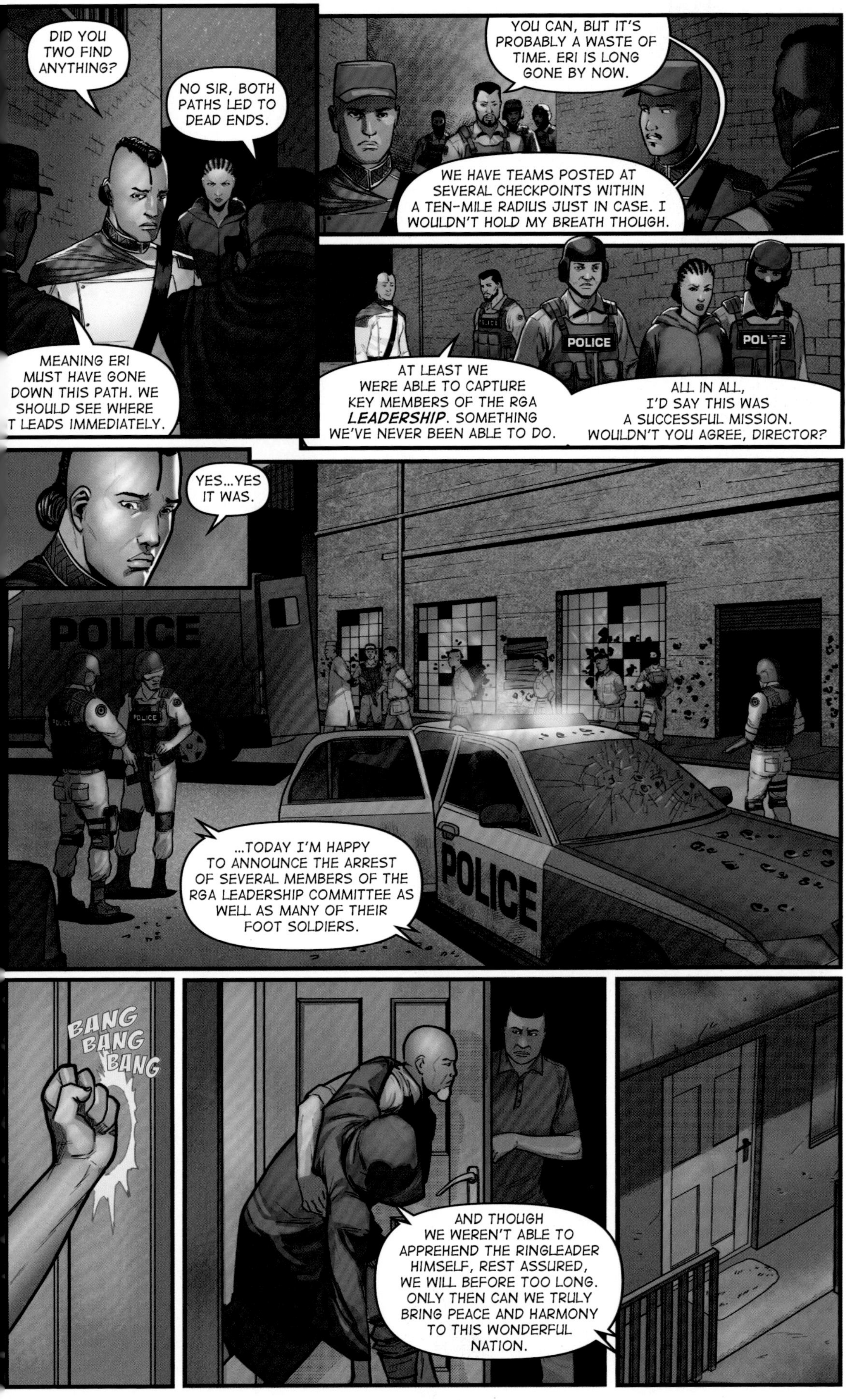
DID YOU TWO FIND ANYTHING?
NO SIR, BOTH PATHS LED TO DEAD ENDS.
MEANING ERI MUST HAVE GONE DOWN THIS PATH. WE SHOULD SEE WHERE T LEADS IMMEDIATELY.
YOU CAN, BUT IT'S PROBABLY A WASTE OF TIME. ERI IS LONG GONE BY NOW.
WE HAVE TEAMS POSTED AT SEVERAL CHECKPOINTS WITHIN A TEN-MILE RADIUS JUST IN CASE. I WOULDN'T HOLD MY BREATH THOUGH.
POLICE
POLICE
AT LEAST WE WERE ABLE TO CAPTURE KEY MEMBERS OF THE RGA *LEADERSHIP*. SOMETHING WE'VE NEVER BEEN ABLE TO DO.
ALL IN ALL, I'D SAY THIS WAS A SUCCESSFUL MISSION. WOULDN'T YOU AGREE, DIRECTOR?
YES...YES IT WAS.
POLICE
POLICE
...TODAY I'M HAPPY TO ANNOUNCE THE ARREST OF SEVERAL MEMBERS OF THE RGA LEADERSHIP COMMITTEE AS WELL AS MANY OF THEIR FOOT SOLDIERS.
BANG BANG BANG
AND THOUGH WE WEREN'T ABLE TO APPREHEND THE RINGLEADER HIMSELF, REST ASSURED, WE WILL BEFORE TOO LONG. ONLY THEN CAN WE TRULY BRING PEACE AND HARMONY TO THIS WONDERFUL NATION.

CHAPTER FIVE

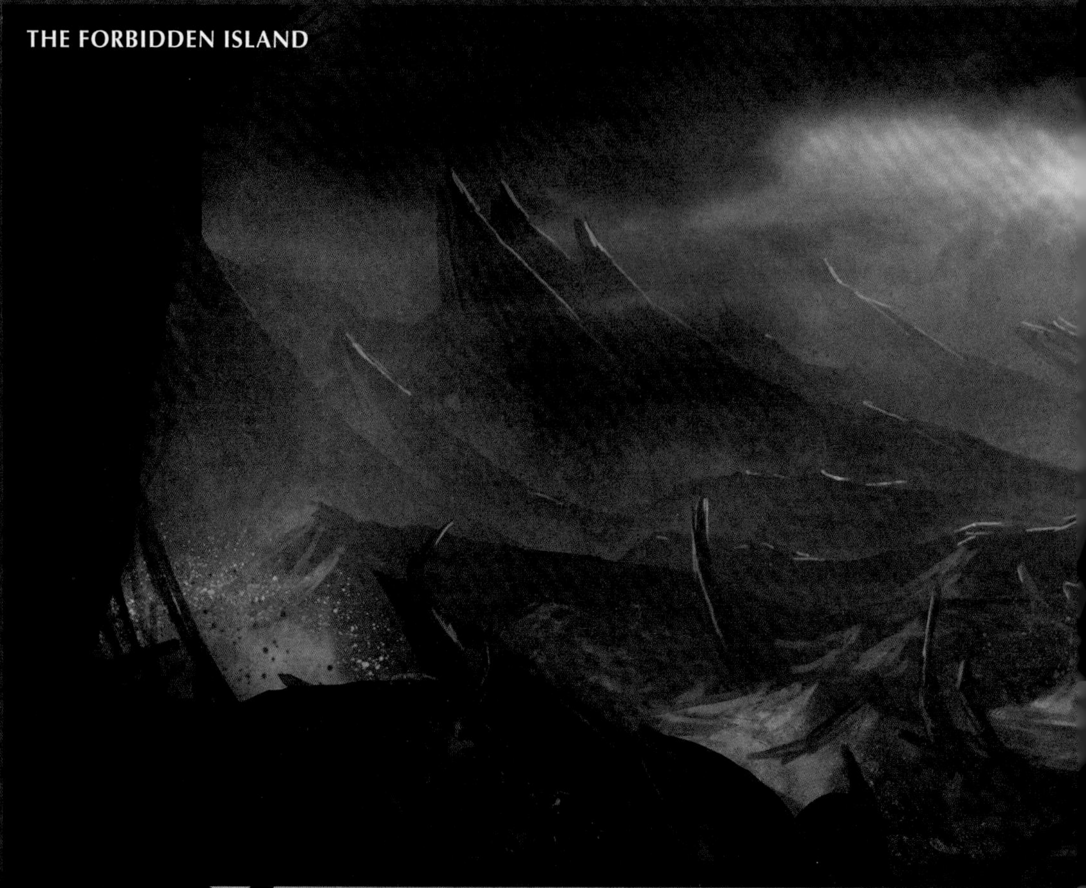
THE FORBIDDEN ISLAND

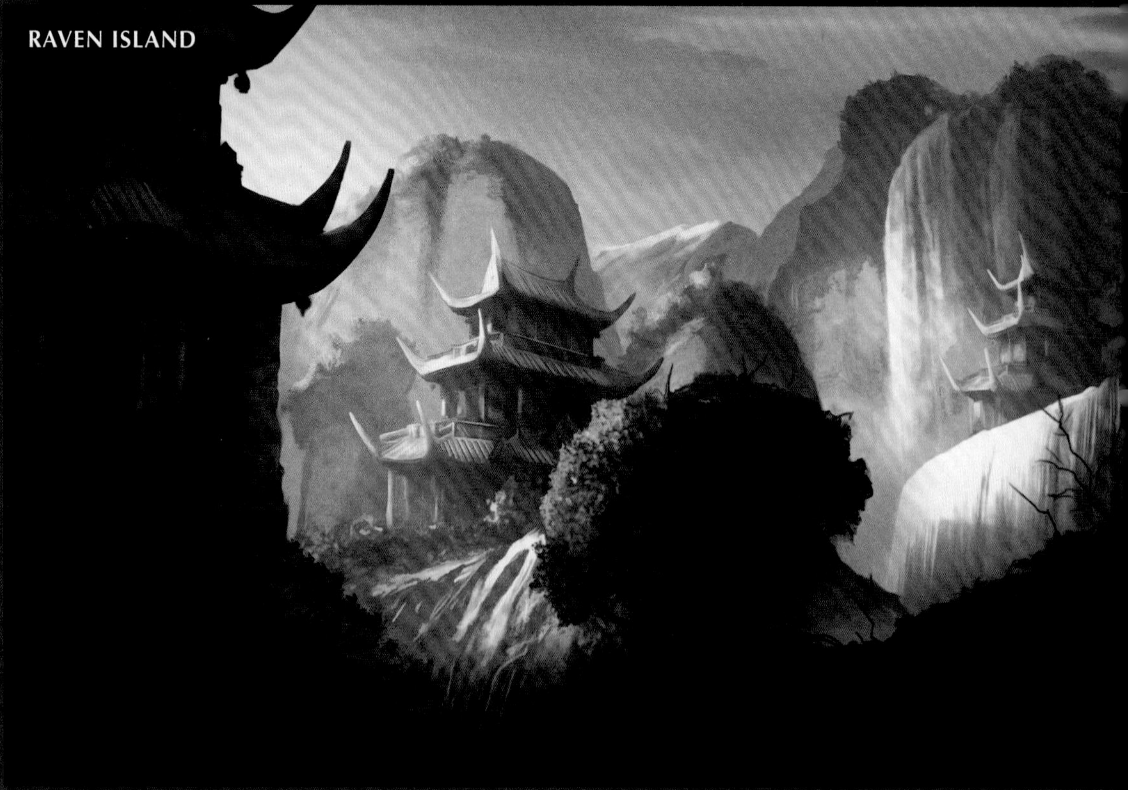
RAVEN ISLAND

ART BY GODWIN AKPAN

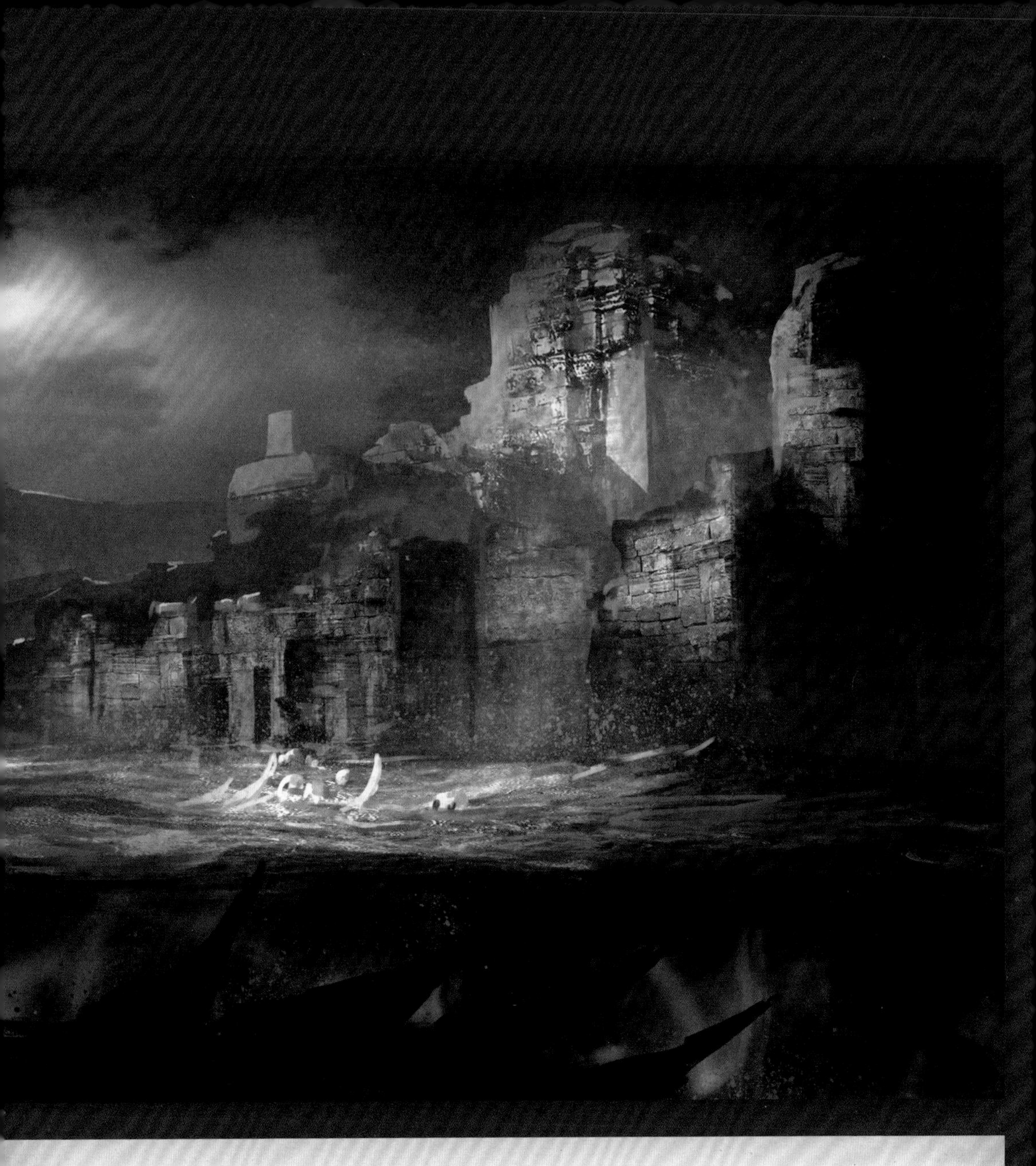

The Forbidden Island

Cursed by the frequent use of dark magic, the Forbidden Island is home to the Olon Jin—a group of dark deities that Atala and the Divine Ones exiled due to their obsession with dark magic. With rebellion embedded deep within their souls, the Olon Jin have once again begun to plot a treacherous plan to secure their freedom. Part of their tactics being using dark magic to conceal and move the entire Forbidden Island frequently to avoid capture.

Raven Island

Historically, Raven Island was home to the Elders of the ancient Kingdom of Atala. It was an island where Atala himself, king of the Divine Ones, frequently mediated and, as such, is considered holy ground.

Today, Raven Island is the home of the Dark Ravens—a separatist group of assassins that splintered off from the original Red Ravens due to their radical ideologies.

THE ISLAND OF THE FROST

ART BY GODWIN AKPAN

The Island of the Frost

Home to the highest mountains known to man, the Island of the Frost is a sight to behold. In a way, it is a mountain protruding out of the ocean with mountains on it. Which is why it is also commonly referred to as the "mountain of mountains." At such a high elevation, the freezing temperatures are unbearable for most life forms, making it the perfect home for the Frost Dragon during the time of dragons.

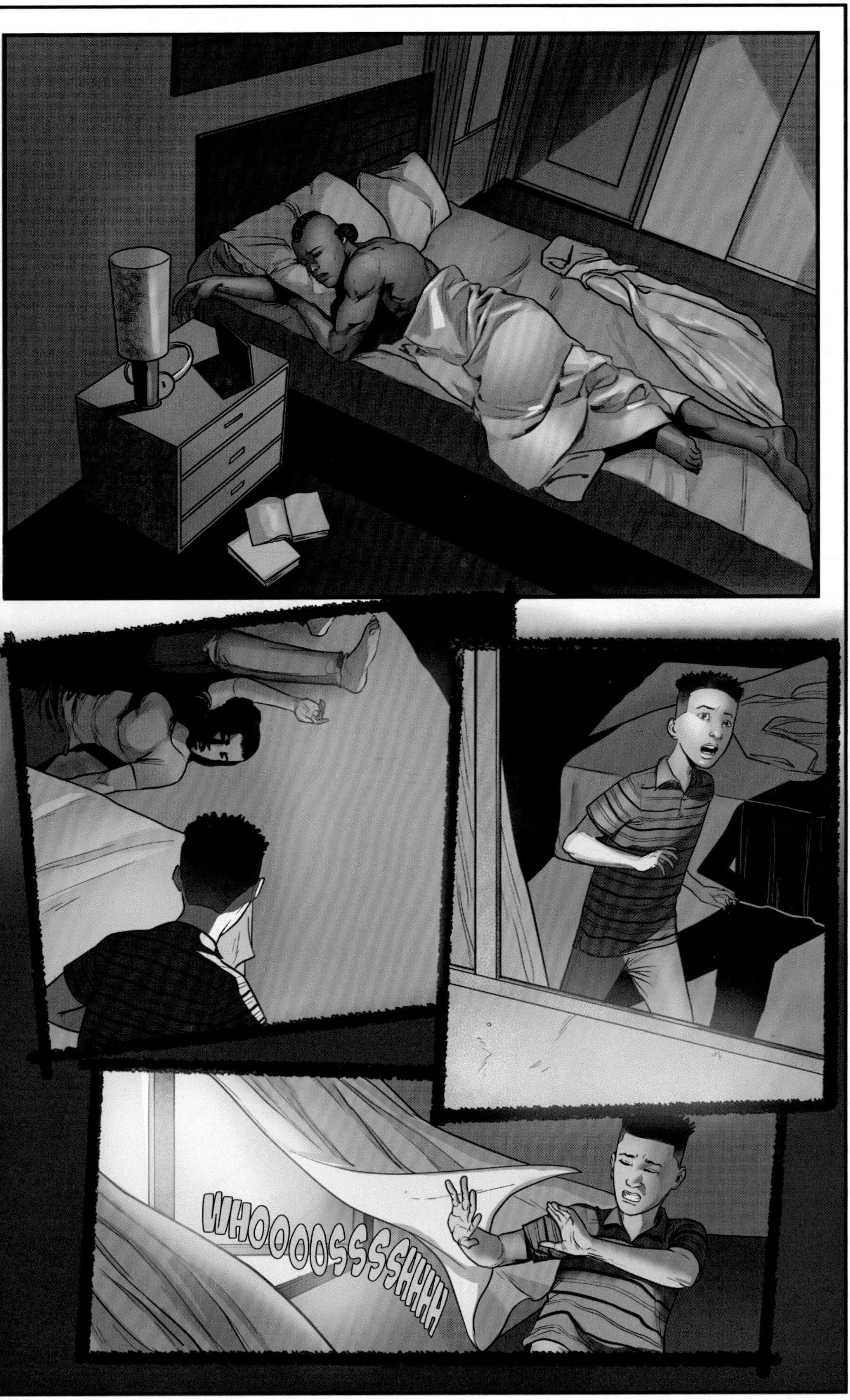
WHOOOOSSSSHHHH

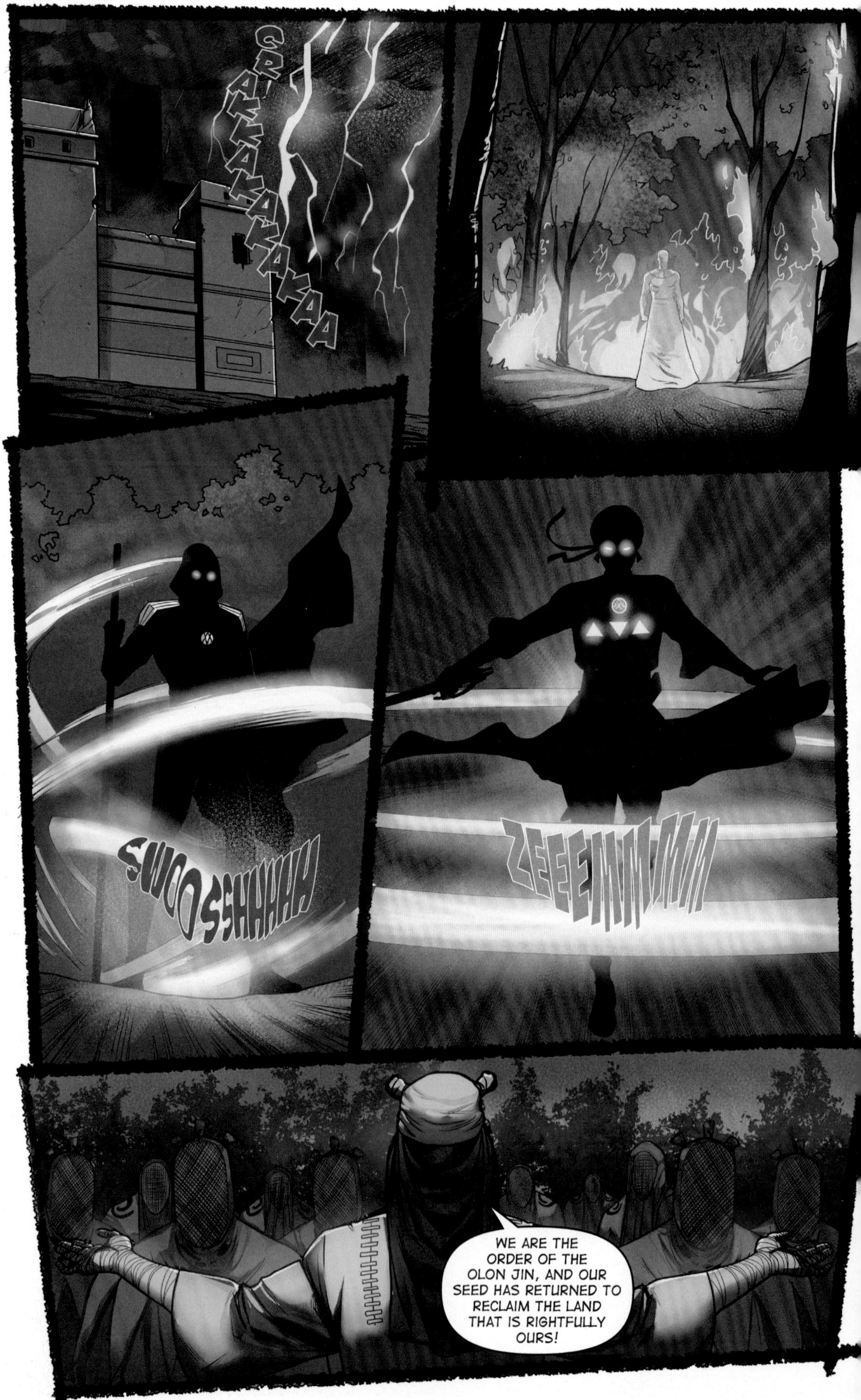

CRAKAKAKAYAA
SWOOSSHHHHH
ZEEEMMMMMM
WE ARE THE ORDER OF THE OLON JIN, AND OUR SEED HAS RETURNED TO RECLAIM THE LAND THAT IS RIGHTFULLY OURS!

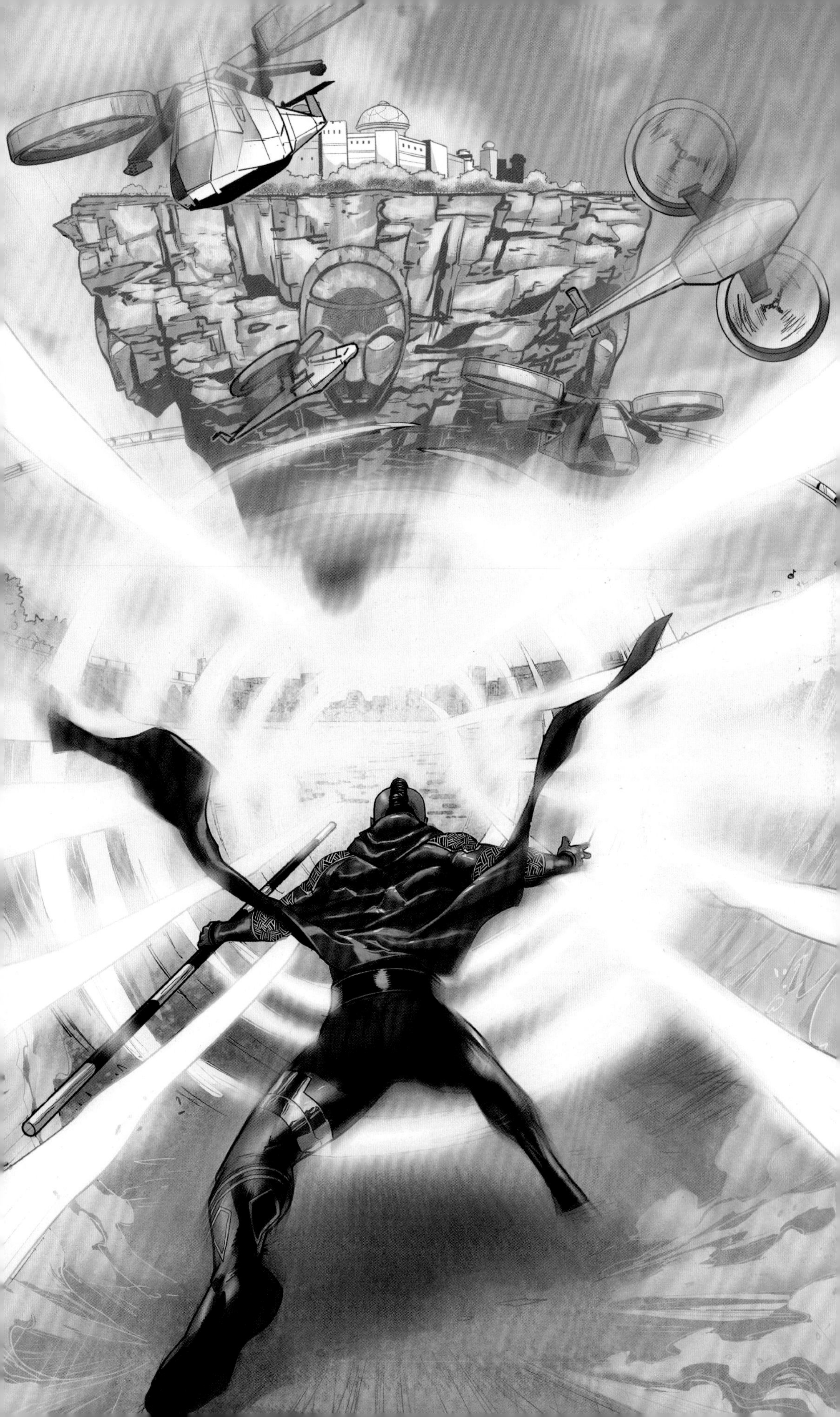

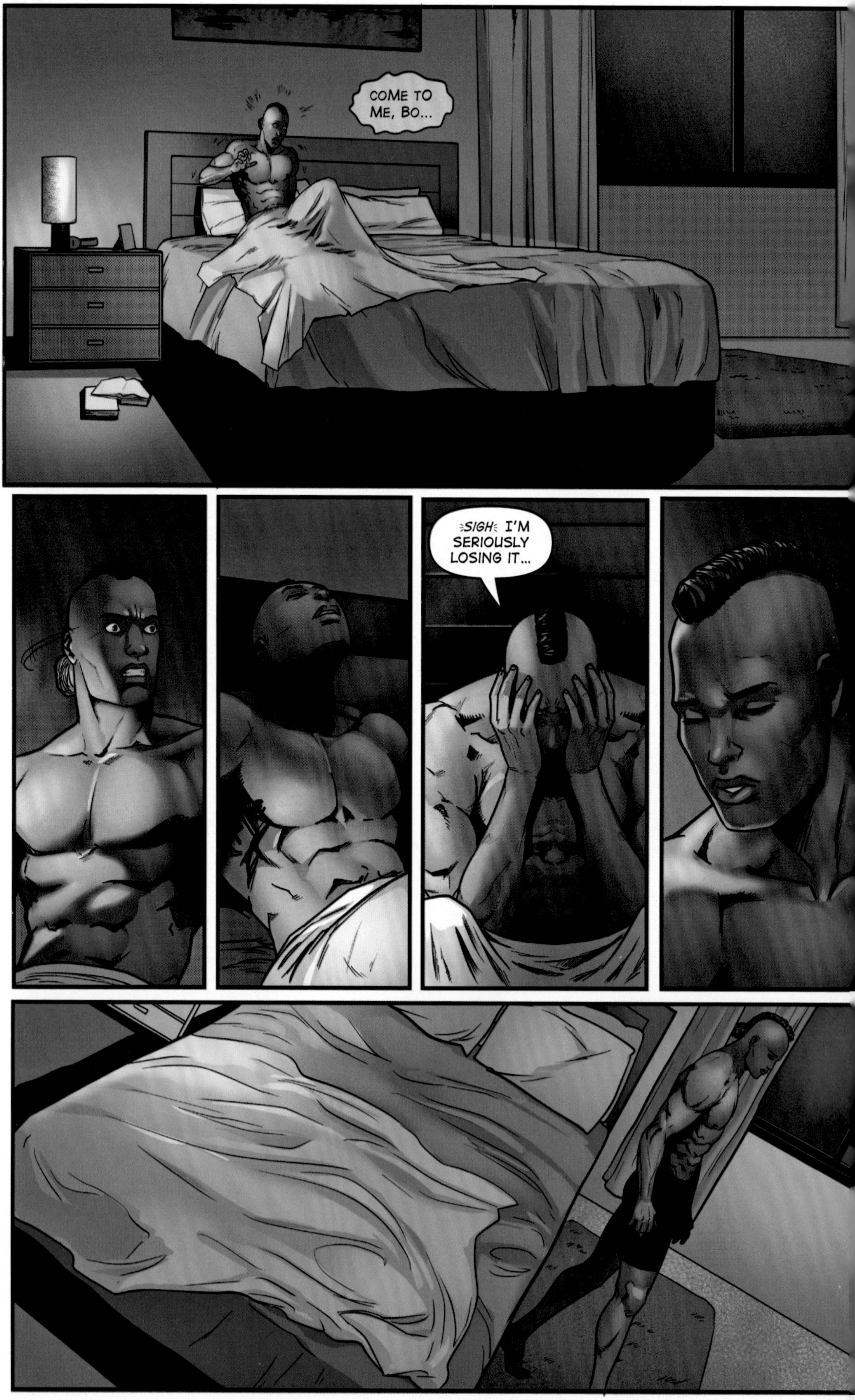
COME TO ME, BO...
SIGH I'M SERIOUSLY LOSING IT...

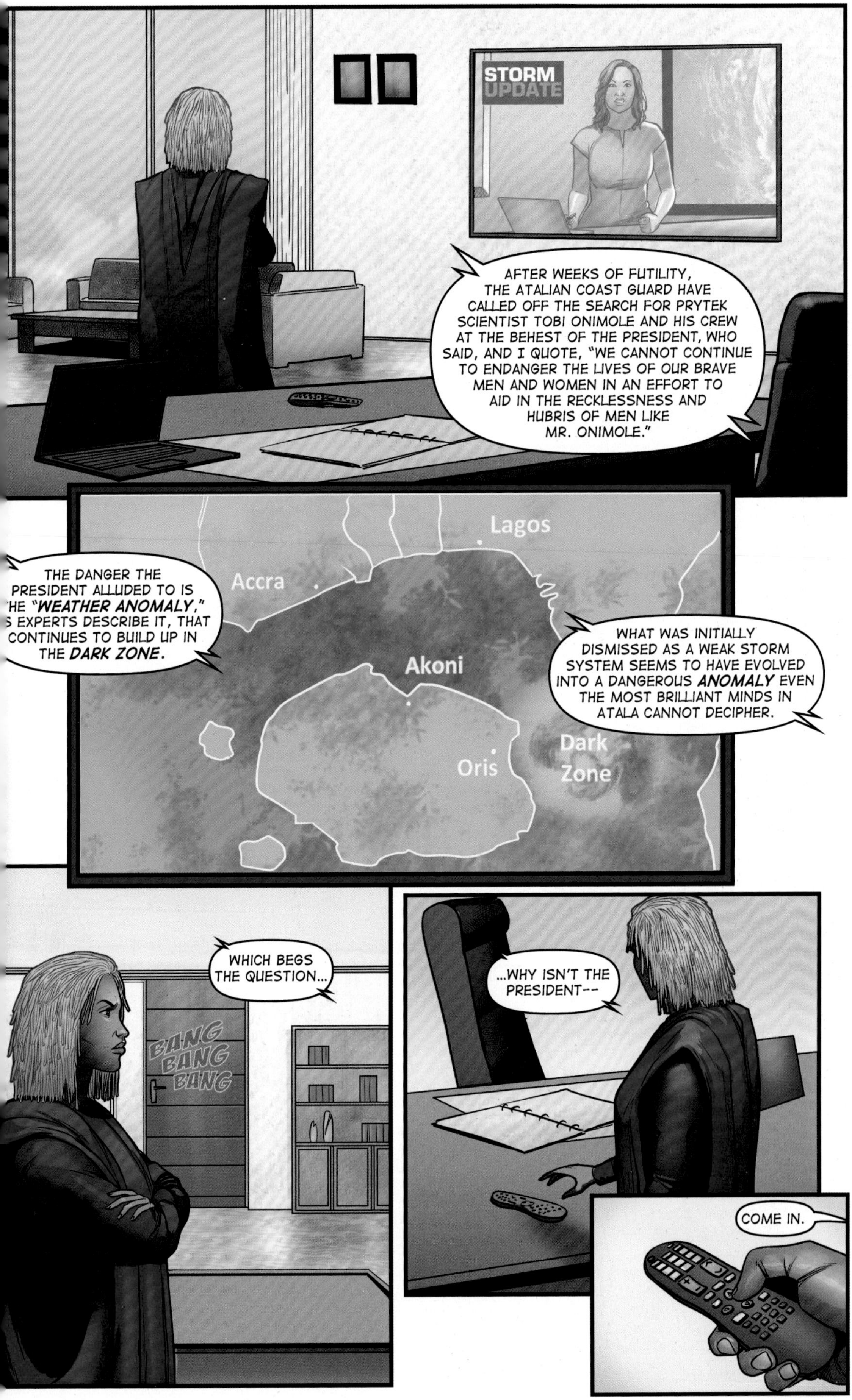
STORM UPDATE
AFTER WEEKS OF FUTILITY, THE ATALIAN COAST GUARD HAVE CALLED OFF THE SEARCH FOR PRYTEK SCIENTIST TOBI ONIMOLE AND HIS CREW AT THE BEHEST OF THE PRESIDENT, WHO SAID, AND I QUOTE, "WE CANNOT CONTINUE TO ENDANGER THE LIVES OF OUR BRAVE MEN AND WOMEN IN AN EFFORT TO AID IN THE RECKLESSNESS AND HUBRIS OF MEN LIKE MR. ONIMOLE."
Lagos
Accra
Akoni
Oris
Dark Zone
THE DANGER THE PRESIDENT ALLUDED TO IS HE "WEATHER ANOMALY," S EXPERTS DESCRIBE IT, THAT CONTINUES TO BUILD UP IN THE DARK ZONE.
WHAT WAS INITIALLY DISMISSED AS A WEAK STORM SYSTEM SEEMS TO HAVE EVOLVED INTO A DANGEROUS ANOMALY EVEN THE MOST BRILLIANT MINDS IN ATALA CANNOT DECIPHER.
WHICH BEGS THE QUESTION...
BANG BANG BANG
...WHY ISN'T THE PRESIDENT--
COME IN.

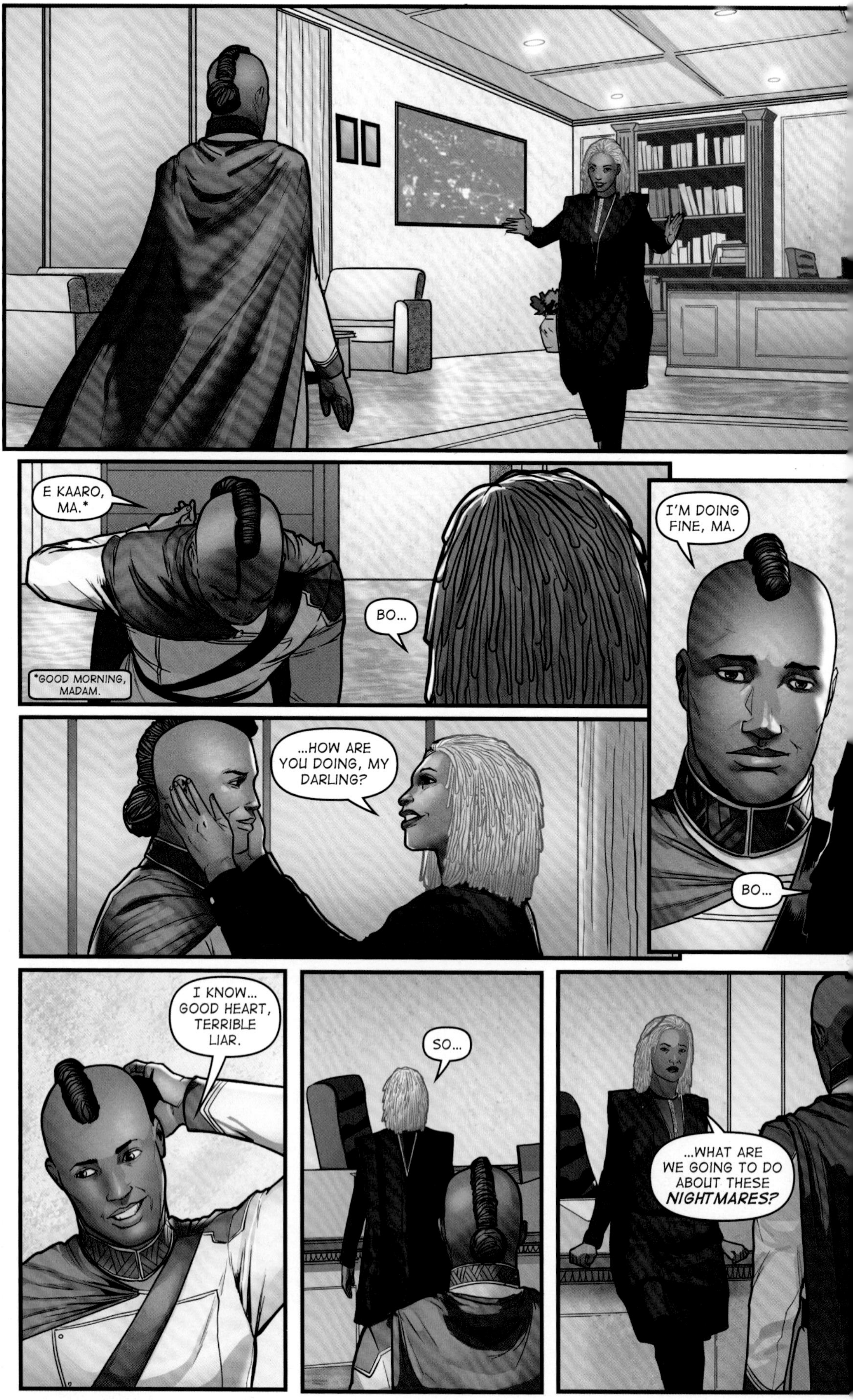
E KAARO, MA.*
*GOOD MORNING, MADAM.
BO...
I'M DOING FINE, MA.
...HOW ARE YOU DOING, MY DARLING?
BO...
I KNOW... GOOD HEART, TERRIBLE LIAR.
SO...
...WHAT ARE WE GOING TO DO ABOUT THESE *NIGHTMARES?*

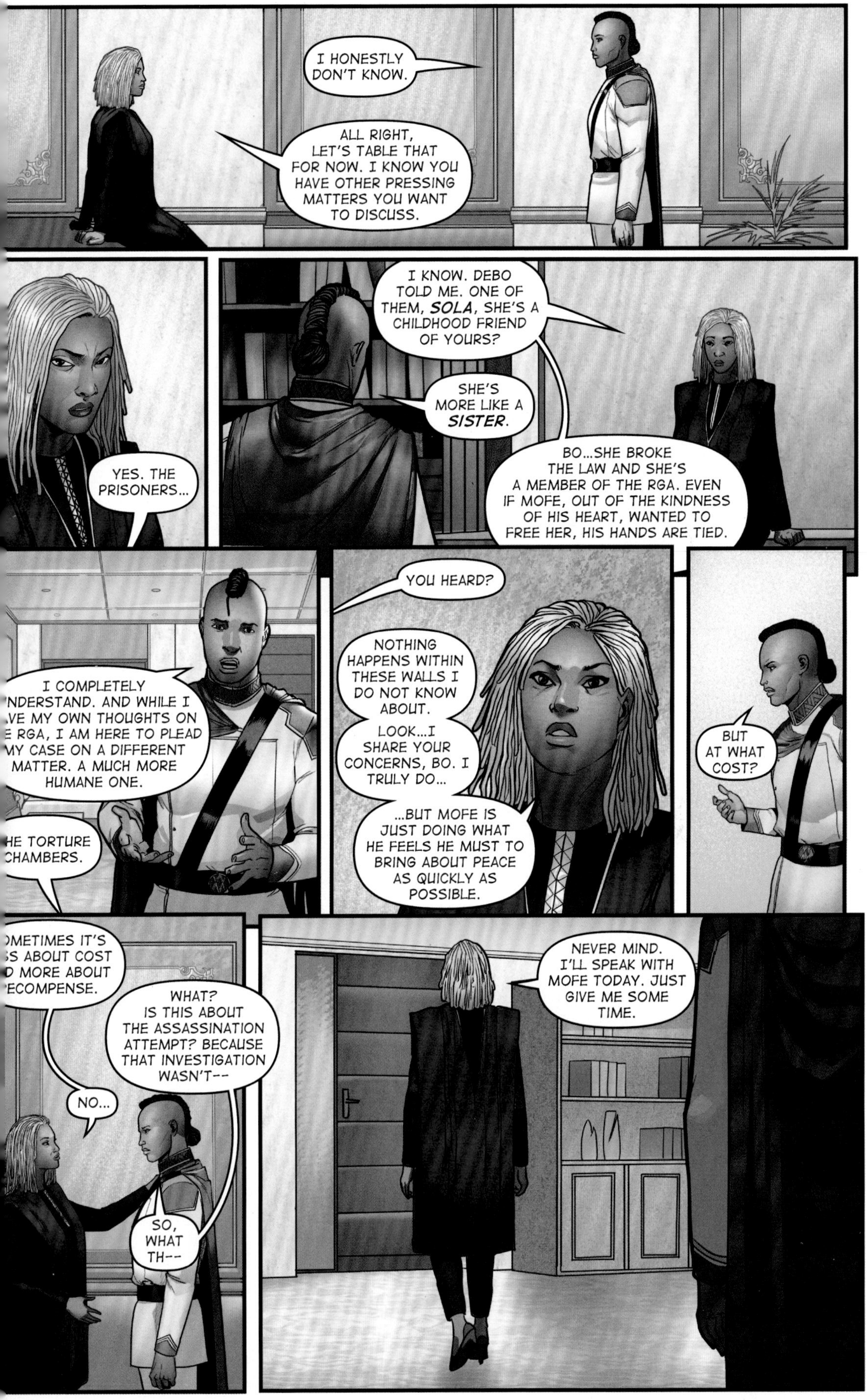
I HONESTLY DON'T KNOW.
ALL RIGHT, LET'S TABLE THAT FOR NOW. I KNOW YOU HAVE OTHER PRESSING MATTERS YOU WANT TO DISCUSS.
YES. THE PRISONERS...
I KNOW. DEBO TOLD ME. ONE OF THEM, SOLA, SHE'S A CHILDHOOD FRIEND OF YOURS?
SHE'S MORE LIKE A SISTER.
BO...SHE BROKE THE LAW AND SHE'S A MEMBER OF THE RGA. EVEN IF MOFE, OUT OF THE KINDNESS OF HIS HEART, WANTED TO FREE HER, HIS HANDS ARE TIED.
NDERSTAND. AND WHILE I
VE MY OWN THOUGHTS ON
E RGA, I AM HERE TO PLEAD
MY CASE ON A DIFFERENT MATTER. A MUCH MORE HUMANE ONE.
HE TORTURE CHAMBERS.
YOU HEARD?
NOTHING HAPPENS WITHIN THESE WALLS I DO NOT KNOW ABOUT.
LOOK...I SHARE YOUR CONCERNS, BO. I TRULY DO...
...BUT MOFE IS JUST DOING WHAT HE FEELS HE MUST TO BRING ABOUT PEACE AS QUICKLY AS POSSIBLE.
BUT AT WHAT COST?
OMETIMES IT'S
S ABOUT COST
D MORE ABOUT
ECOMPENSE.
WHAT? IS THIS ABOUT THE ASSASSINATION ATTEMPT? BECAUSE THAT INVESTIGATION WASN'T--
NO...
SO, WHAT TH--
NEVER MIND. I'LL SPEAK WITH MOFE TODAY. JUST GIVE ME SOME TIME.

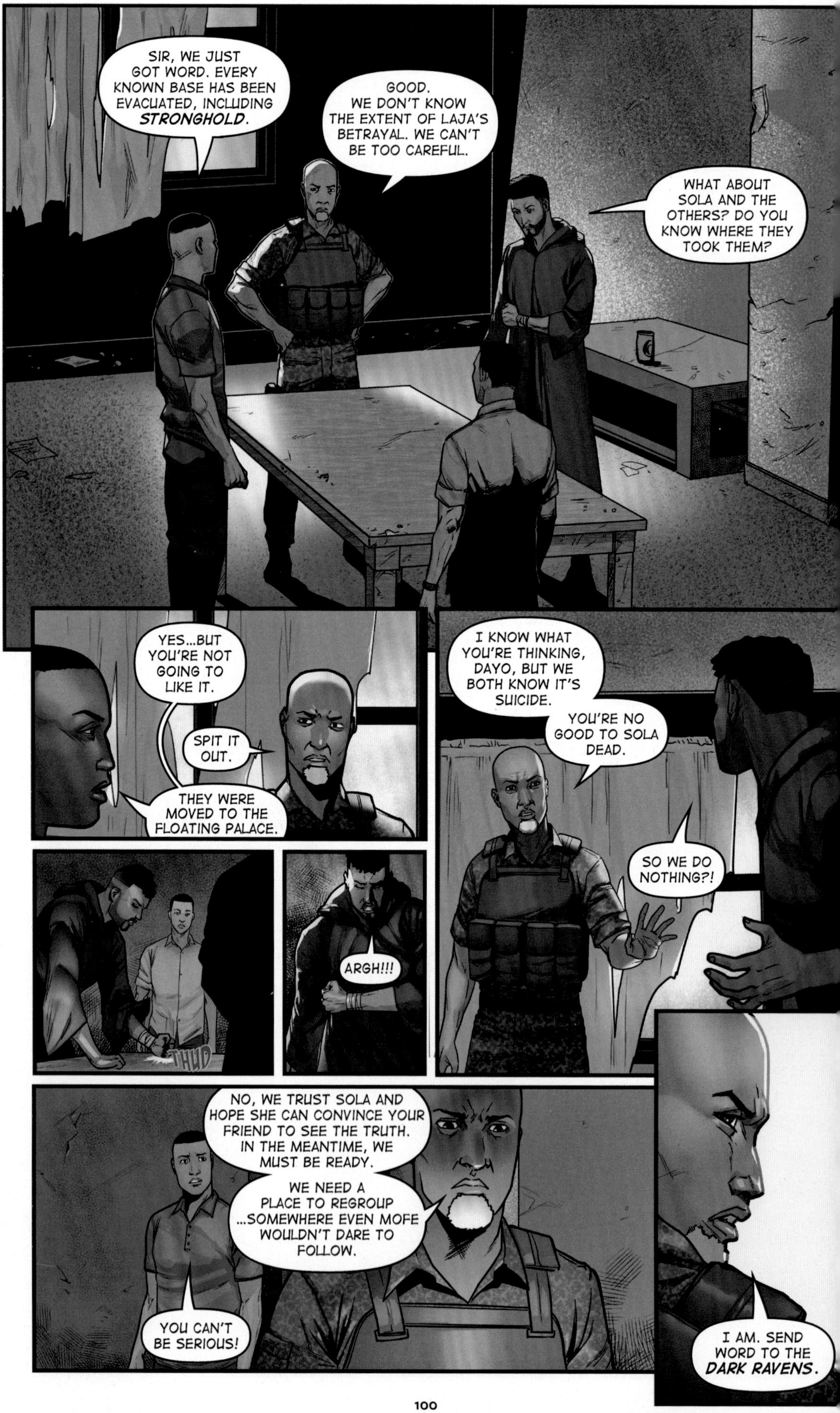
SIR, WE JUST GOT WORD. EVERY KNOWN BASE HAS BEEN EVACUATED, INCLUDING STRONGHOLD.
GOOD. WE DON'T KNOW THE EXTENT OF LAJA'S BETRAYAL. WE CAN'T BE TOO CAREFUL.
WHAT ABOUT SOLA AND THE OTHERS? DO YOU KNOW WHERE THEY TOOK THEM?
YES...BUT YOU'RE NOT GOING TO LIKE IT.
SPIT IT OUT.
THEY WERE MOVED TO THE FLOATING PALACE.
I KNOW WHAT YOU'RE THINKING, DAYO, BUT WE BOTH KNOW IT'S SUICIDE.
YOU'RE NO GOOD TO SOLA DEAD.
SO WE DO NOTHING?!
THUD
ARGH!!!
NO, WE TRUST SOLA AND HOPE SHE CAN CONVINCE YOUR FRIEND TO SEE THE TRUTH. IN THE MEANTIME, WE MUST BE READY.
WE NEED A PLACE TO REGROUP ...SOMEWHERE EVEN MOFE WOULDN'T DARE TO FOLLOW.
YOU CAN'T BE SERIOUS!
I AM. SEND WORD TO THE DARK RAVENS.

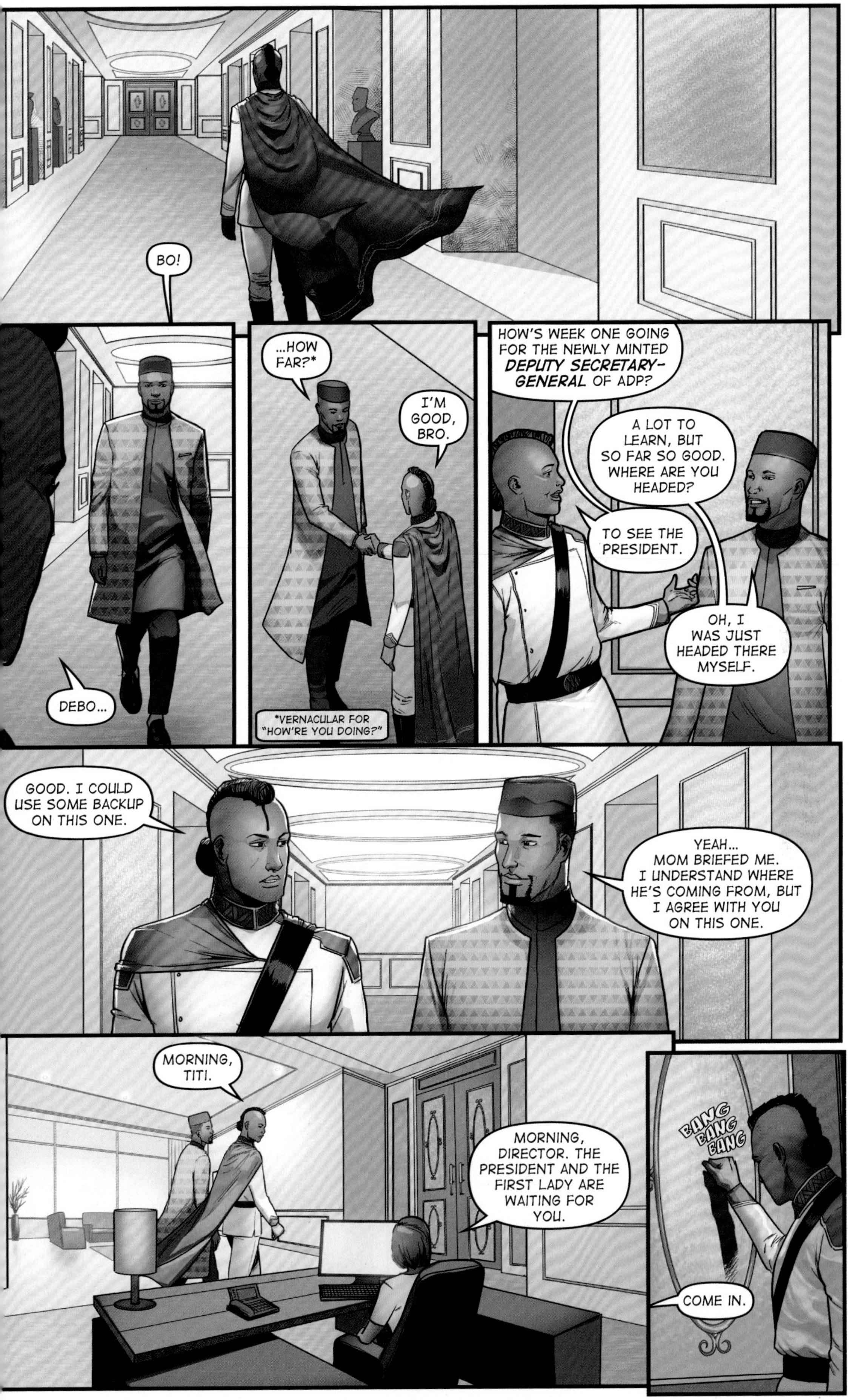
BO!
DEBO...
...HOW FAR?*
I'M GOOD, BRO.
*VERNACULAR FOR "HOW'RE YOU DOING?"
HOW'S WEEK ONE GOING FOR THE NEWLY MINTED *DEPUTY SECRETARY-GENERAL* OF ADP?
A LOT TO LEARN, BUT SO FAR SO GOOD. WHERE ARE YOU HEADED?
TO SEE THE PRESIDENT.
OH, I WAS JUST HEADED THERE MYSELF.
GOOD. I COULD USE SOME BACKUP ON THIS ONE.
YEAH... MOM BRIEFED ME. I UNDERSTAND WHERE HE'S COMING FROM, BUT I AGREE WITH YOU ON THIS ONE.
MORNING, TITI.
MORNING, DIRECTOR. THE PRESIDENT AND THE FIRST LADY ARE WAITING FOR YOU.
BANG BANG BANG
COME IN.

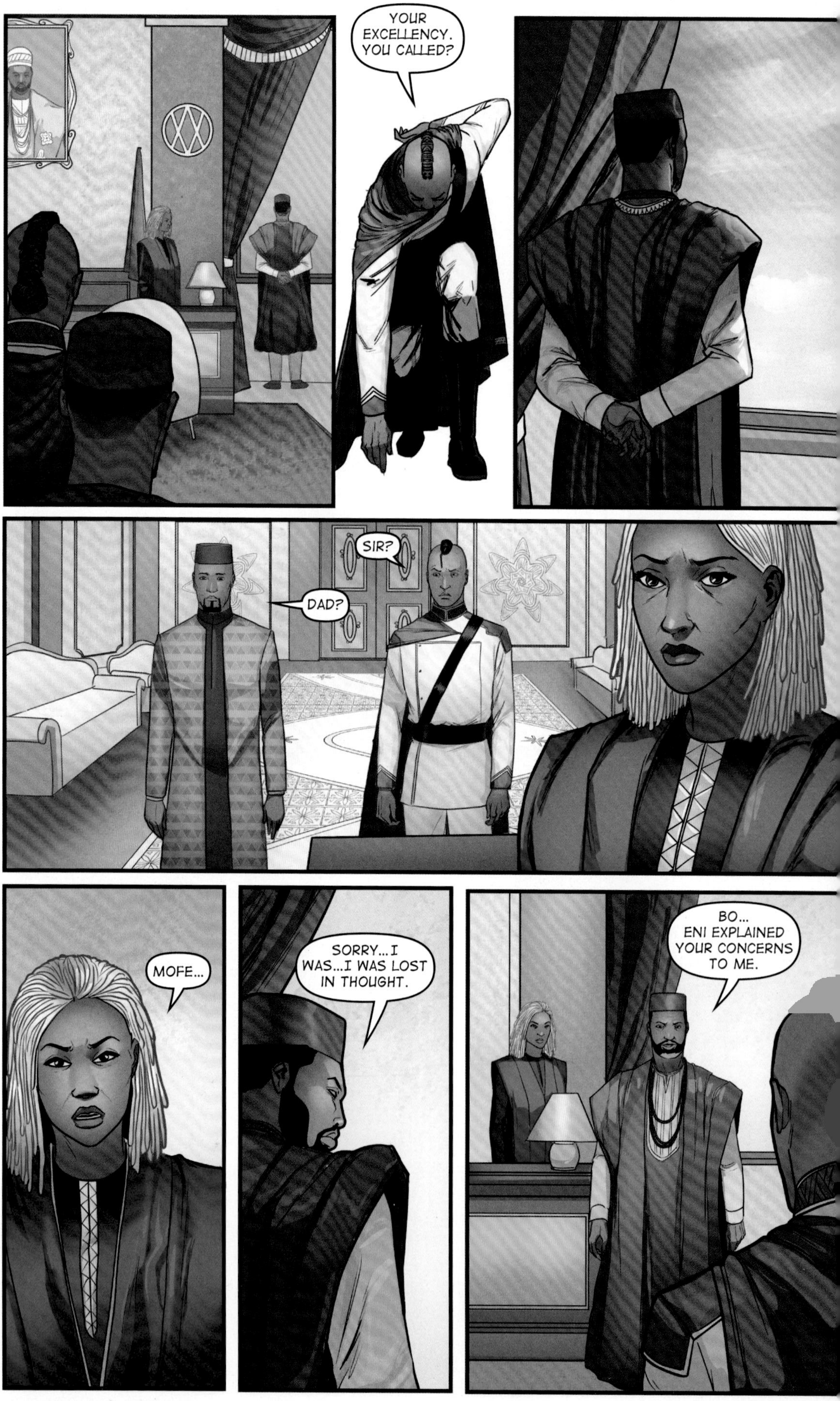
YOUR EXCELLENCY. YOU CALLED?
SIR?
DAD?
MOFE...
SORRY... I WAS...I WAS LOST IN THOUGHT.
BO... ENI EXPLAINED YOUR CONCERNS TO ME.

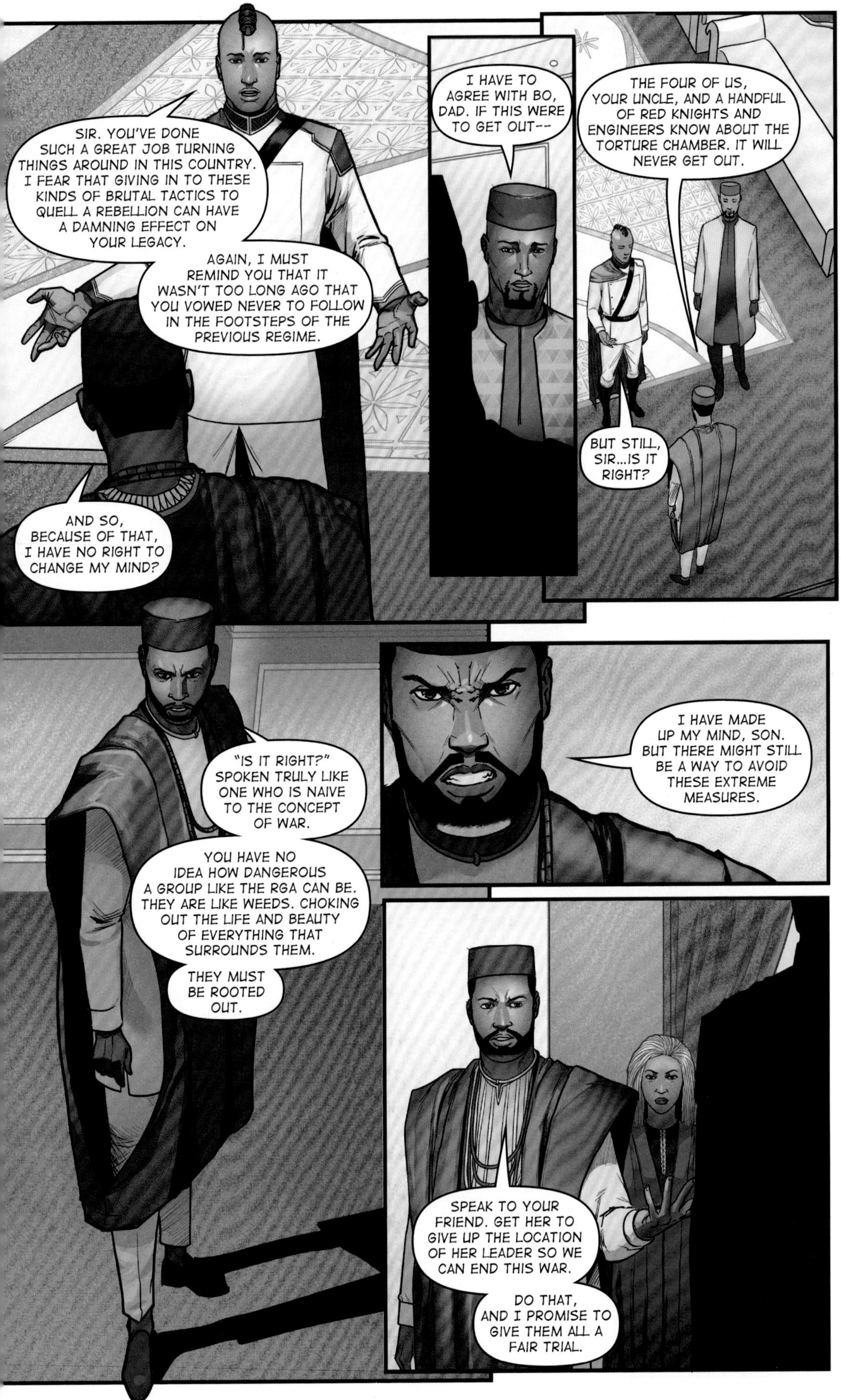
SIR. YOU'VE DONE SUCH A GREAT JOB TURNING THINGS AROUND IN THIS COUNTRY. I FEAR THAT GIVING IN TO THESE KINDS OF BRUTAL TACTICS TO QUELL A REBELLION CAN HAVE A DAMNING EFFECT ON YOUR LEGACY.
AGAIN, I MUST REMIND YOU THAT IT WASN'T TOO LONG AGO THAT YOU VOWED NEVER TO FOLLOW IN THE FOOTSTEPS OF THE PREVIOUS REGIME.
AND SO, BECAUSE OF THAT, I HAVE NO RIGHT TO CHANGE MY MIND?
I HAVE TO AGREE WITH BO, DAD. IF THIS WERE TO GET OUT--
THE FOUR OF US, YOUR UNCLE, AND A HANDFUL OF RED KNIGHTS AND ENGINEERS KNOW ABOUT THE TORTURE CHAMBER. IT WILL NEVER GET OUT.
BUT STILL, SIR...IS IT RIGHT?
"IS IT RIGHT?" SPOKEN TRULY LIKE ONE WHO IS NAIVE TO THE CONCEPT OF WAR.
YOU HAVE NO IDEA HOW DANGEROUS A GROUP LIKE THE RGA CAN BE. THEY ARE LIKE WEEDS. CHOKING OUT THE LIFE AND BEAUTY OF EVERYTHING THAT SURROUNDS THEM.
THEY MUST BE ROOTED OUT.
I HAVE MADE UP MY MIND, SON. BUT THERE MIGHT STILL BE A WAY TO AVOID THESE EXTREME MEASURES.
SPEAK TO YOUR FRIEND. GET HER TO GIVE UP THE LOCATION OF HER LEADER SO WE CAN END THIS WAR.
DO THAT, AND I PROMISE TO GIVE THEM ALL A FAIR TRIAL.

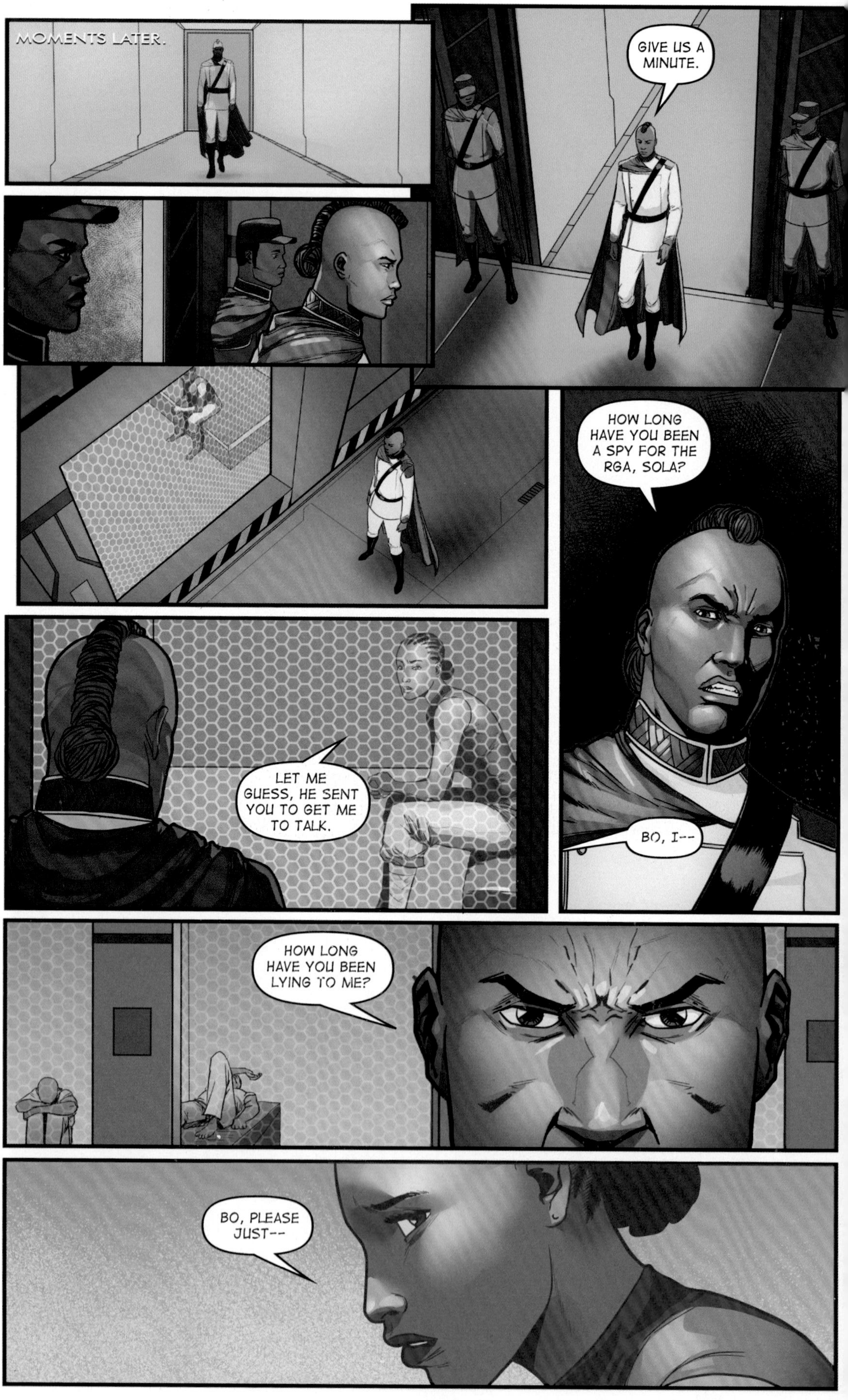
MOMENTS LATER.
GIVE US A MINUTE.
HOW LONG HAVE YOU BEEN A SPY FOR THE RGA, SOLA?
LET ME GUESS, HE SENT YOU TO GET ME TO TALK.
BO, I--
HOW LONG HAVE YOU BEEN LYING TO ME?
BO, PLEASE JUST--

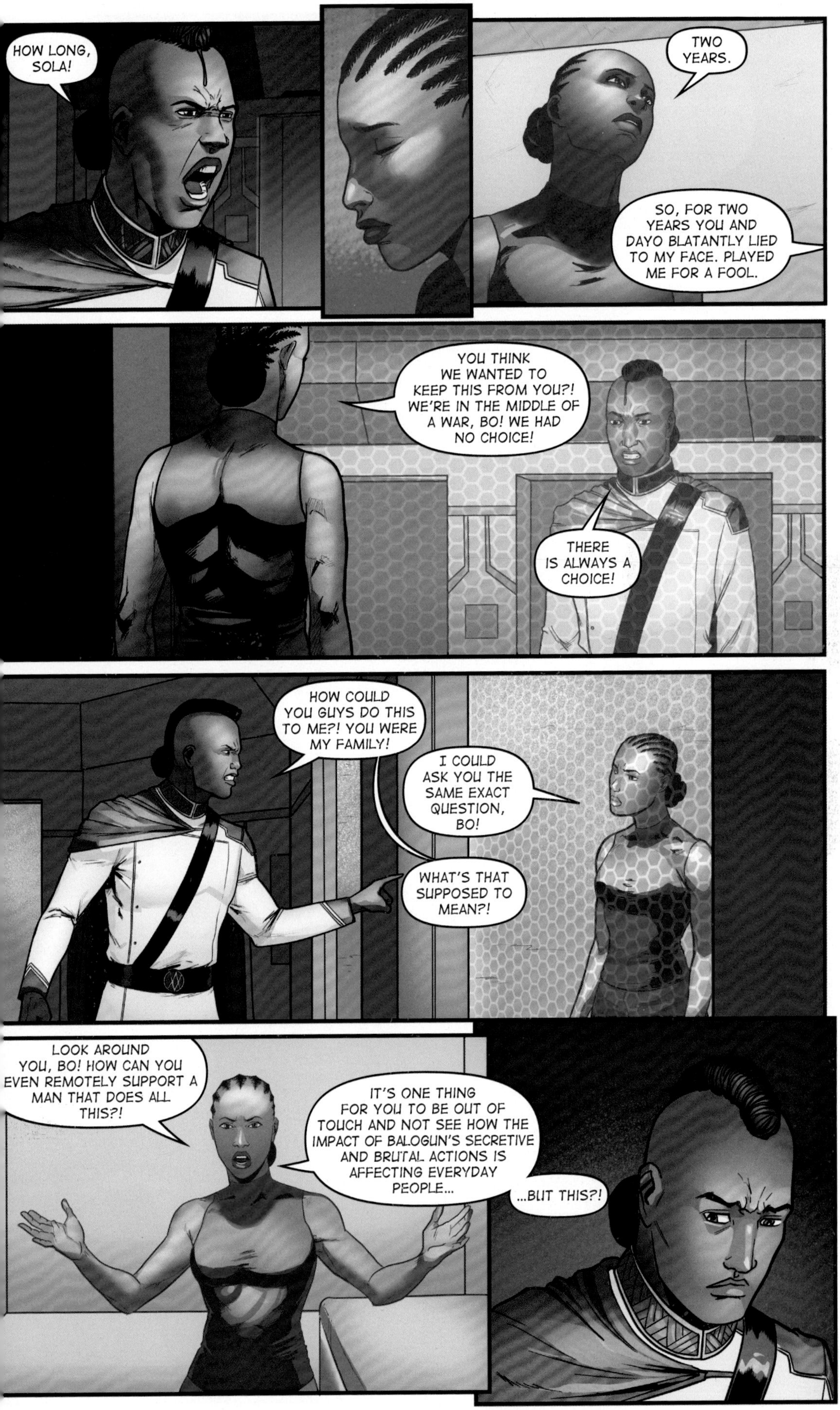
HOW LONG, SOLA!
TWO YEARS.
SO, FOR TWO YEARS YOU AND DAYO BLATANTLY LIED TO MY FACE. PLAYED ME FOR A FOOL.
YOU THINK WE WANTED TO KEEP THIS FROM YOU?! WE'RE IN THE MIDDLE OF A WAR, BO! WE HAD NO CHOICE!
THERE IS ALWAYS A CHOICE!
HOW COULD YOU GUYS DO THIS TO ME?! YOU WERE MY FAMILY!
I COULD ASK YOU THE SAME EXACT QUESTION, BO!
WHAT'S THAT SUPPOSED TO MEAN?!
LOOK AROUND YOU, BO! HOW CAN YOU EVEN REMOTELY SUPPORT A MAN THAT DOES ALL THIS?!
IT'S ONE THING FOR YOU TO BE OUT OF TOUCH AND NOT SEE HOW THE IMPACT OF BALOGUN'S SECRETIVE AND BRUTAL ACTIONS IS AFFECTING EVERYDAY PEOPLE...
...BUT THIS?!

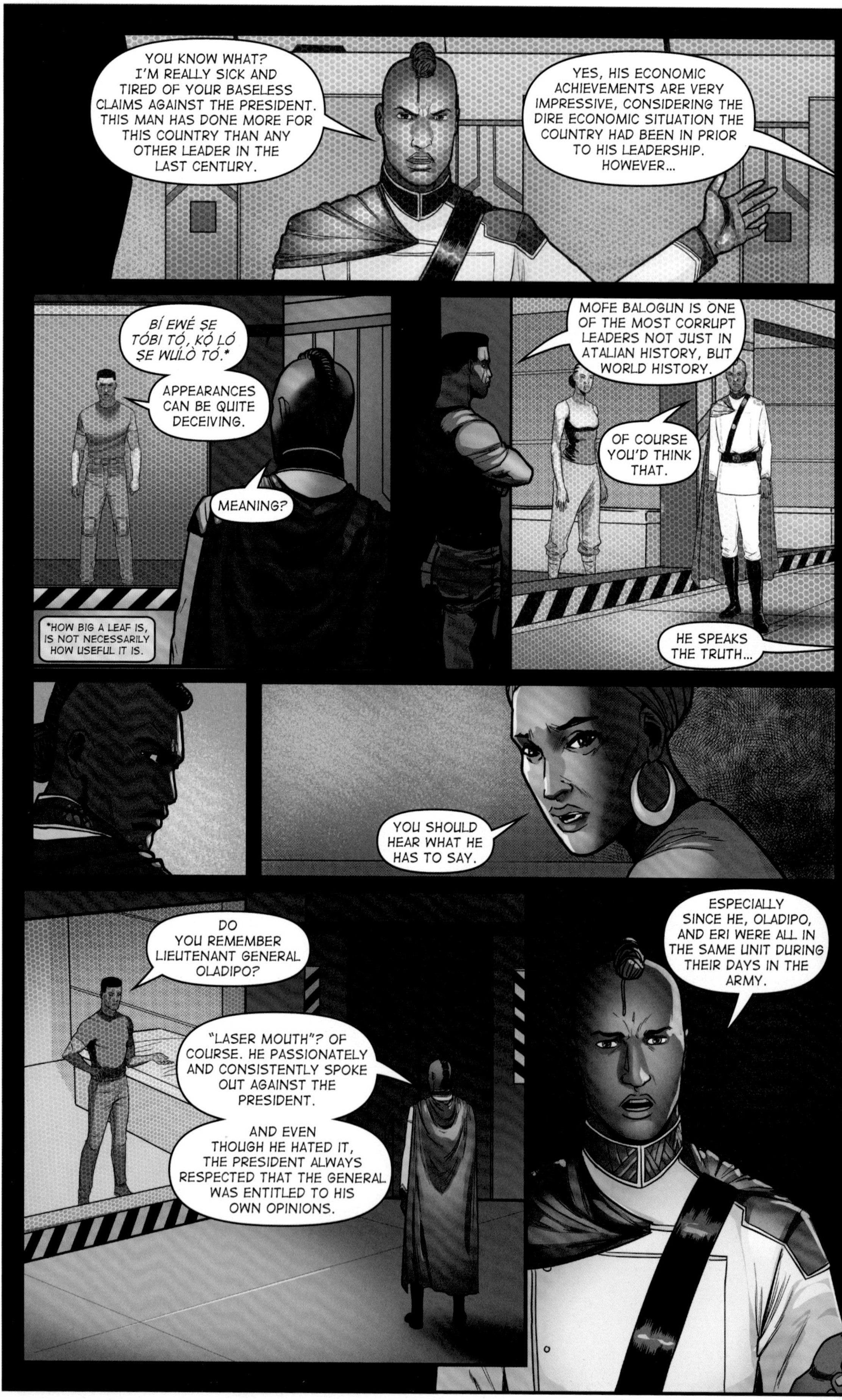

YOU KNOW WHAT? I'M REALLY SICK AND TIRED OF YOUR BASELESS CLAIMS AGAINST THE PRESIDENT. THIS MAN HAS DONE MORE FOR THIS COUNTRY THAN ANY OTHER LEADER IN THE LAST CENTURY.
YES, HIS ECONOMIC ACHIEVEMENTS ARE VERY IMPRESSIVE, CONSIDERING THE DIRE ECONOMIC SITUATION THE COUNTRY HAD BEEN IN PRIOR TO HIS LEADERSHIP. HOWEVER...
BÍ EWÉ ṢE TÓBI TÓ, KỌ́ LÓ ṢE WÚLÒ TÓ.*
APPEARANCES CAN BE QUITE DECEIVING.
*HOW BIG A LEAF IS, IS NOT NECESSARILY HOW USEFUL IT IS.
MEANING?
MOFE BALOGUN IS ONE OF THE MOST CORRUPT LEADERS NOT JUST IN ATALIAN HISTORY, BUT WORLD HISTORY.
OF COURSE YOU'D THINK THAT.
HE SPEAKS THE TRUTH...
YOU SHOULD HEAR WHAT HE HAS TO SAY.
DO YOU REMEMBER LIEUTENANT GENERAL OLADIPO?
"LASER MOUTH"? OF COURSE. HE PASSIONATELY AND CONSISTENTLY SPOKE OUT AGAINST THE PRESIDENT.
AND EVEN THOUGH HE HATED IT, THE PRESIDENT ALWAYS RESPECTED THAT THE GENERAL WAS ENTITLED TO HIS OWN OPINIONS.
ESPECIALLY SINCE HE, OLADIPO, AND ERI WERE ALL IN THE SAME UNIT DURING THEIR DAYS IN THE ARMY.

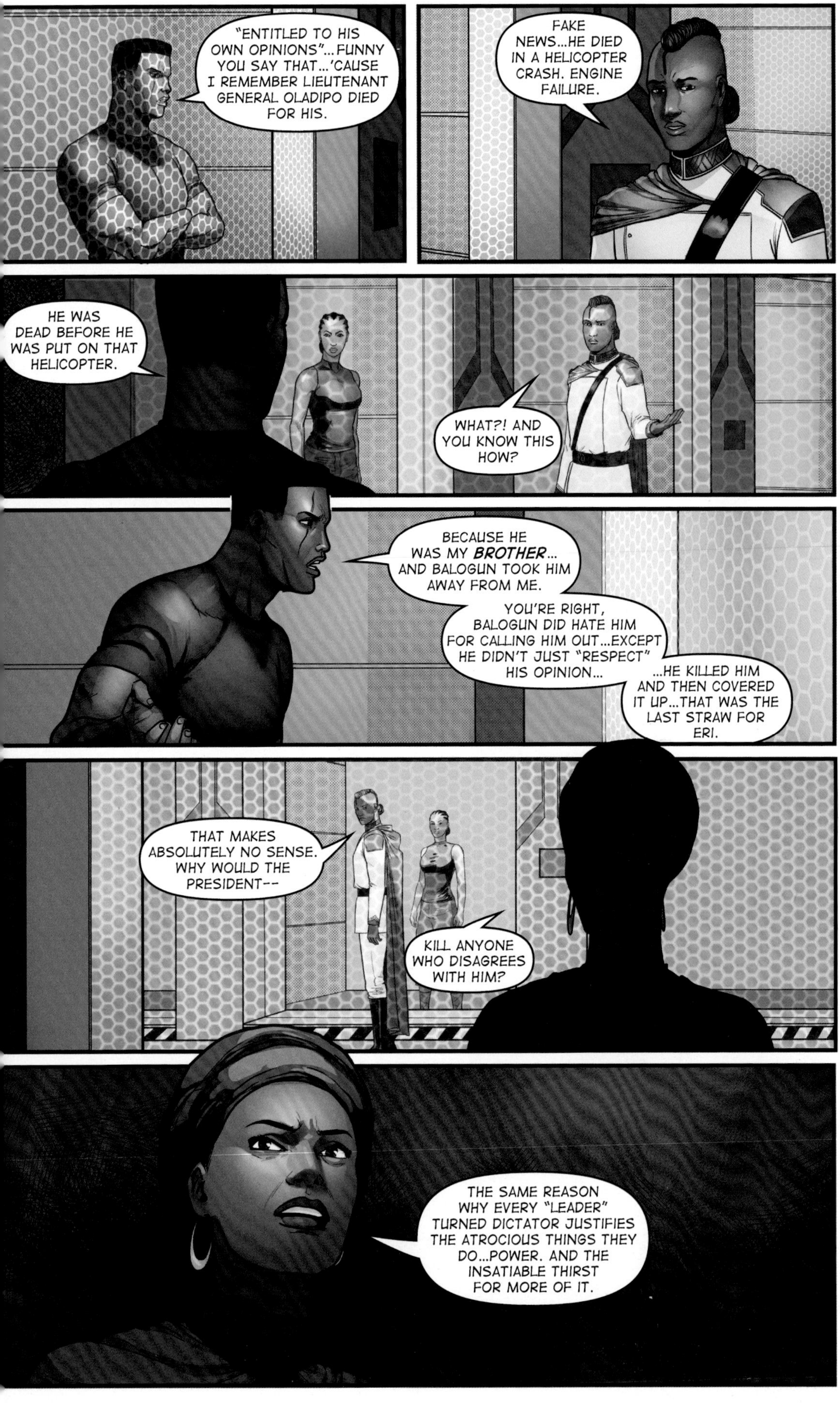
"ENTITLED TO HIS OWN OPINIONS"...FUNNY YOU SAY THAT...'CAUSE I REMEMBER LIEUTENANT GENERAL OLADIPO DIED FOR HIS.
FAKE NEWS...HE DIED IN A HELICOPTER CRASH. ENGINE FAILURE.
HE WAS DEAD BEFORE HE WAS PUT ON THAT HELICOPTER.
WHAT?! AND YOU KNOW THIS HOW?
BECAUSE HE WAS MY BROTHER... AND BALOGUN TOOK HIM AWAY FROM ME.
YOU'RE RIGHT, BALOGUN DID HATE HIM FOR CALLING HIM OUT...EXCEPT HE DIDN'T JUST "RESPECT" HIS OPINION...
...HE KILLED HIM AND THEN COVERED IT UP...THAT WAS THE LAST STRAW FOR ERI.
THAT MAKES ABSOLUTELY NO SENSE. WHY WOULD THE PRESIDENT--
KILL ANYONE WHO DISAGREES WITH HIM?
THE SAME REASON WHY EVERY "LEADER" TURNED DICTATOR JUSTIFIES THE ATROCIOUS THINGS THEY DO...POWER. AND THE INSATIABLE THIRST FOR MORE OF IT.

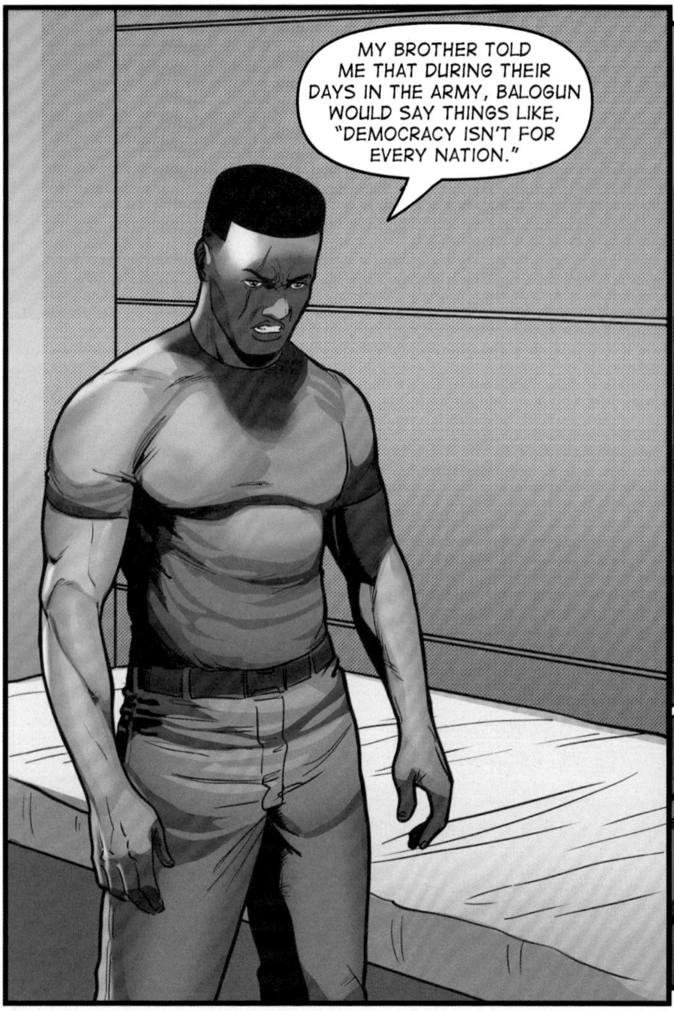
MY BROTHER TOLD ME THAT DURING THEIR DAYS IN THE ARMY, BALOGUN WOULD SAY THINGS LIKE, "DEMOCRACY ISN'T FOR EVERY NATION."

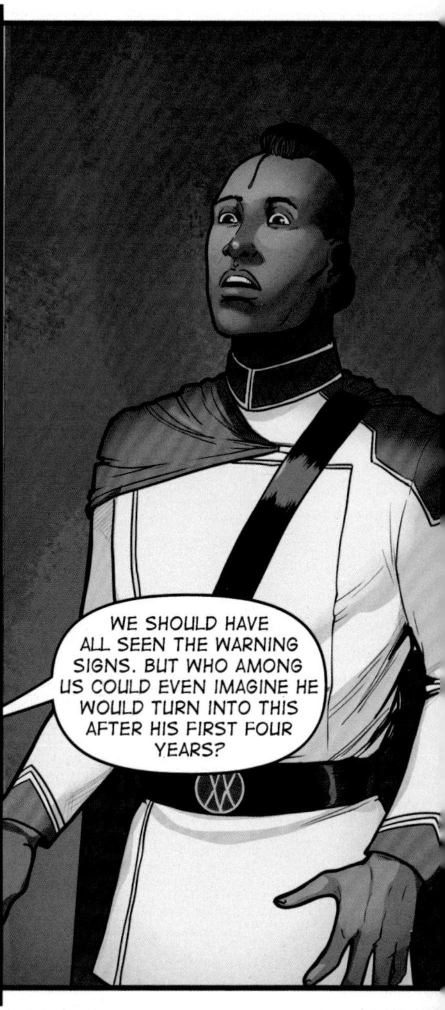
WE SHOULD HAVE ALL SEEN THE WARNING SIGNS. BUT WHO AMONG US COULD EVEN IMAGINE HE WOULD TURN INTO THIS AFTER HIS FIRST FOUR YEARS?

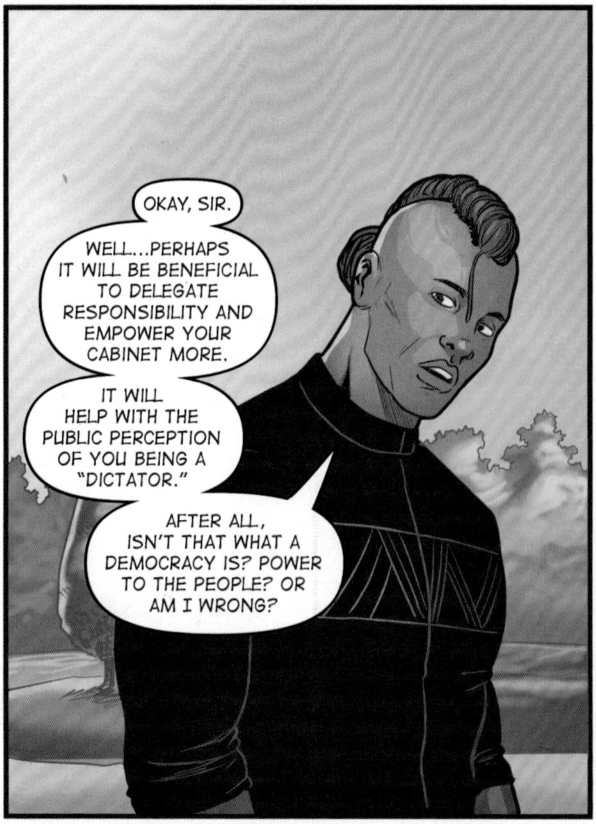
OKAY, SIR.
WELL...PERHAPS IT WILL BE BENEFICIAL TO DELEGATE RESPONSIBILITY AND EMPOWER YOUR CABINET MORE.
IT WILL HELP WITH THE PUBLIC PERCEPTION OF YOU BEING A "DICTATOR."
AFTER ALL, ISN'T THAT WHAT A DEMOCRACY IS? POWER TO THE PEOPLE? OR AM I WRONG?

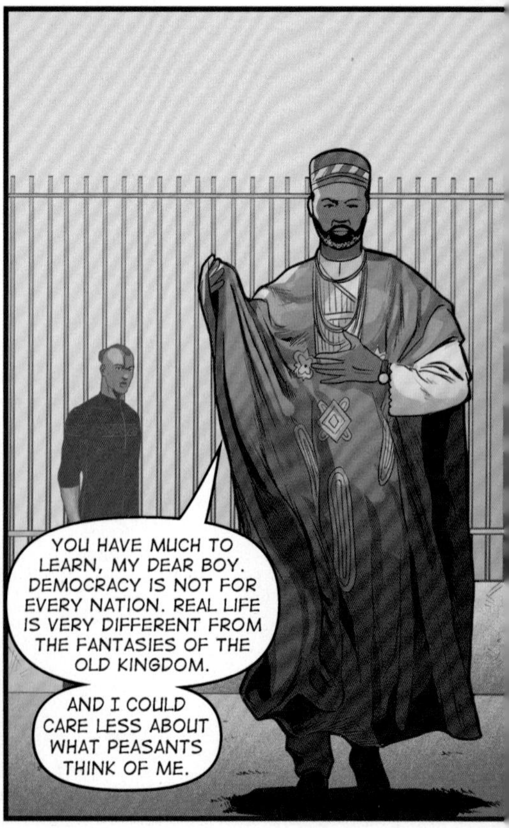
YOU HAVE MUCH TO LEARN, MY DEAR BOY. DEMOCRACY IS NOT FOR EVERY NATION. REAL LIFE IS VERY DIFFERENT FROM THE FANTASIES OF THE OLD KINGDOM.
AND I COULD CARE LESS ABOUT WHAT PEASANTS THINK OF ME.

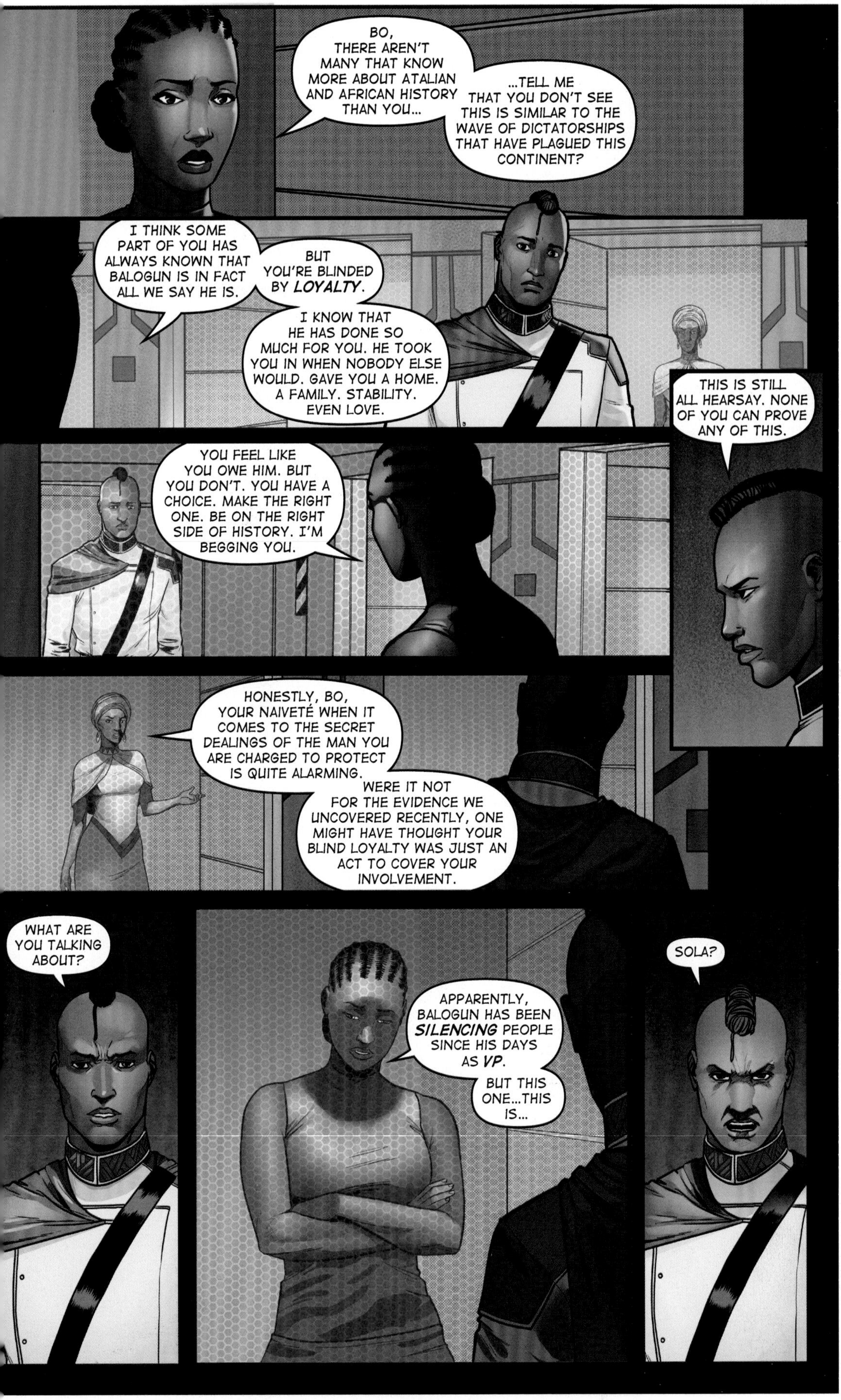
BO, THERE AREN'T MANY THAT KNOW MORE ABOUT ATALIAN AND AFRICAN HISTORY THAN YOU...
...TELL ME THAT YOU DON'T SEE THIS IS SIMILAR TO THE WAVE OF DICTATORSHIPS THAT HAVE PLAGUED THIS CONTINENT?
I THINK SOME PART OF YOU HAS ALWAYS KNOWN THAT BALOGUN IS IN FACT ALL WE SAY HE IS.
BUT YOU'RE BLINDED BY LOYALTY.
I KNOW THAT HE HAS DONE SO MUCH FOR YOU. HE TOOK YOU IN WHEN NOBODY ELSE WOULD. GAVE YOU A HOME. A FAMILY. STABILITY. EVEN LOVE.
YOU FEEL LIKE YOU OWE HIM. BUT YOU DON'T. YOU HAVE A CHOICE. MAKE THE RIGHT ONE. BE ON THE RIGHT SIDE OF HISTORY. I'M BEGGING YOU.
THIS IS STILL ALL HEARSAY. NONE OF YOU CAN PROVE ANY OF THIS.
HONESTLY, BO, YOUR NAIVETÉ WHEN IT COMES TO THE SECRET DEALINGS OF THE MAN YOU ARE CHARGED TO PROTECT IS QUITE ALARMING.
WERE IT NOT FOR THE EVIDENCE WE UNCOVERED RECENTLY, ONE MIGHT HAVE THOUGHT YOUR BLIND LOYALTY WAS JUST AN ACT TO COVER YOUR INVOLVEMENT.
WHAT ARE YOU TALKING ABOUT?
APPARENTLY, BALOGUN HAS BEEN SILENCING PEOPLE SINCE HIS DAYS AS VP.
BUT THIS ONE...THIS IS...
SOLA?

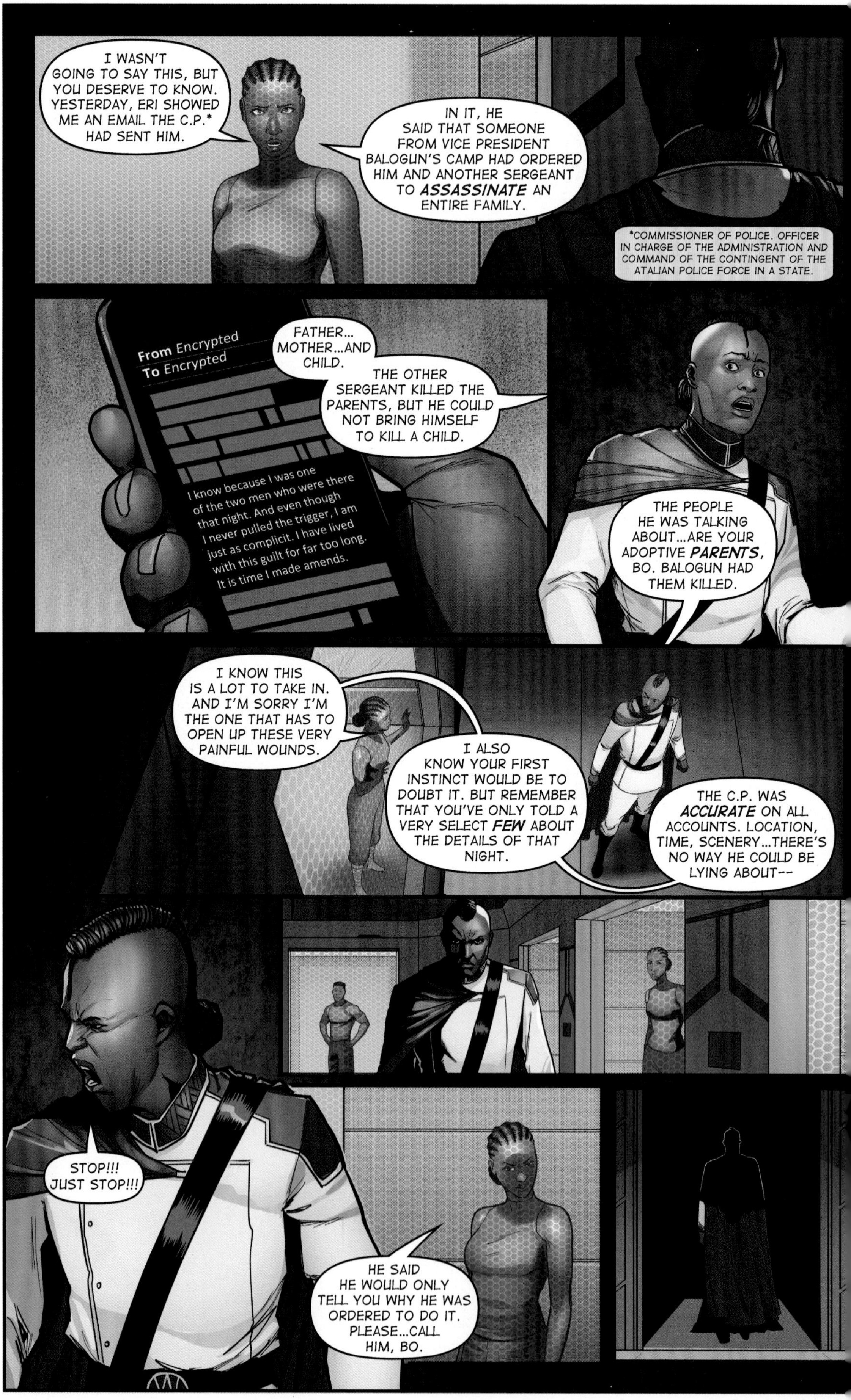

I WASN'T GOING TO SAY THIS, BUT YOU DESERVE TO KNOW. YESTERDAY, ERI SHOWED ME AN EMAIL THE C.P.* HAD SENT HIM.
IN IT, HE SAID THAT SOMEONE FROM VICE PRESIDENT BALOGUN'S CAMP HAD ORDERED HIM AND ANOTHER SERGEANT TO ASSASSINATE AN ENTIRE FAMILY.
*COMMISSIONER OF POLICE. OFFICER IN CHARGE OF THE ADMINISTRATION AND COMMAND OF THE CONTINGENT OF THE ATALIAN POLICE FORCE IN A STATE.
From Encrypted
To Encrypted
I know because I was one of the two men who were there that night. And even though I never pulled the trigger, I am just as complicit. I have lived with this guilt for far too long. It is time I made amends.
FATHER... MOTHER...AND CHILD.
THE OTHER SERGEANT KILLED THE PARENTS, BUT HE COULD NOT BRING HIMSELF TO KILL A CHILD.
THE PEOPLE HE WAS TALKING ABOUT...ARE YOUR ADOPTIVE PARENTS, BO. BALOGUN HAD THEM KILLED.
I KNOW THIS IS A LOT TO TAKE IN. AND I'M SORRY I'M THE ONE THAT HAS TO OPEN UP THESE VERY PAINFUL WOUNDS.
I ALSO KNOW YOUR FIRST INSTINCT WOULD BE TO DOUBT IT. BUT REMEMBER THAT YOU'VE ONLY TOLD A VERY SELECT FEW ABOUT THE DETAILS OF THAT NIGHT.
THE C.P. WAS ACCURATE ON ALL ACCOUNTS. LOCATION, TIME, SCENERY...THERE'S NO WAY HE COULD BE LYING ABOUT--
STOP!!! JUST STOP!!!
HE SAID HE WOULD ONLY TELL YOU WHY HE WAS ORDERED TO DO IT. PLEASE...CALL HIM, BO.

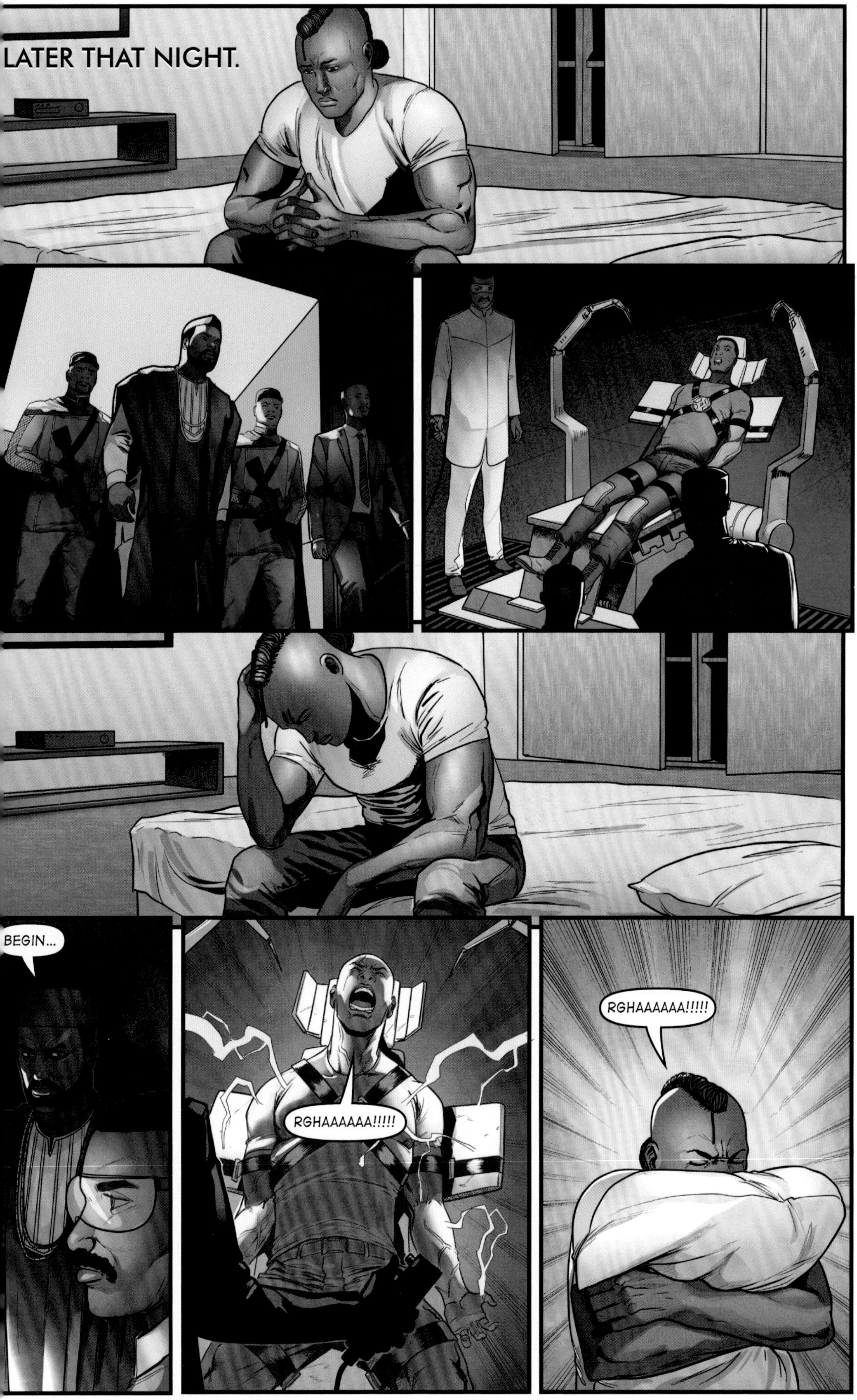
LATER THAT NIGHT.
BEGIN...
RGHAAAAAA!!!!!
RGHAAAAAA!!!!!

CHAPTER SIX

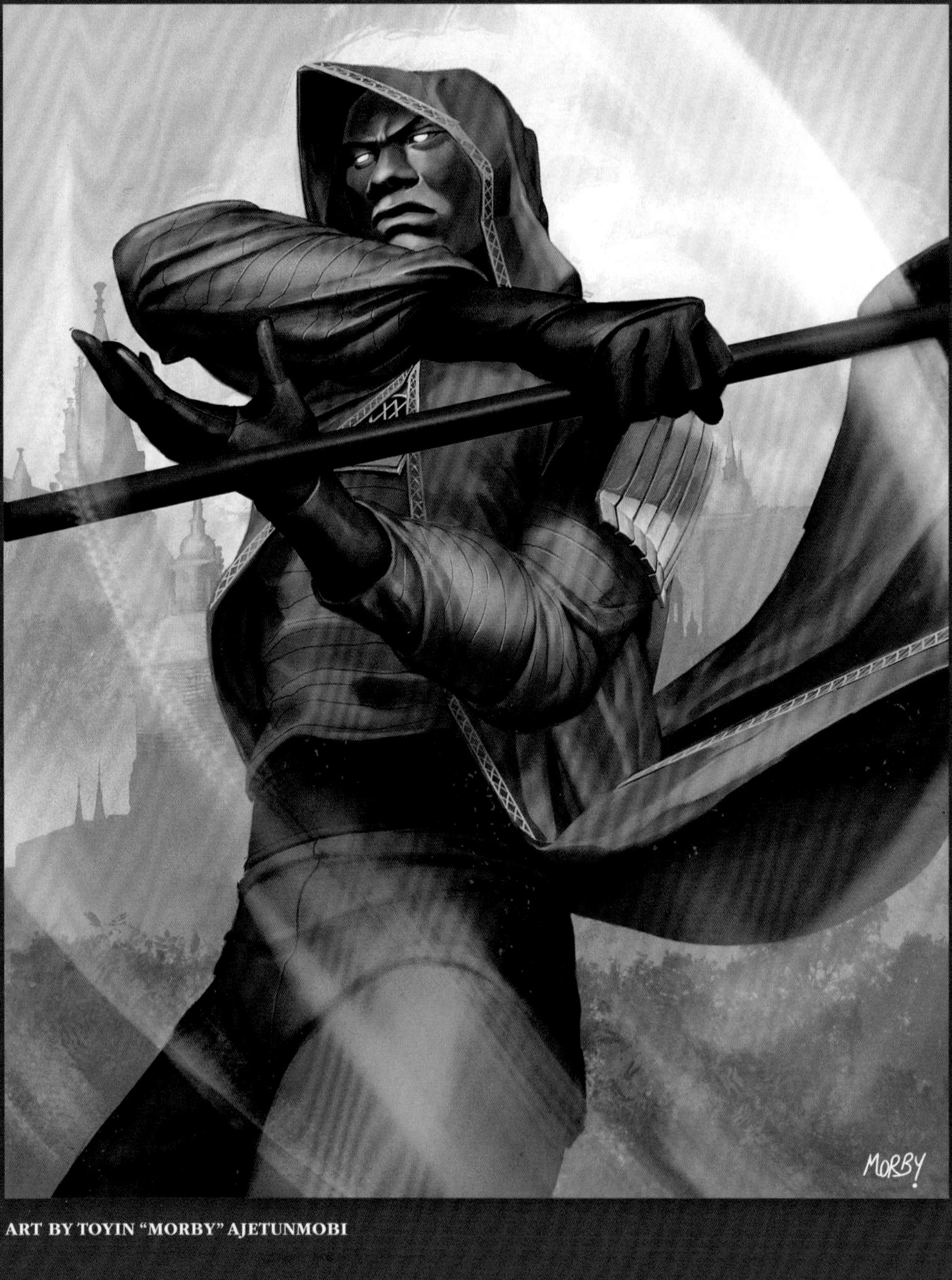
MORBY

ART BY TOYIN "MORBY" AJETUNMOBI

Ever the curious warrior, Bass found one of the ancient Atalian relics and became the first WindMaker. With his newfound powers to manipulate the wind as well as his Red Raven Army, Bass would go on to drive the rouge general Cheng and his forces away from Atala. His victory would go on to earn him the honor of being crowned the first-ever King of Atala.

FUN FACT: As I mentioned previously, Bass and his kingdom, Atala (which would later become the Republic of Atala you see in this book), are both heavily influenced by Yoruba culture, the Yoruba being one of the three major tribes in Nigeria. While Atala itself is a fictional nation, its history pulls several tidbits from Yoruba lore, one being that the Atalians (in our YouNiverse) are direct descendants of actual Yoruba people that emigrated from Ife, an ancient Yoruba city in southwestern Nigeria. Hence Atala (fictional) is made up of (real) Yoruba people.

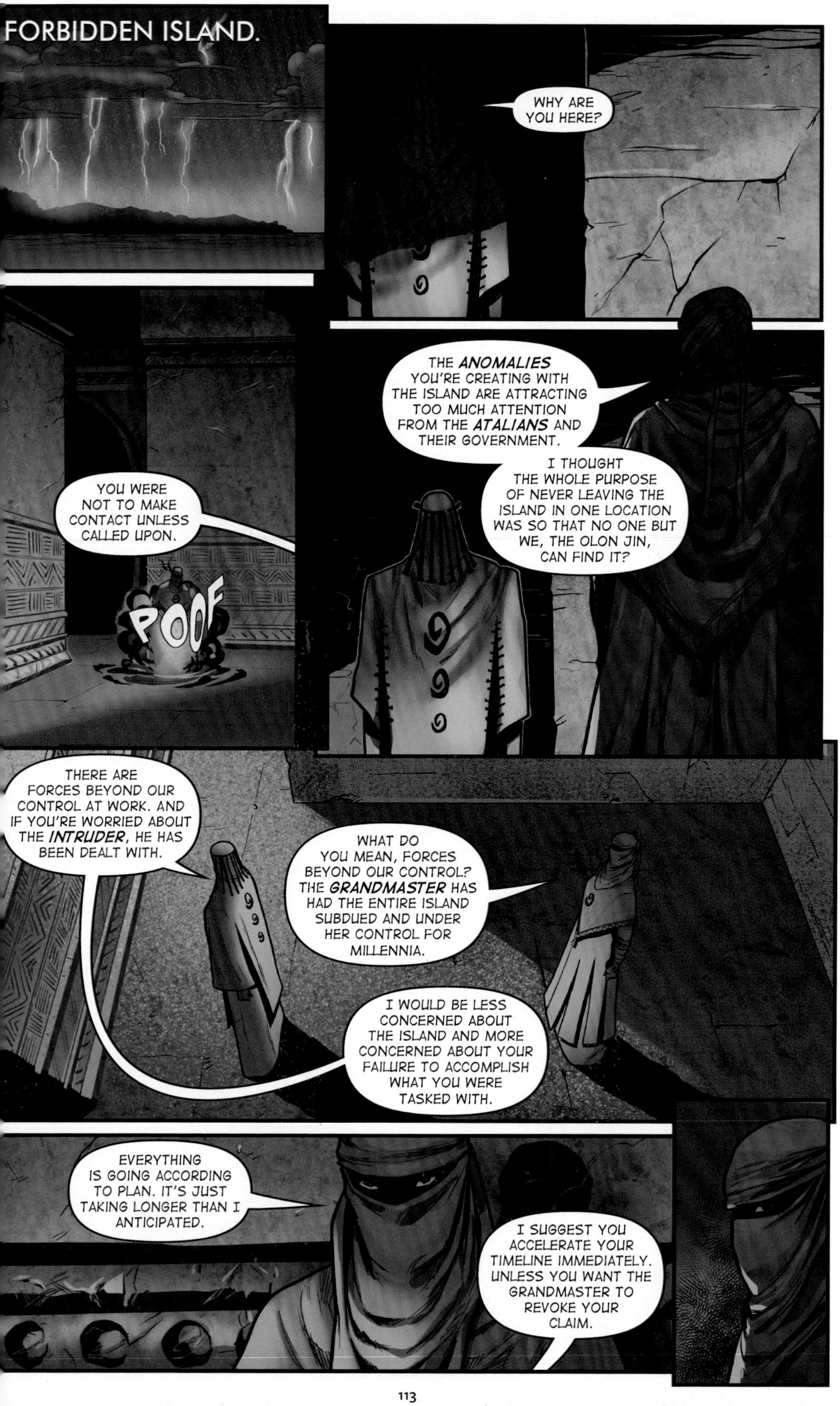
FORBIDDEN ISLAND.
WHY ARE YOU HERE?
YOU WERE NOT TO MAKE CONTACT UNLESS CALLED UPON.
POOF
THE ANOMALIES YOU'RE CREATING WITH THE ISLAND ARE ATTRACTING TOO MUCH ATTENTION FROM THE ATALIANS AND THEIR GOVERNMENT.
I THOUGHT THE WHOLE PURPOSE OF NEVER LEAVING THE ISLAND IN ONE LOCATION WAS SO THAT NO ONE BUT WE, THE OLON JIN, CAN FIND IT?
THERE ARE FORCES BEYOND OUR CONTROL AT WORK. AND IF YOU'RE WORRIED ABOUT THE INTRUDER, HE HAS BEEN DEALT WITH.
WHAT DO YOU MEAN, FORCES BEYOND OUR CONTROL? THE GRANDMASTER HAS HAD THE ENTIRE ISLAND SUBDUED AND UNDER HER CONTROL FOR MILLENNIA.
I WOULD BE LESS CONCERNED ABOUT THE ISLAND AND MORE CONCERNED ABOUT YOUR FAILURE TO ACCOMPLISH WHAT YOU WERE TASKED WITH.
EVERYTHING IS GOING ACCORDING TO PLAN. IT'S JUST TAKING LONGER THAN I ANTICIPATED.
I SUGGEST YOU ACCELERATE YOUR TIMELINE IMMEDIATELY. UNLESS YOU WANT THE GRANDMASTER TO REVOKE YOUR CLAIM.

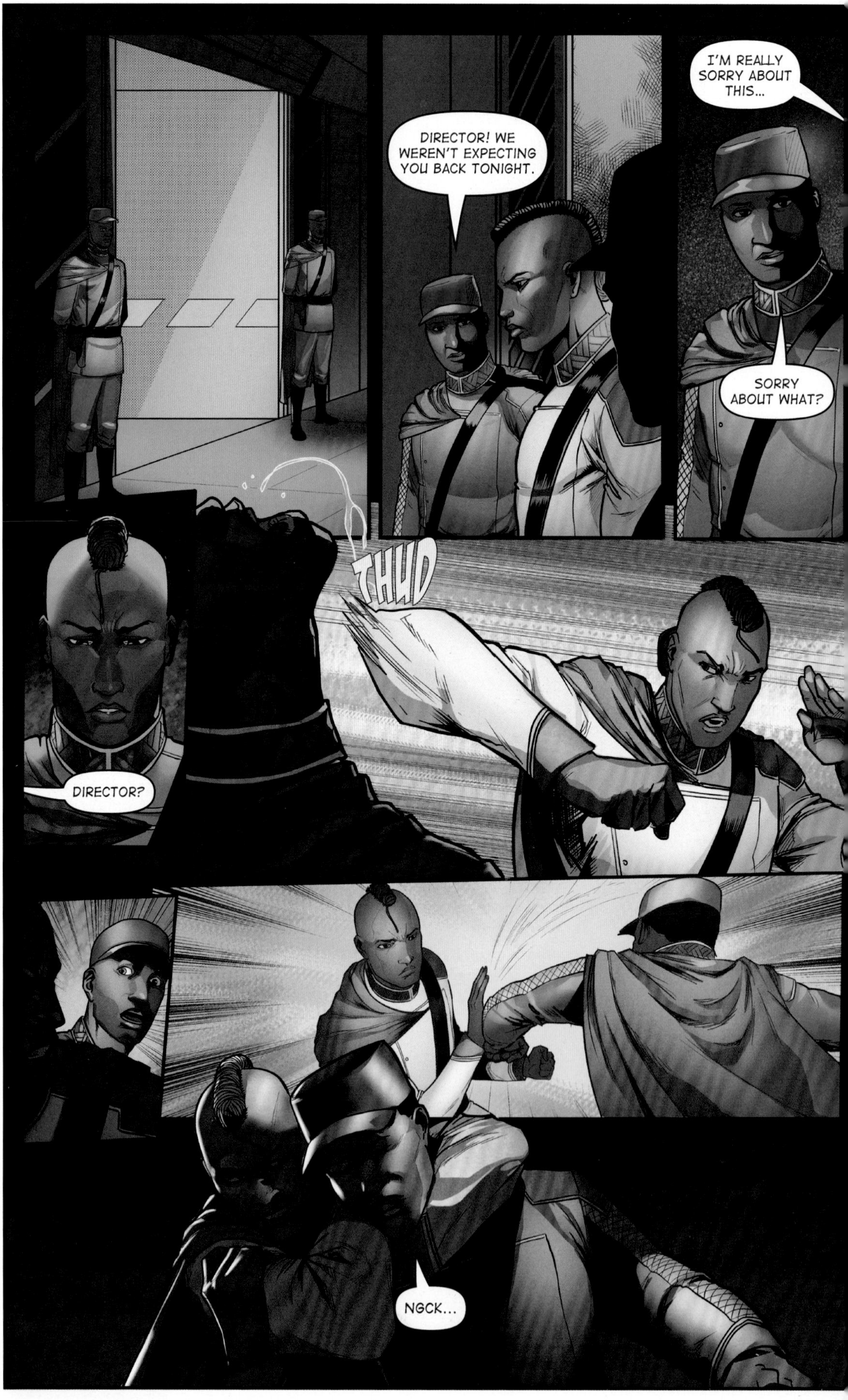
DIRECTOR! WE WEREN'T EXPECTING YOU BACK TONIGHT.
I'M REALLY SORRY ABOUT THIS...
SORRY ABOUT WHAT?
DIRECTOR?
THUD
NGCK...

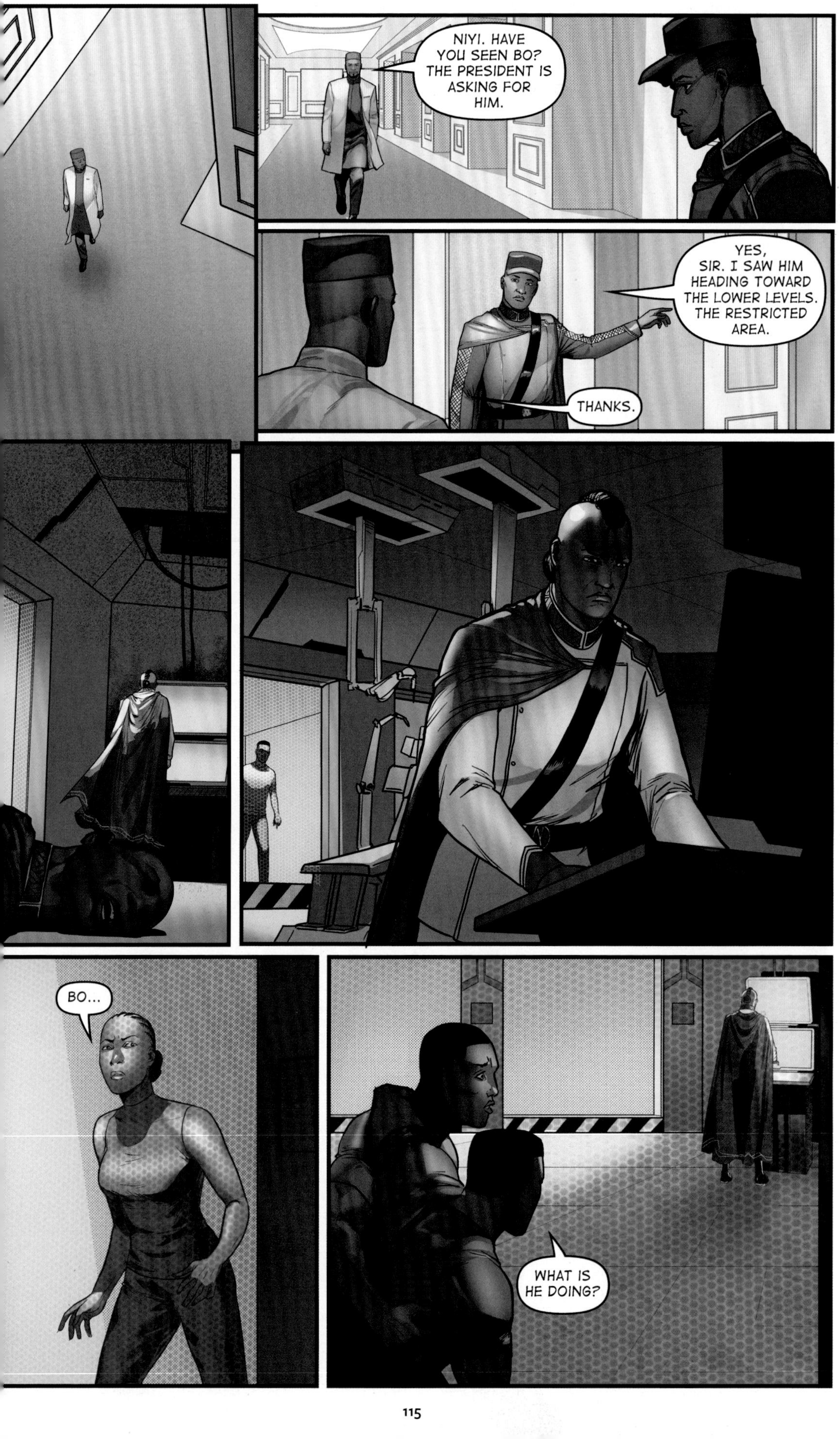
NIYI. HAVE YOU SEEN BO? THE PRESIDENT IS ASKING FOR HIM.
YES, SIR. I SAW HIM HEADING TOWARD THE LOWER LEVELS. THE RESTRICTED AREA.
THANKS.
BO...
WHAT IS HE DOING?

BOOOMMM!!!

HURRY... WE DON'T HAVE MUCH TIME.

YOU CALLED HIM, DIDN'T YOU? WHAT DID HE TELL YOU?

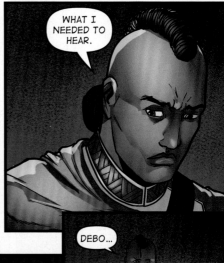

WHAT I NEEDED TO HEAR.

DEBO...

LISTEN, SOLA...I HAD NO IDEA ABOUT THIS PLACE UNTIL IT WAS TOO LATE. I WOULD HAVE--

I KNOW.

WE HAVE INCOMING.

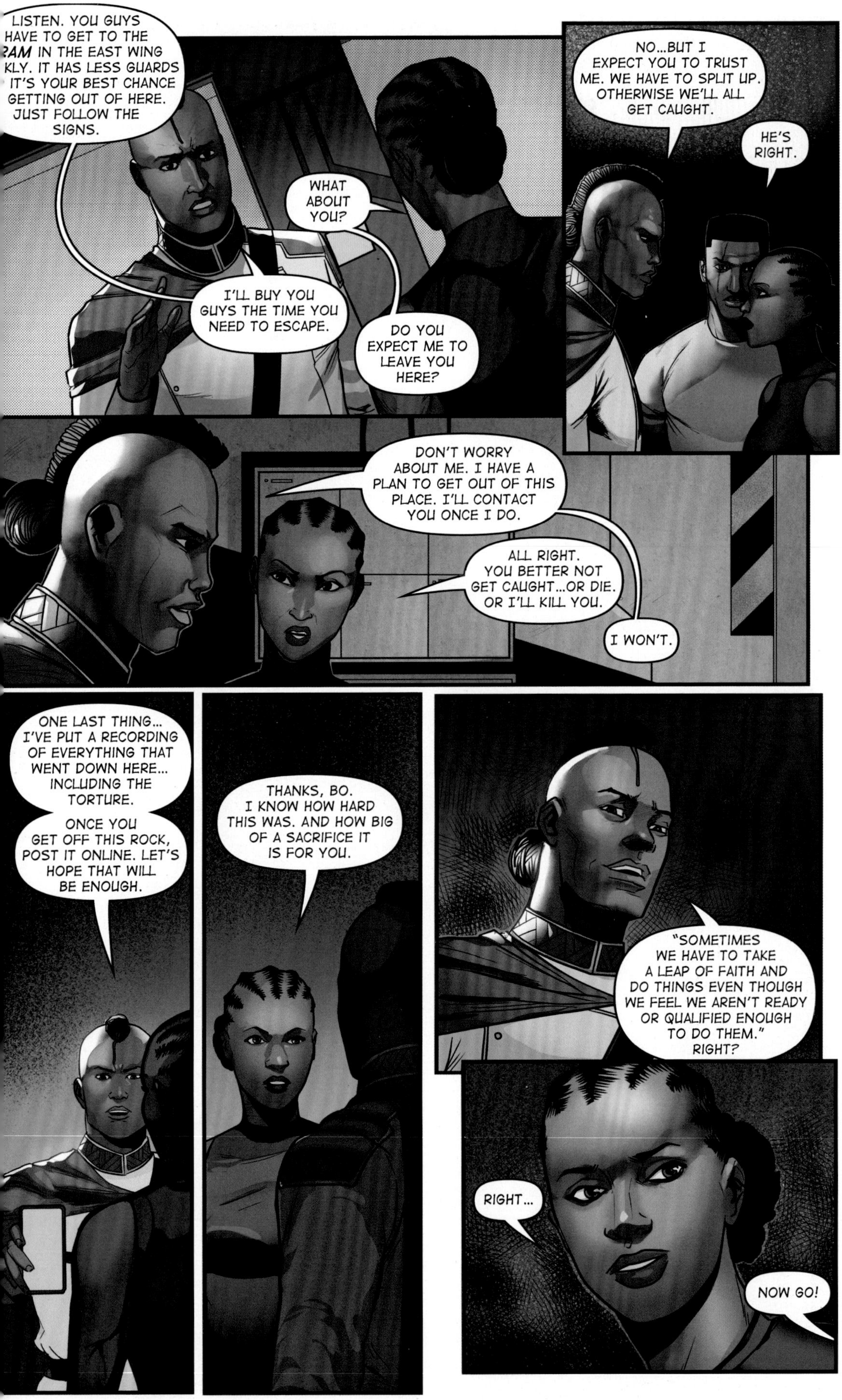
LISTEN. YOU GUYS HAVE TO GET TO THE RAM IN THE EAST WING KLY. IT HAS LESS GUARDS IT'S YOUR BEST CHANCE GETTING OUT OF HERE. JUST FOLLOW THE SIGNS.
WHAT ABOUT YOU?
I'LL BUY YOU GUYS THE TIME YOU NEED TO ESCAPE.
DO YOU EXPECT ME TO LEAVE YOU HERE?
NO...BUT I EXPECT YOU TO TRUST ME. WE HAVE TO SPLIT UP. OTHERWISE WE'LL ALL GET CAUGHT.
HE'S RIGHT.
DON'T WORRY ABOUT ME. I HAVE A PLAN TO GET OUT OF THIS PLACE. I'LL CONTACT YOU ONCE I DO.
ALL RIGHT. YOU BETTER NOT GET CAUGHT...OR DIE. OR I'LL KILL YOU.
I WON'T.
ONE LAST THING... I'VE PUT A RECORDING OF EVERYTHING THAT WENT DOWN HERE... INCLUDING THE TORTURE.
ONCE YOU GET OFF THIS ROCK, POST IT ONLINE. LET'S HOPE THAT WILL BE ENOUGH.
THANKS, BO. I KNOW HOW HARD THIS WAS. AND HOW BIG OF A SACRIFICE IT IS FOR YOU.
"SOMETIMES WE HAVE TO TAKE A LEAP OF FAITH AND DO THINGS EVEN THOUGH WE FEEL WE AREN'T READY OR QUALIFIED ENOUGH TO DO THEM." RIGHT?
RIGHT...
NOW GO!

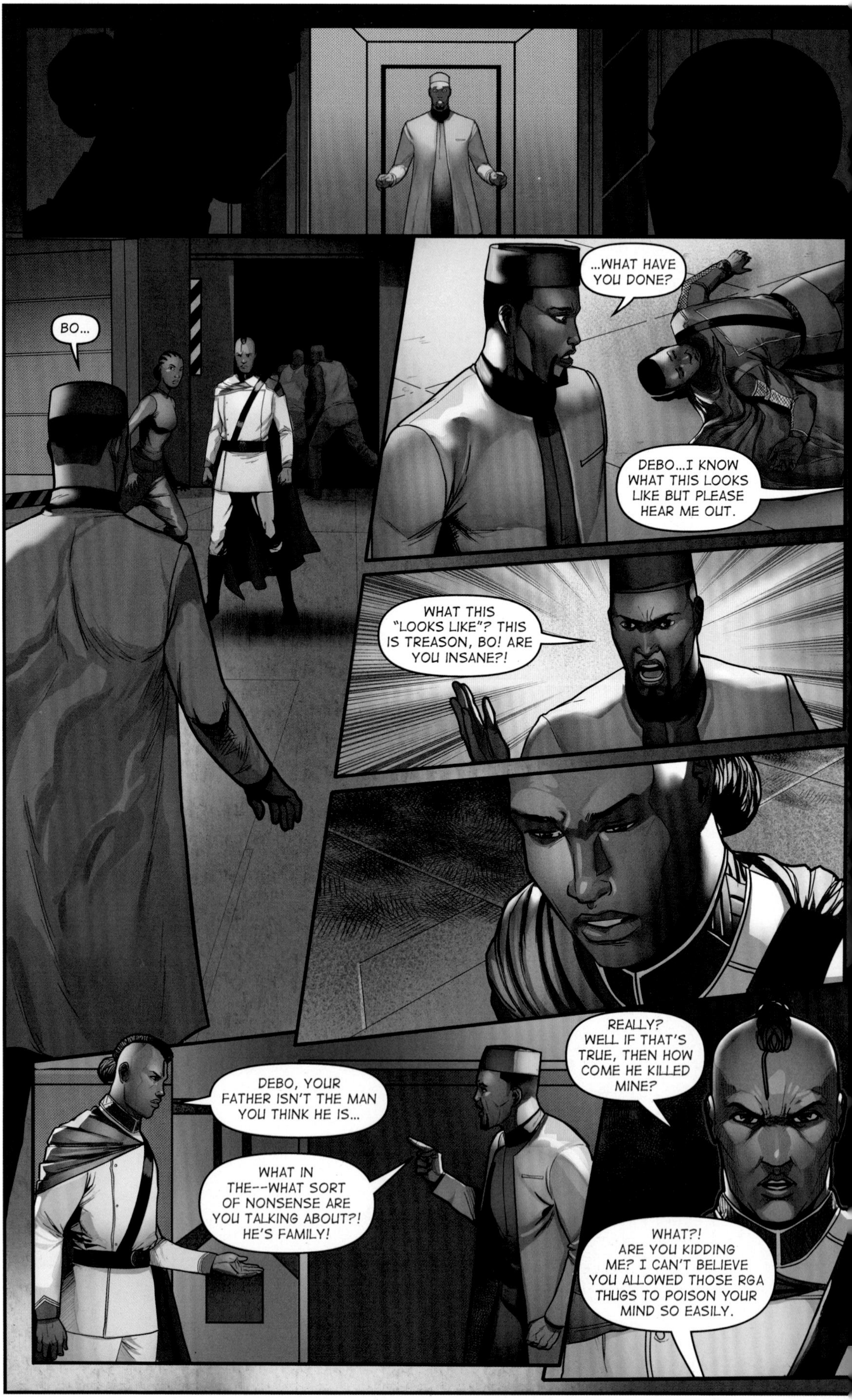

BO...
...WHAT HAVE YOU DONE?
DEBO...I KNOW WHAT THIS LOOKS LIKE BUT PLEASE HEAR ME OUT.
WHAT THIS "LOOKS LIKE"? THIS IS TREASON, BO! ARE YOU INSANE?!
DEBO, YOUR FATHER ISN'T THE MAN YOU THINK HE IS...
WHAT IN THE--WHAT SORT OF NONSENSE ARE YOU TALKING ABOUT?! HE'S FAMILY!
REALLY? WELL IF THAT'S TRUE, THEN HOW COME HE KILLED MINE?
WHAT?! ARE YOU KIDDING ME? I CAN'T BELIEVE YOU ALLOWED THOSE RGA THUGS TO POISON YOUR MIND SO EASILY.

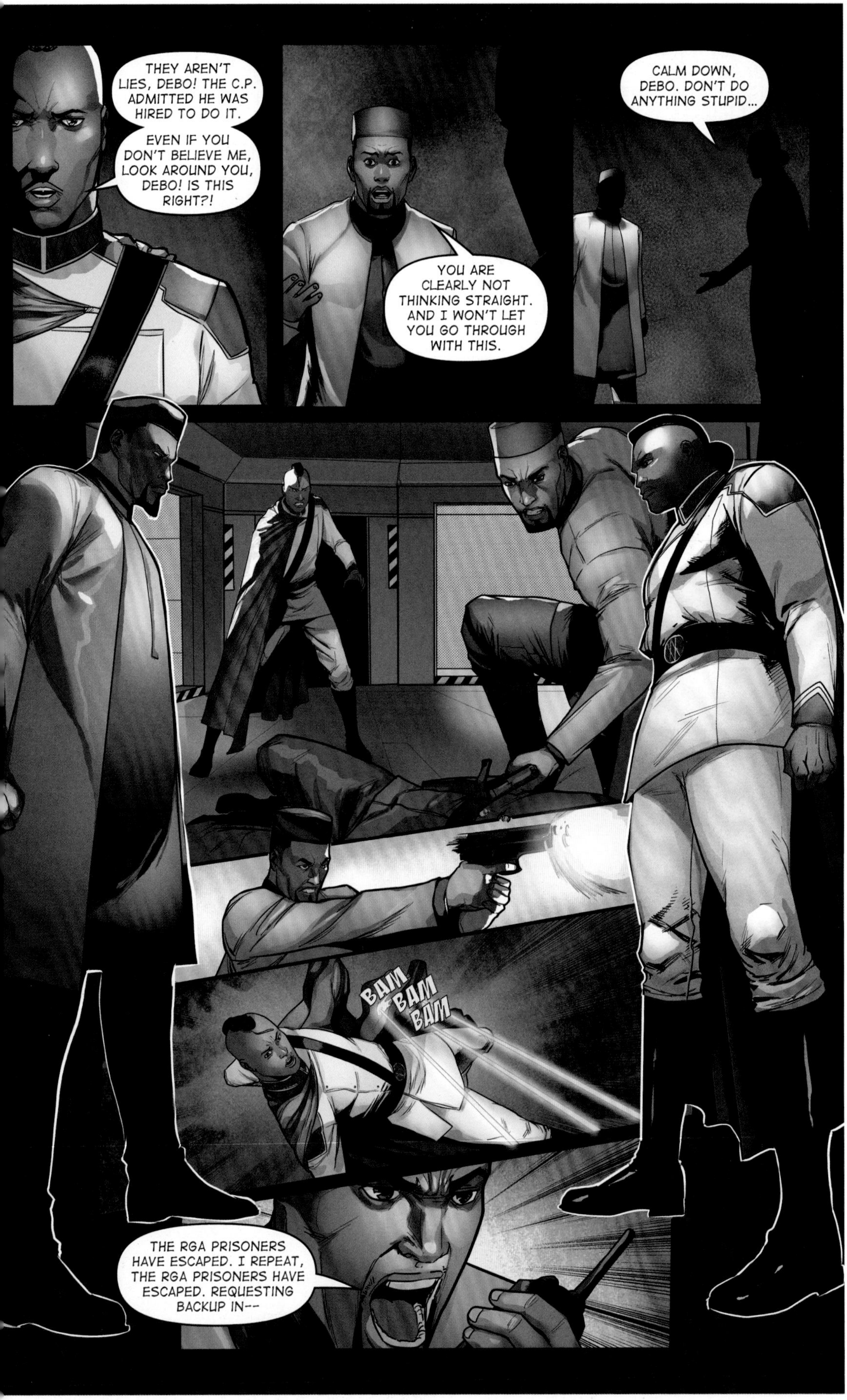
THEY AREN'T LIES, DEBO! THE C.P. ADMITTED HE WAS HIRED TO DO IT.
EVEN IF YOU DON'T BELIEVE ME, LOOK AROUND YOU, DEBO! IS THIS RIGHT?!
YOU ARE CLEARLY NOT THINKING STRAIGHT. AND I WON'T LET YOU GO THROUGH WITH THIS.
CALM DOWN, DEBO. DON'T DO ANYTHING STUPID...
BAM BAM BAM
THE RGA PRISONERS HAVE ESCAPED. I REPEAT, THE RGA PRISONERS HAVE ESCAPED. REQUESTING BACKUP IN--

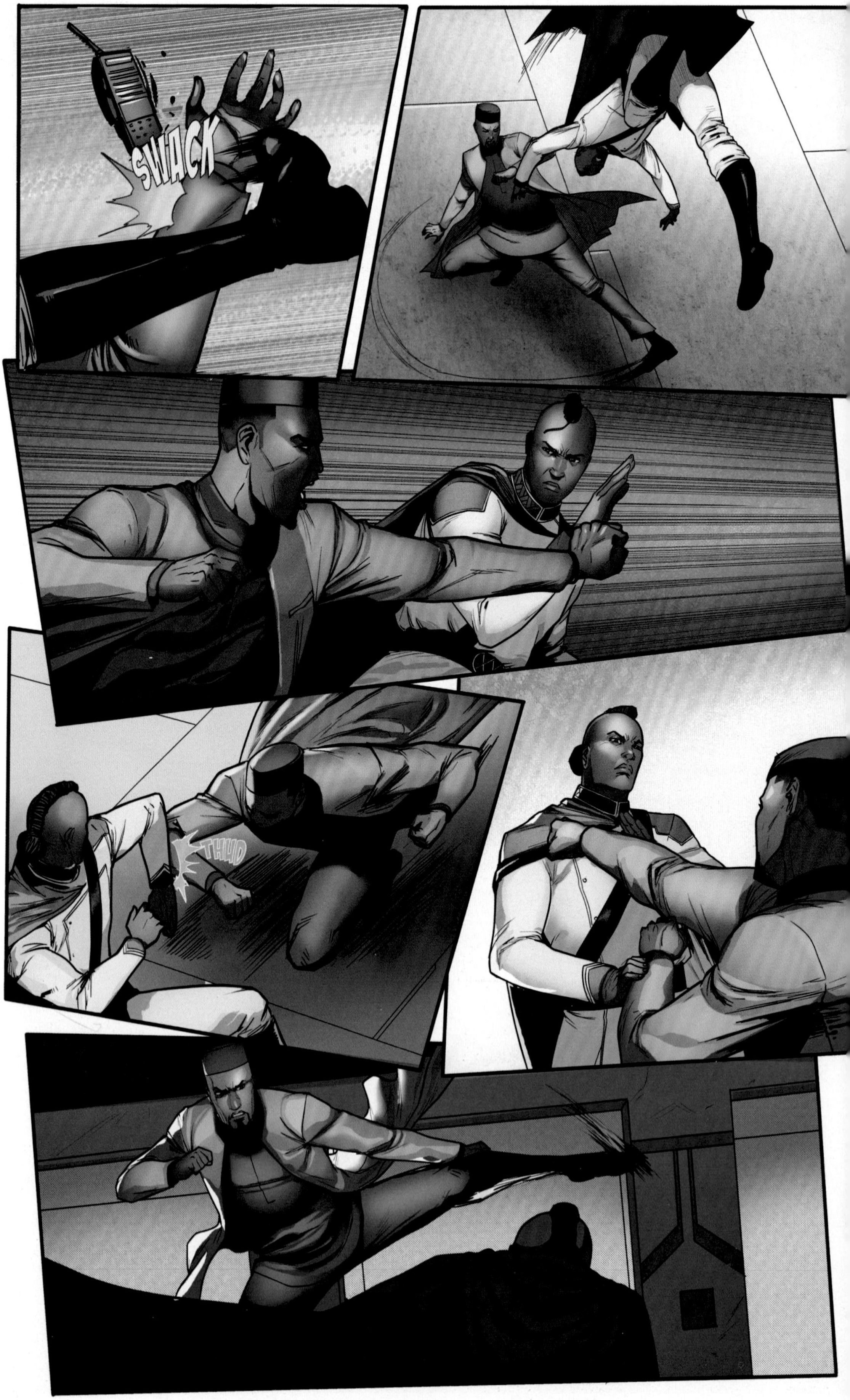
SWACK
THUD

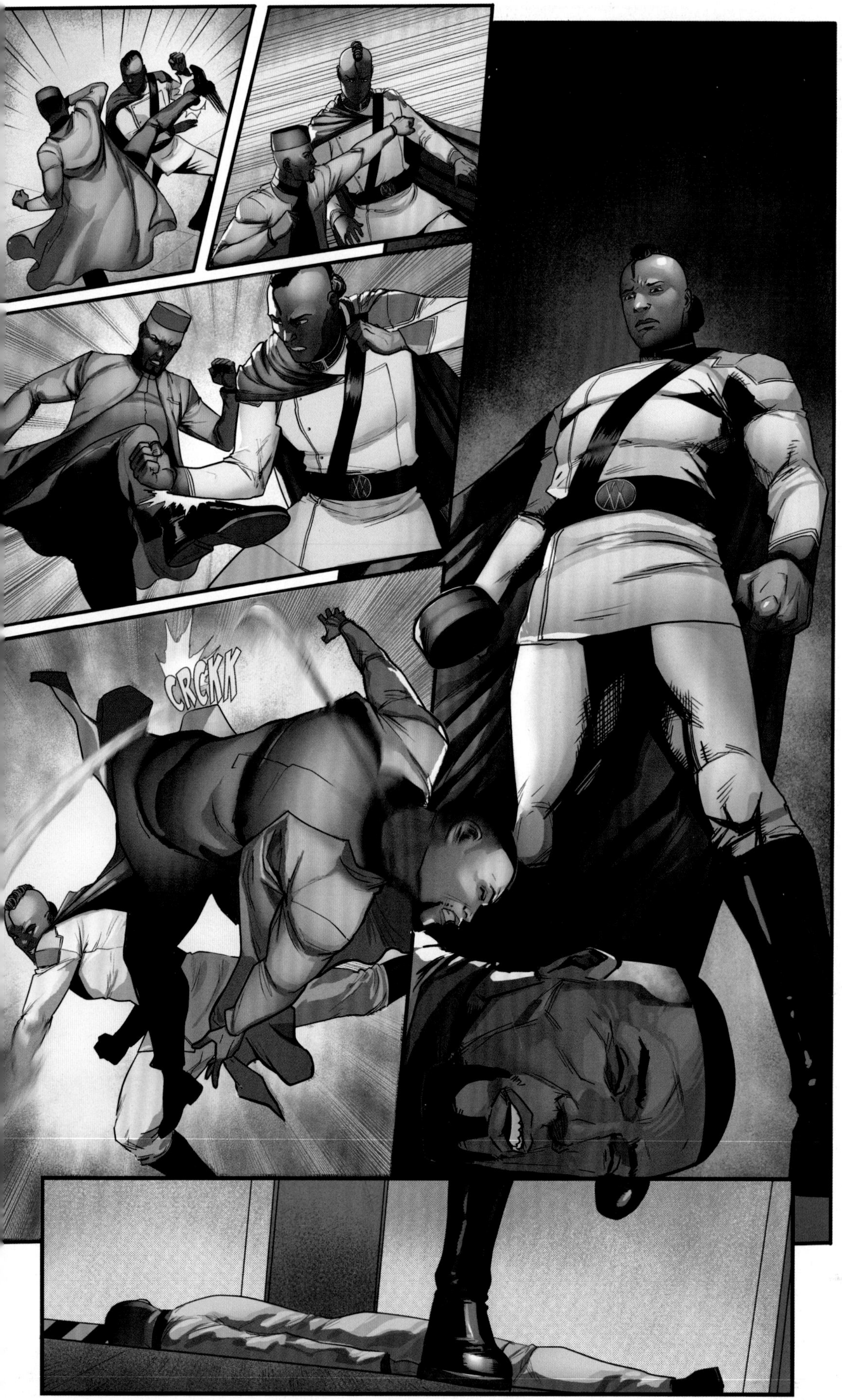
CRCKK

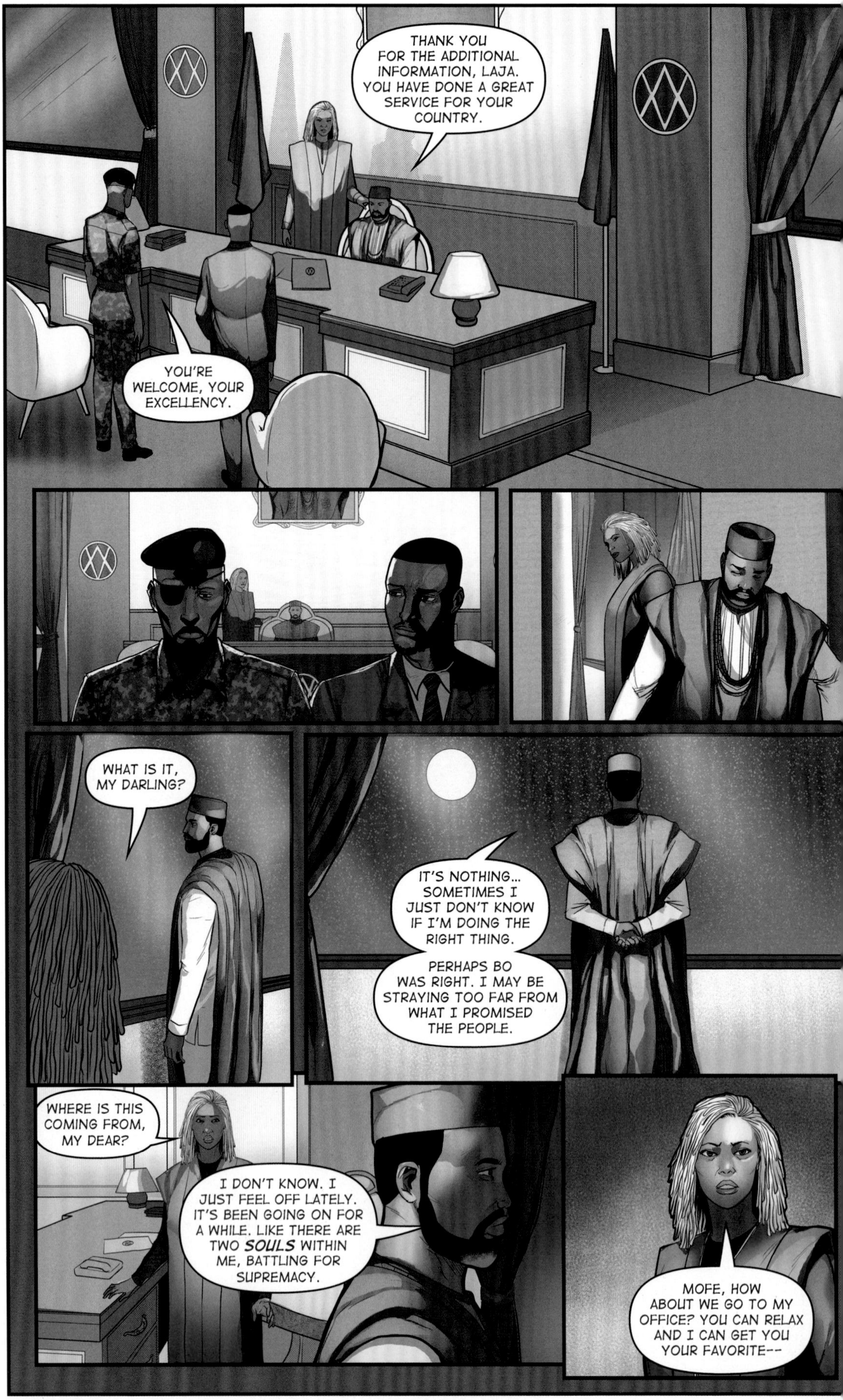
THANK YOU FOR THE ADDITIONAL INFORMATION, LAJA. YOU HAVE DONE A GREAT SERVICE FOR YOUR COUNTRY.
YOU'RE WELCOME, YOUR EXCELLENCY.
WHAT IS IT, MY DARLING?
IT'S NOTHING... SOMETIMES I JUST DON'T KNOW IF I'M DOING THE RIGHT THING.
PERHAPS BO WAS RIGHT. I MAY BE STRAYING TOO FAR FROM WHAT I PROMISED THE PEOPLE.
WHERE IS THIS COMING FROM, MY DEAR?
I DON'T KNOW. I JUST FEEL OFF LATELY. IT'S BEEN GOING ON FOR A WHILE. LIKE THERE ARE TWO ***SOULS*** WITHIN ME, BATTLING FOR SUPREMACY.
MOFE, HOW ABOUT WE GO TO MY OFFICE? YOU CAN RELAX AND I CAN GET YOU YOUR FAVORITE--

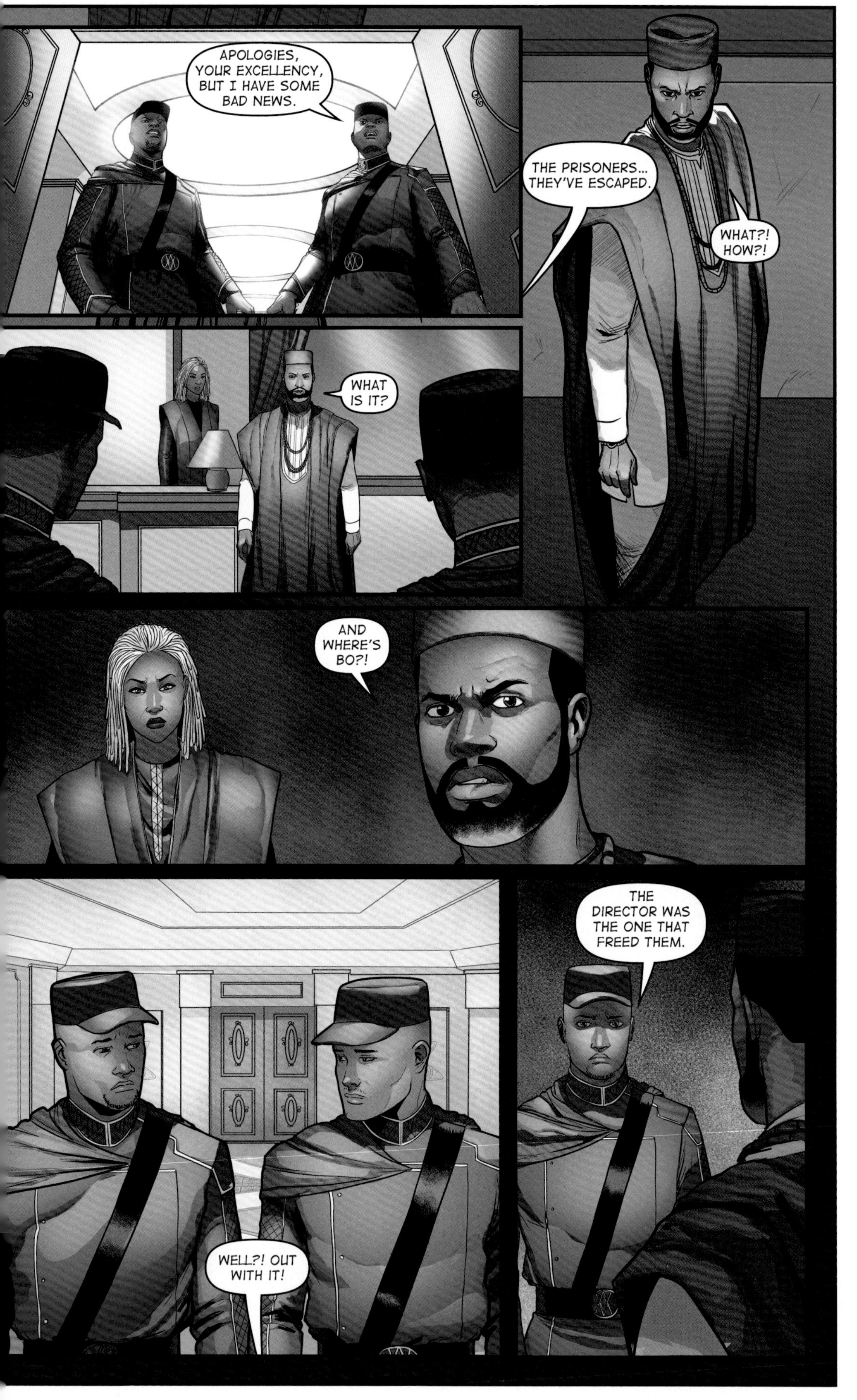
APOLOGIES, YOUR EXCELLENCY, BUT I HAVE SOME BAD NEWS.
WHAT IS IT?
THE PRISONERS... THEY'VE ESCAPED.
WHAT?! HOW?!
AND WHERE'S BO?!
WELL?! OUT WITH IT!
THE DIRECTOR WAS THE ONE THAT FREED THEM.

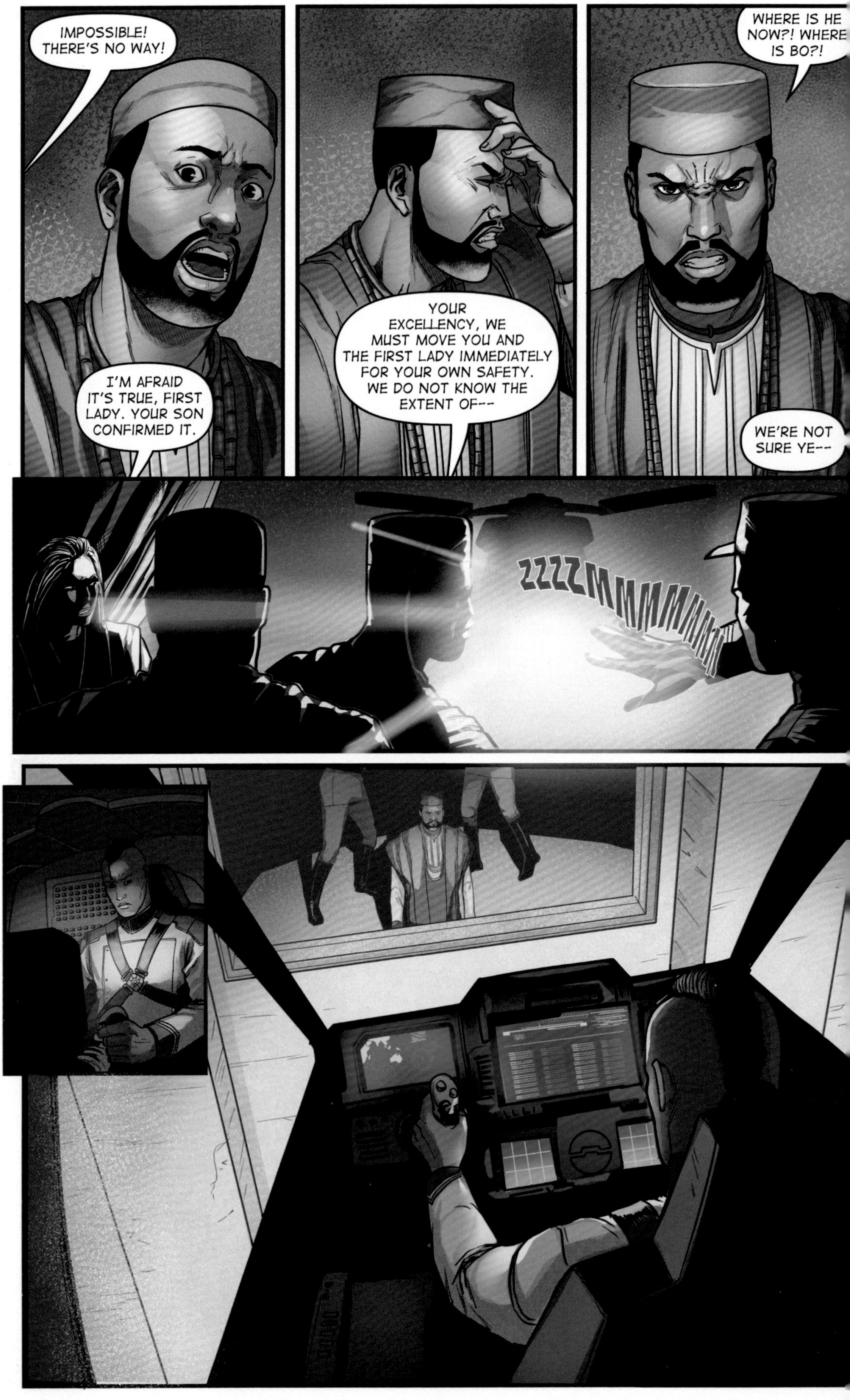

IMPOSSIBLE! THERE'S NO WAY!
I'M AFRAID IT'S TRUE, FIRST LADY. YOUR SON CONFIRMED IT.
YOUR EXCELLENCY, WE MUST MOVE YOU AND THE FIRST LADY IMMEDIATELY FOR YOUR OWN SAFETY. WE DO NOT KNOW THE EXTENT OF--
WHERE IS HE NOW?! WHERE IS BO?!
WE'RE NOT SURE YE--
ZZZZMMMMMMNNN

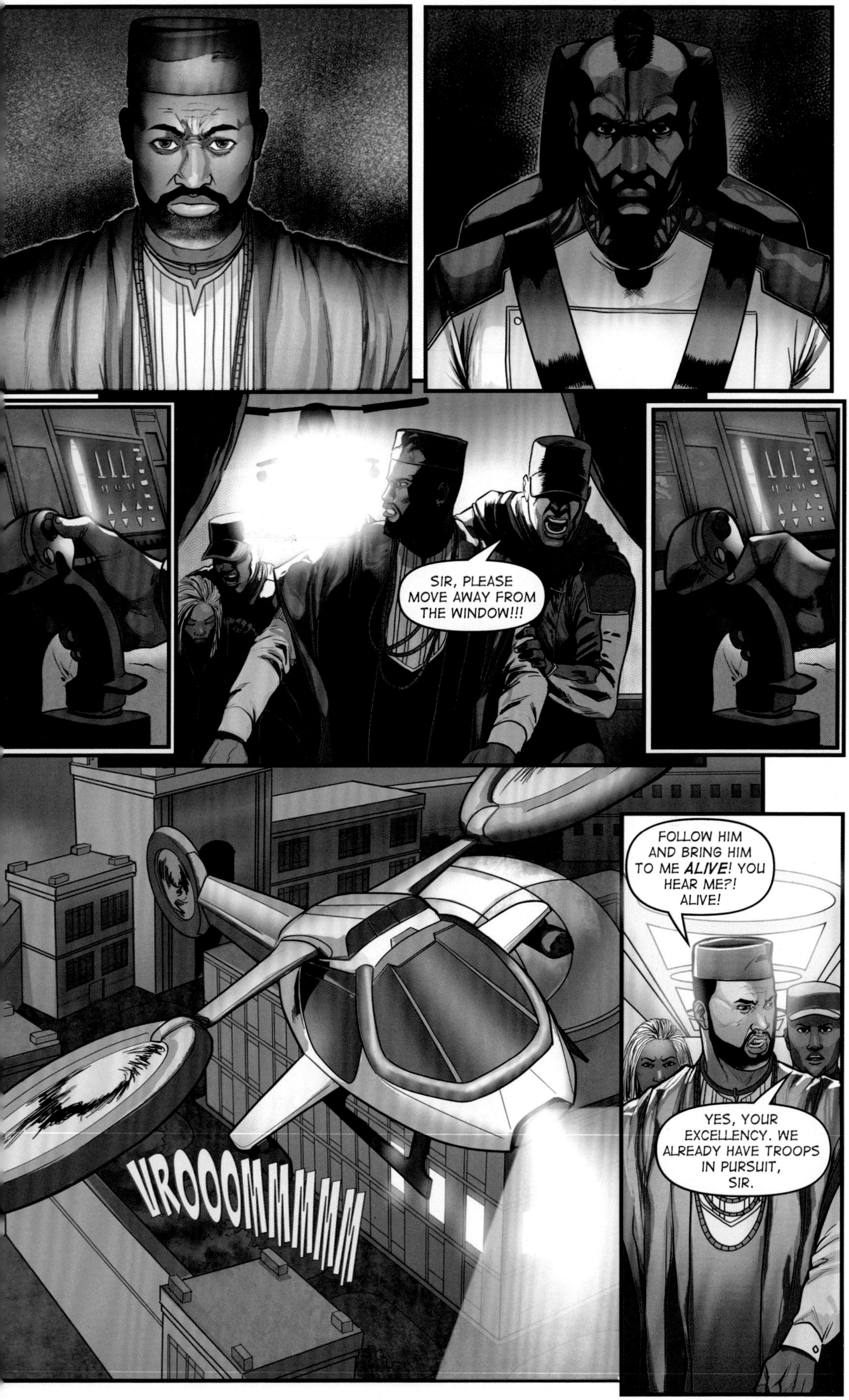
SIR, PLEASE MOVE AWAY FROM THE WINDOW!!!
VROOOMMMMM
FOLLOW HIM AND BRING HIM TO ME *ALIVE*! YOU HEAR ME?! ALIVE!
YES, YOUR EXCELLENCY. WE ALREADY HAVE TROOPS IN PURSUIT, SIR.

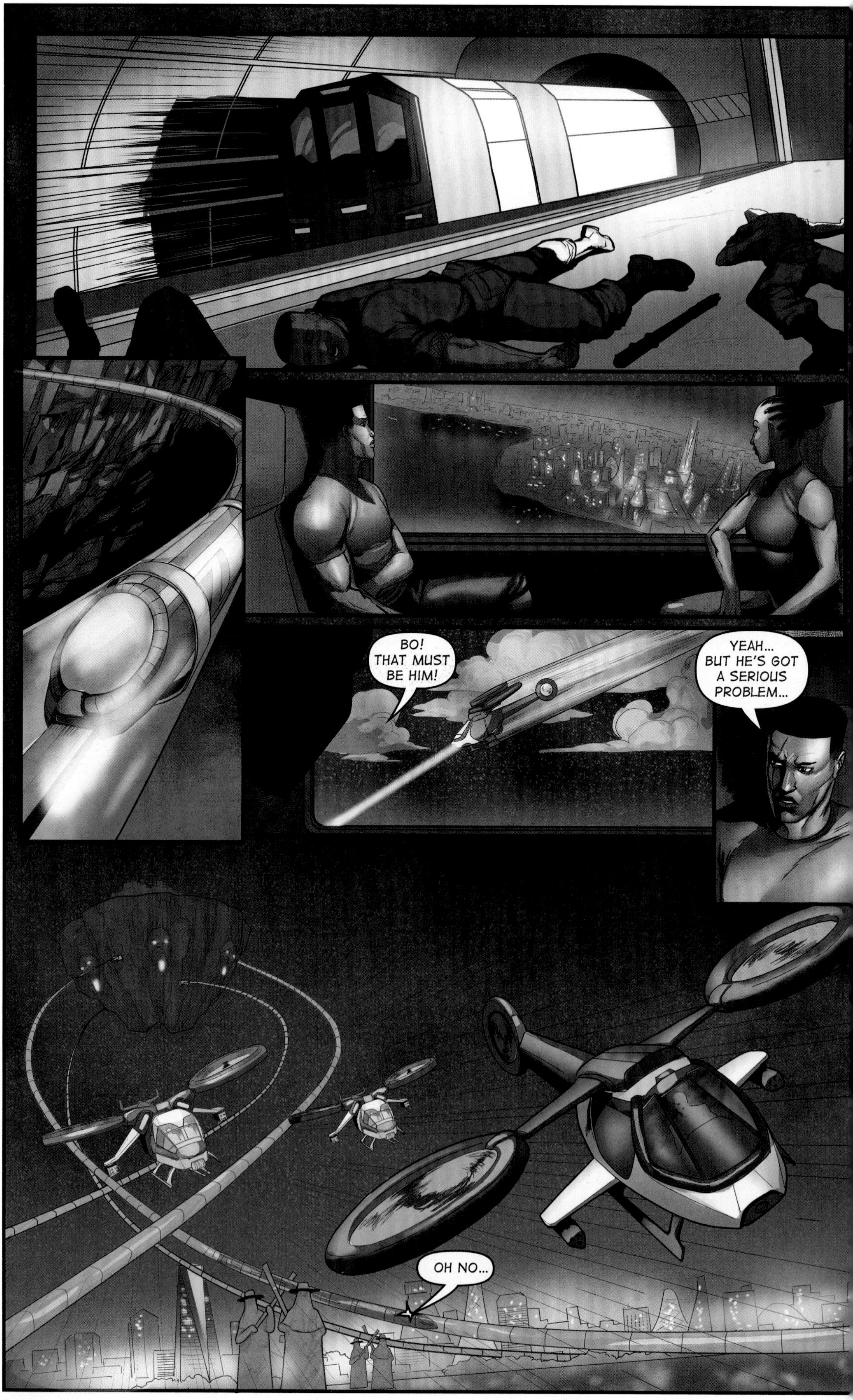
BO!
THAT MUST
BE HIM!
YEAH...
BUT HE'S GOT
A SERIOUS
PROBLEM...
OH NO...

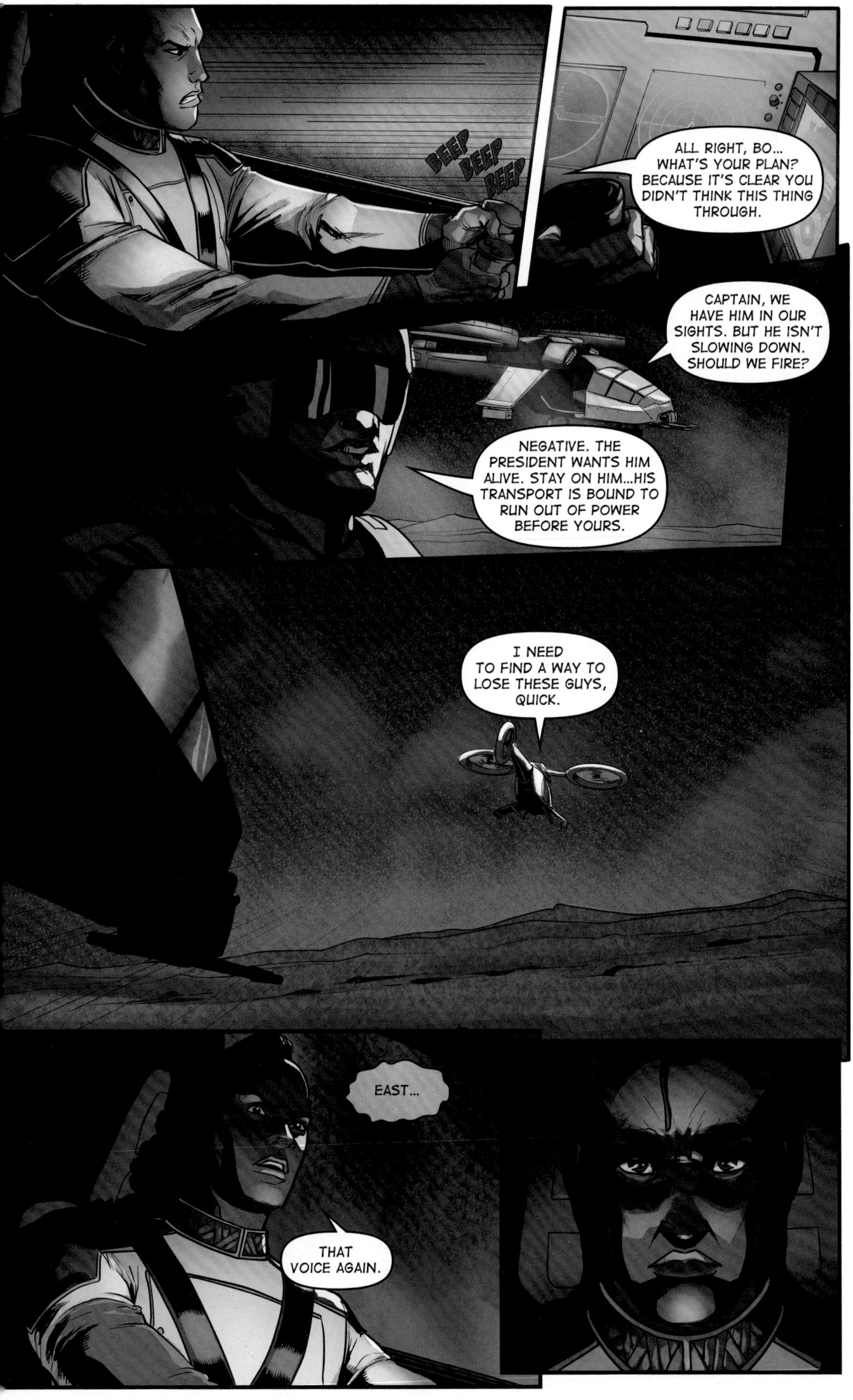
BEEP BEEP BEEP
ALL RIGHT, BO... WHAT'S YOUR PLAN? BECAUSE IT'S CLEAR YOU DIDN'T THINK THIS THING THROUGH.
CAPTAIN, WE HAVE HIM IN OUR SIGHTS. BUT HE ISN'T SLOWING DOWN. SHOULD WE FIRE?
NEGATIVE. THE PRESIDENT WANTS HIM ALIVE. STAY ON HIM...HIS TRANSPORT IS BOUND TO RUN OUT OF POWER BEFORE YOURS.
I NEED TO FIND A WAY TO LOSE THESE GUYS, QUICK.
EAST...
THAT VOICE AGAIN.

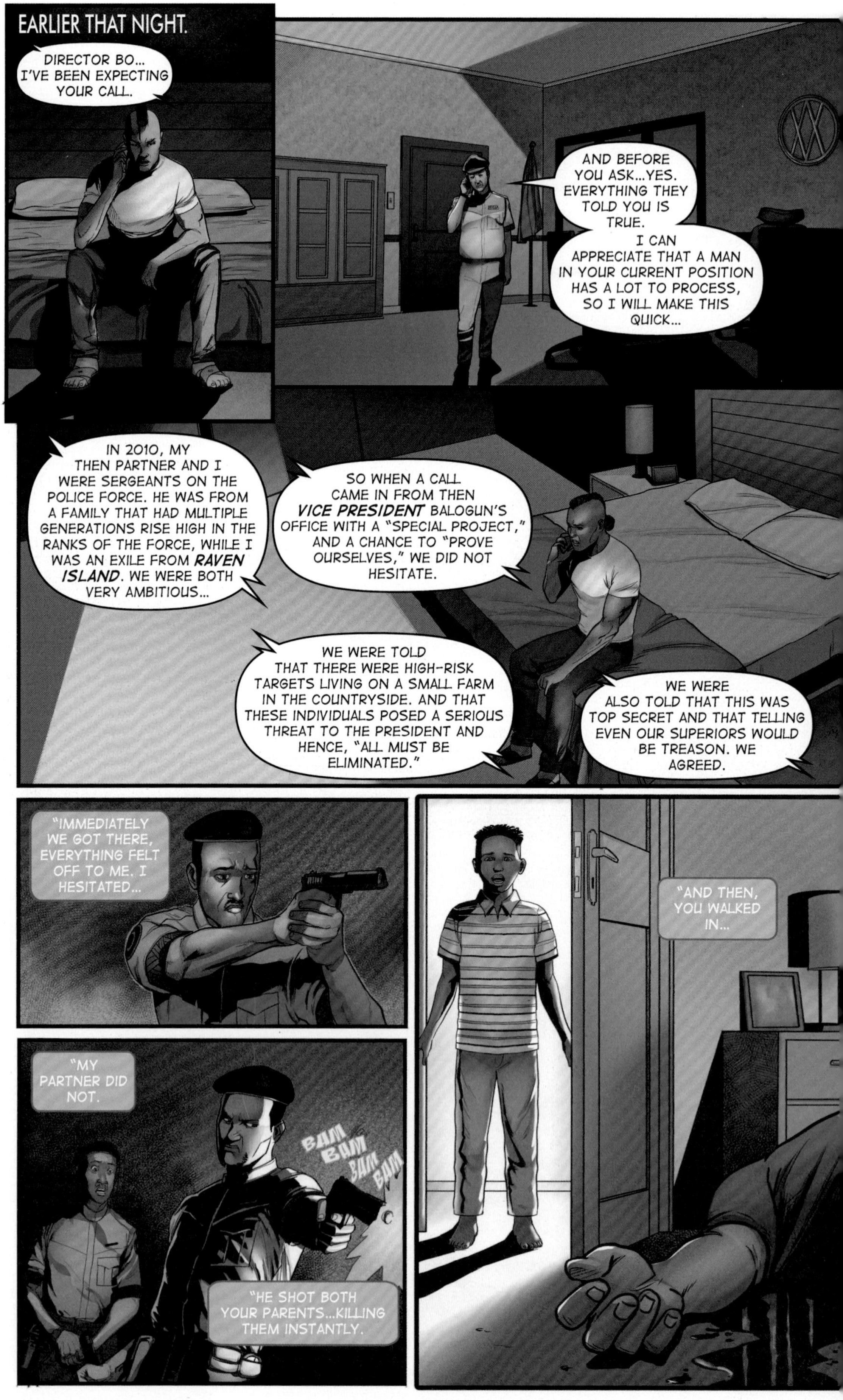
EARLIER THAT NIGHT.
DIRECTOR BO... I'VE BEEN EXPECTING YOUR CALL.
AND BEFORE YOU ASK...YES. EVERYTHING THEY TOLD YOU IS TRUE.
I CAN APPRECIATE THAT A MAN IN YOUR CURRENT POSITION HAS A LOT TO PROCESS, SO I WILL MAKE THIS QUICK...
IN 2010, MY THEN PARTNER AND I WERE SERGEANTS ON THE POLICE FORCE. HE WAS FROM A FAMILY THAT HAD MULTIPLE GENERATIONS RISE HIGH IN THE RANKS OF THE FORCE, WHILE I WAS AN EXILE FROM RAVEN ISLAND. WE WERE BOTH VERY AMBITIOUS...
SO WHEN A CALL CAME IN FROM THEN VICE PRESIDENT BALOGUN'S OFFICE WITH A "SPECIAL PROJECT," AND A CHANCE TO "PROVE OURSELVES," WE DID NOT HESITATE.
WE WERE TOLD THAT THERE WERE HIGH-RISK TARGETS LIVING ON A SMALL FARM IN THE COUNTRYSIDE. AND THAT THESE INDIVIDUALS POSED A SERIOUS THREAT TO THE PRESIDENT AND HENCE, "ALL MUST BE ELIMINATED."
WE WERE ALSO TOLD THAT THIS WAS TOP SECRET AND THAT TELLING EVEN OUR SUPERIORS WOULD BE TREASON. WE AGREED.
"IMMEDIATELY WE GOT THERE, EVERYTHING FELT OFF TO ME. I HESITATED...
"MY PARTNER DID NOT.
BAM BAM BAM BAM
"HE SHOT BOTH YOUR PARENTS...KILLING THEM INSTANTLY.
"AND THEN, YOU WALKED IN...

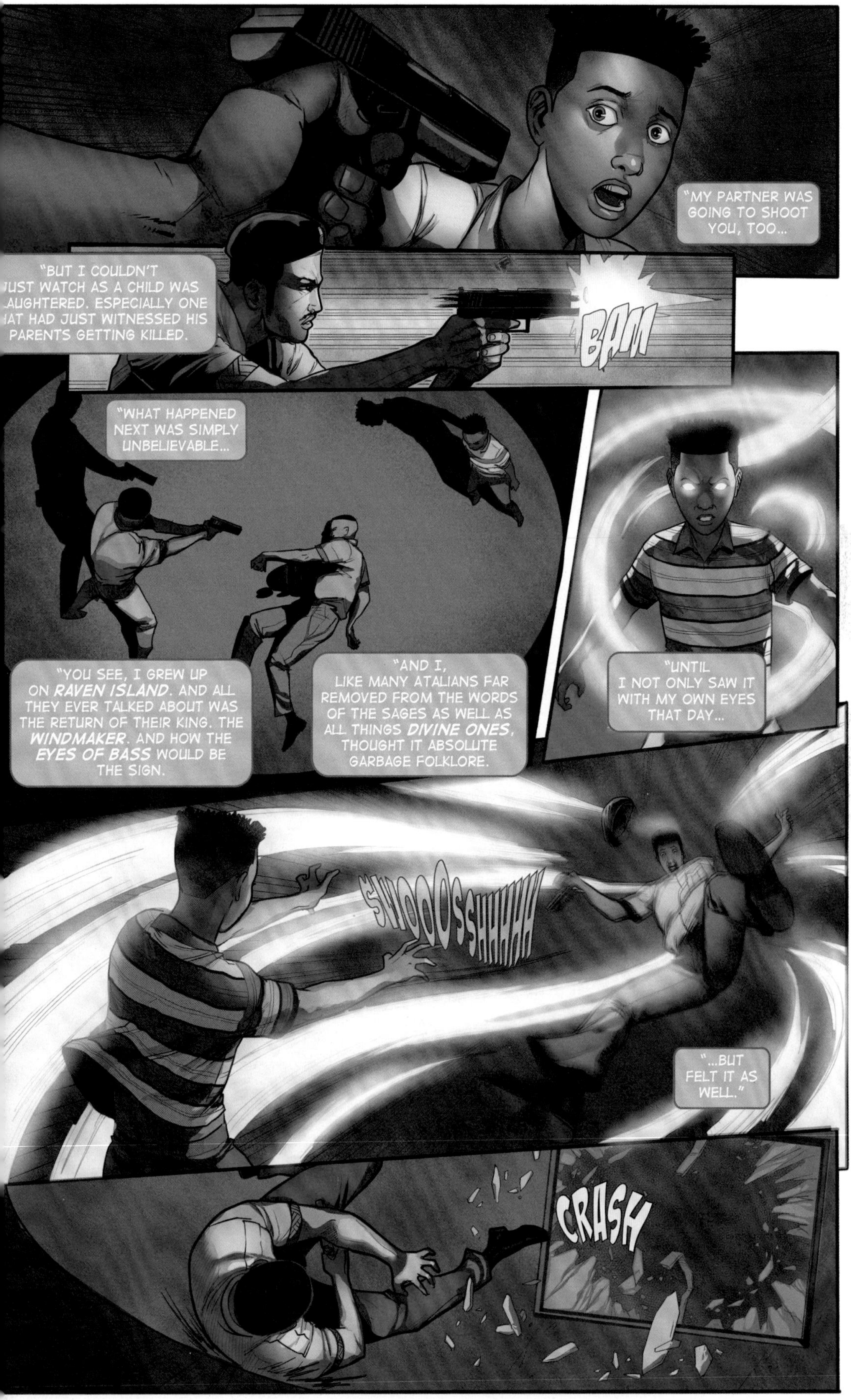
"MY PARTNER WAS GOING TO SHOOT YOU, TOO...
"BUT I COULDN'T UST WATCH AS A CHILD WAS LAUGHTERED. ESPECIALLY ONE HAT HAD JUST WITNESSED HIS PARENTS GETTING KILLED.
BAM
"WHAT HAPPENED NEXT WAS SIMPLY UNBELIEVABLE...
"YOU SEE, I GREW UP ON *RAVEN ISLAND*. AND ALL THEY EVER TALKED ABOUT WAS THE RETURN OF THEIR KING. THE *WINDMAKER*. AND HOW THE *EYES OF BASS* WOULD BE THE SIGN.
"AND I, LIKE MANY ATALIANS FAR REMOVED FROM THE WORDS OF THE SAGES AS WELL AS ALL THINGS *DIVINE ONES*, THOUGHT IT ABSOLUTE GARBAGE FOLKLORE.
"UNTIL I NOT ONLY SAW IT WITH MY OWN EYES THAT DAY...
SHOOOSSHHHHH
"...BUT FELT IT AS WELL."
CRASH

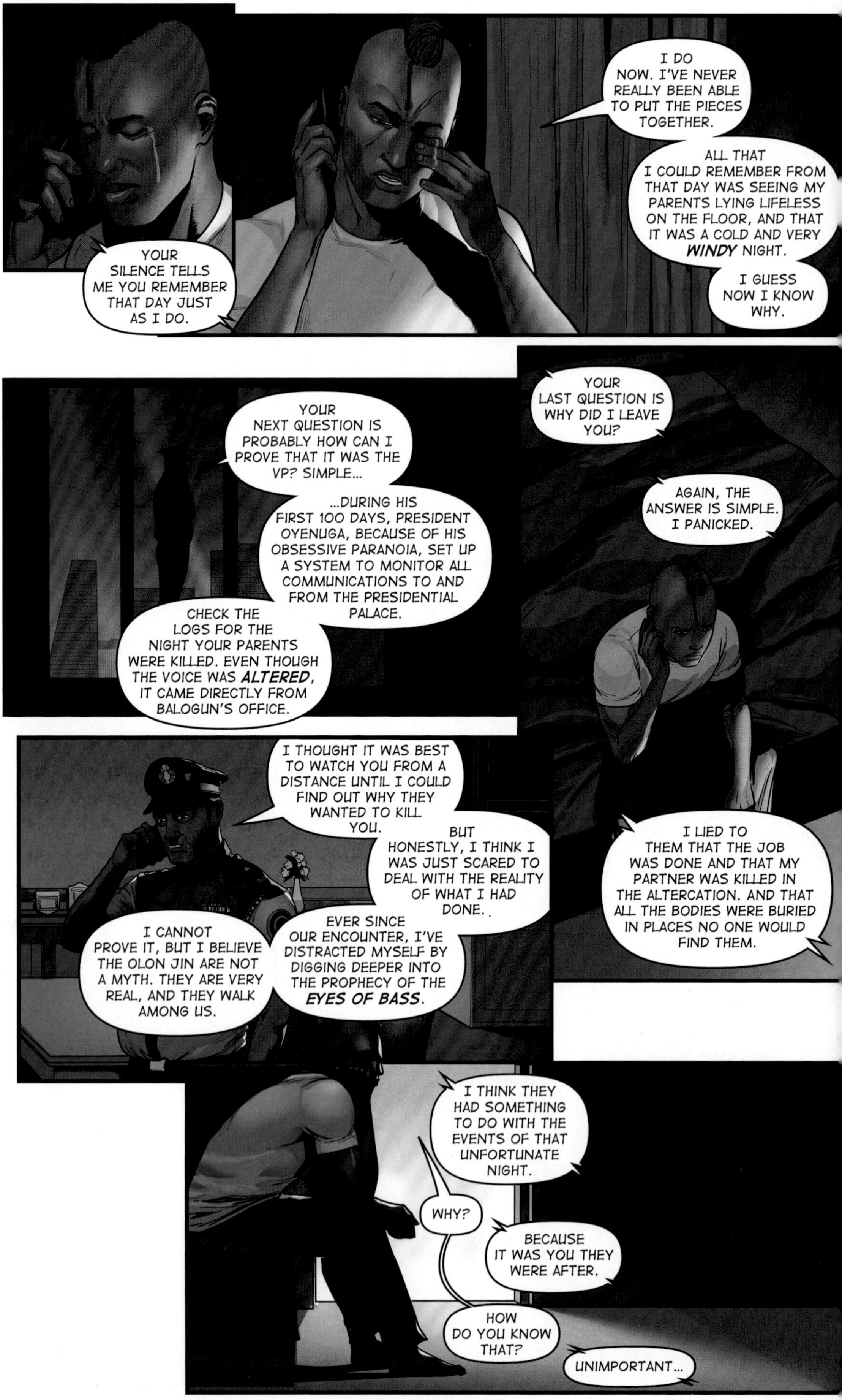
I DO NOW. I'VE NEVER REALLY BEEN ABLE TO PUT THE PIECES TOGETHER.
ALL THAT I COULD REMEMBER FROM THAT DAY WAS SEEING MY PARENTS LYING LIFELESS ON THE FLOOR, AND THAT IT WAS A COLD AND VERY *WINDY* NIGHT.
I GUESS NOW I KNOW WHY.
YOUR SILENCE TELLS ME YOU REMEMBER THAT DAY JUST AS I DO.
YOUR NEXT QUESTION IS PROBABLY HOW CAN I PROVE THAT IT WAS THE VP? SIMPLE...
...DURING HIS FIRST 100 DAYS, PRESIDENT OYENUGA, BECAUSE OF HIS OBSESSIVE PARANOIA, SET UP A SYSTEM TO MONITOR ALL COMMUNICATIONS TO AND FROM THE PRESIDENTIAL PALACE.
CHECK THE LOGS FOR THE NIGHT YOUR PARENTS WERE KILLED. EVEN THOUGH THE VOICE WAS *ALTERED*, IT CAME DIRECTLY FROM BALOGUN'S OFFICE.
YOUR LAST QUESTION IS WHY DID I LEAVE YOU?
AGAIN, THE ANSWER IS SIMPLE. I PANICKED.
I LIED TO THEM THAT THE JOB WAS DONE AND THAT MY PARTNER WAS KILLED IN THE ALTERCATION. AND THAT ALL THE BODIES WERE BURIED IN PLACES NO ONE WOULD FIND THEM.
I THOUGHT IT WAS BEST TO WATCH YOU FROM A DISTANCE UNTIL I COULD FIND OUT WHY THEY WANTED TO KILL YOU.
BUT HONESTLY, I THINK I WAS JUST SCARED TO DEAL WITH THE REALITY OF WHAT I HAD DONE.
EVER SINCE OUR ENCOUNTER, I'VE DISTRACTED MYSELF BY DIGGING DEEPER INTO THE PROPHECY OF THE *EYES OF BASS*.
I CANNOT PROVE IT, BUT I BELIEVE THE OLON JIN ARE NOT A MYTH. THEY ARE VERY REAL, AND THEY WALK AMONG US.
I THINK THEY HAD SOMETHING TO DO WITH THE EVENTS OF THAT UNFORTUNATE NIGHT.
WHY?
BECAUSE IT WAS YOU THEY WERE AFTER.
HOW DO YOU KNOW THAT?
UNIMPORTANT...

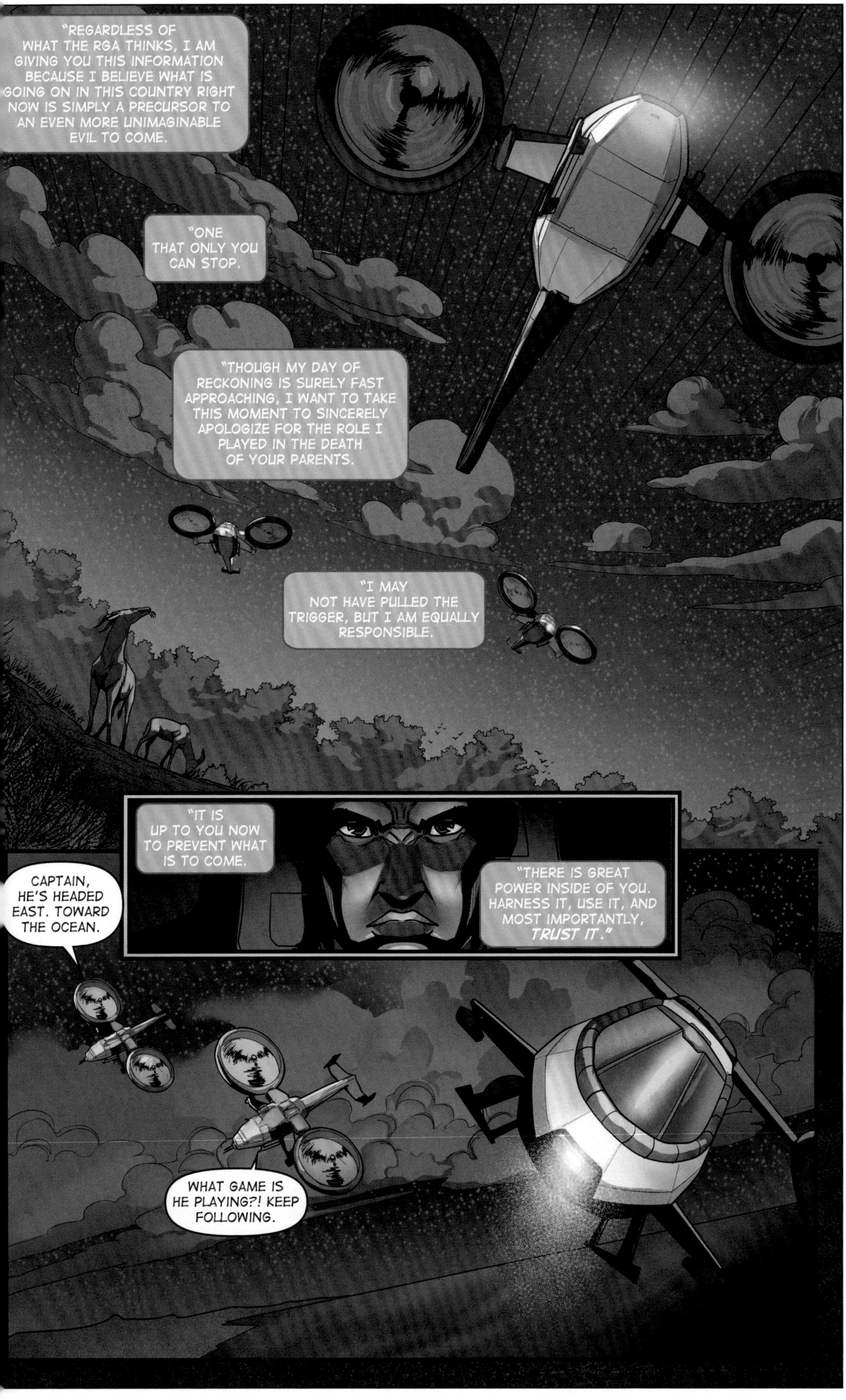
"REGARDLESS OF WHAT THE RGA THINKS, I AM GIVING YOU THIS INFORMATION BECAUSE I BELIEVE WHAT IS GOING ON IN THIS COUNTRY RIGHT NOW IS SIMPLY A PRECURSOR TO AN EVEN MORE UNIMAGINABLE EVIL TO COME.
"ONE THAT ONLY YOU CAN STOP.
"THOUGH MY DAY OF RECKONING IS SURELY FAST APPROACHING, I WANT TO TAKE THIS MOMENT TO SINCERELY APOLOGIZE FOR THE ROLE I PLAYED IN THE DEATH OF YOUR PARENTS.
"I MAY NOT HAVE PULLED THE TRIGGER, BUT I AM EQUALLY RESPONSIBLE.
"IT IS UP TO YOU NOW TO PREVENT WHAT IS TO COME.
"THERE IS GREAT POWER INSIDE OF YOU. HARNESS IT, USE IT, AND MOST IMPORTANTLY, *TRUST IT*."
CAPTAIN, HE'S HEADED EAST. TOWARD THE OCEAN.
WHAT GAME IS HE PLAYING?! KEEP FOLLOWING.

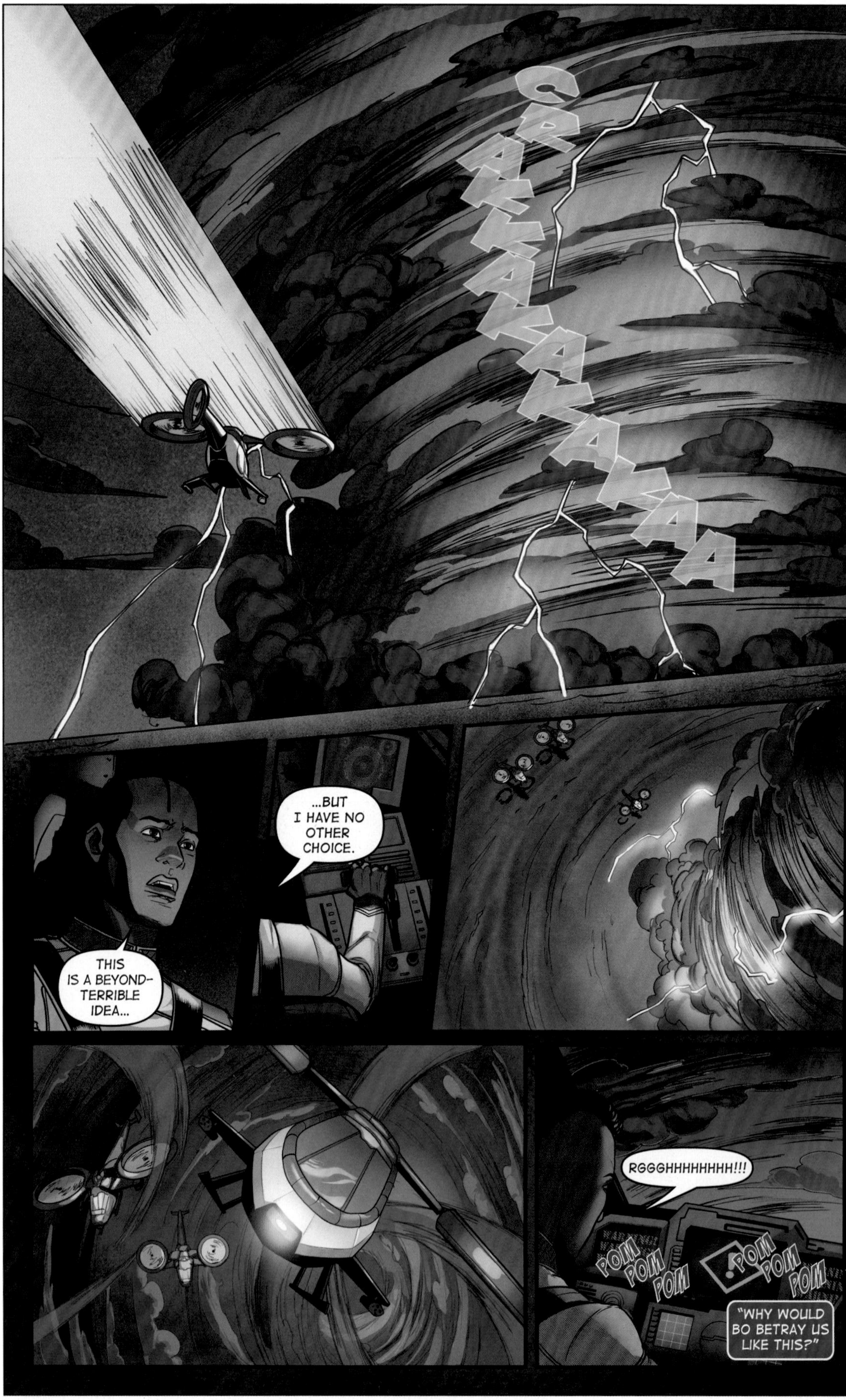
CRAKAKAKAKAKAKAA
...BUT I HAVE NO OTHER CHOICE.
THIS IS A BEYOND-TERRIBLE IDEA...
RGGGHHHHHHHH!!!
POM POM POM
POM POM POM
"WHY WOULD BO BETRAY US LIKE THIS?"

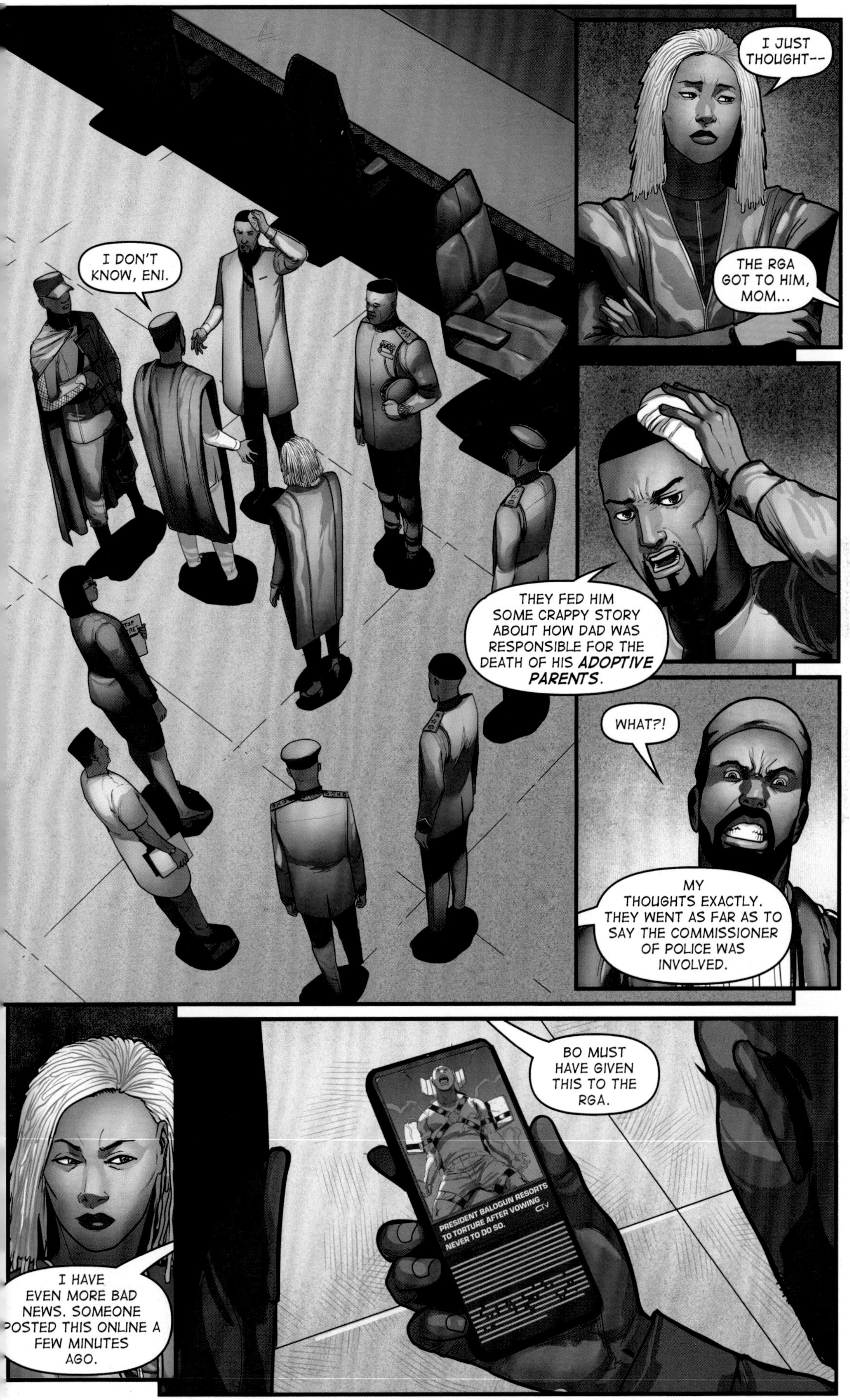
I DON'T KNOW, ENI.
I JUST THOUGHT--
THE RGA GOT TO HIM, MOM...
THEY FED HIM SOME CRAPPY STORY ABOUT HOW DAD WAS RESPONSIBLE FOR THE DEATH OF HIS *ADOPTIVE PARENTS*.
WHAT?!
MY THOUGHTS EXACTLY. THEY WENT AS FAR AS TO SAY THE COMMISSIONER OF POLICE WAS INVOLVED.
I HAVE EVEN MORE BAD NEWS. SOMEONE POSTED THIS ONLINE A FEW MINUTES AGO.
BO MUST HAVE GIVEN THIS TO THE RGA.
PRESIDENT BALOGUN RESORTS TO TORTURE AFTER VOWING NEVER TO DO SO.
CTV

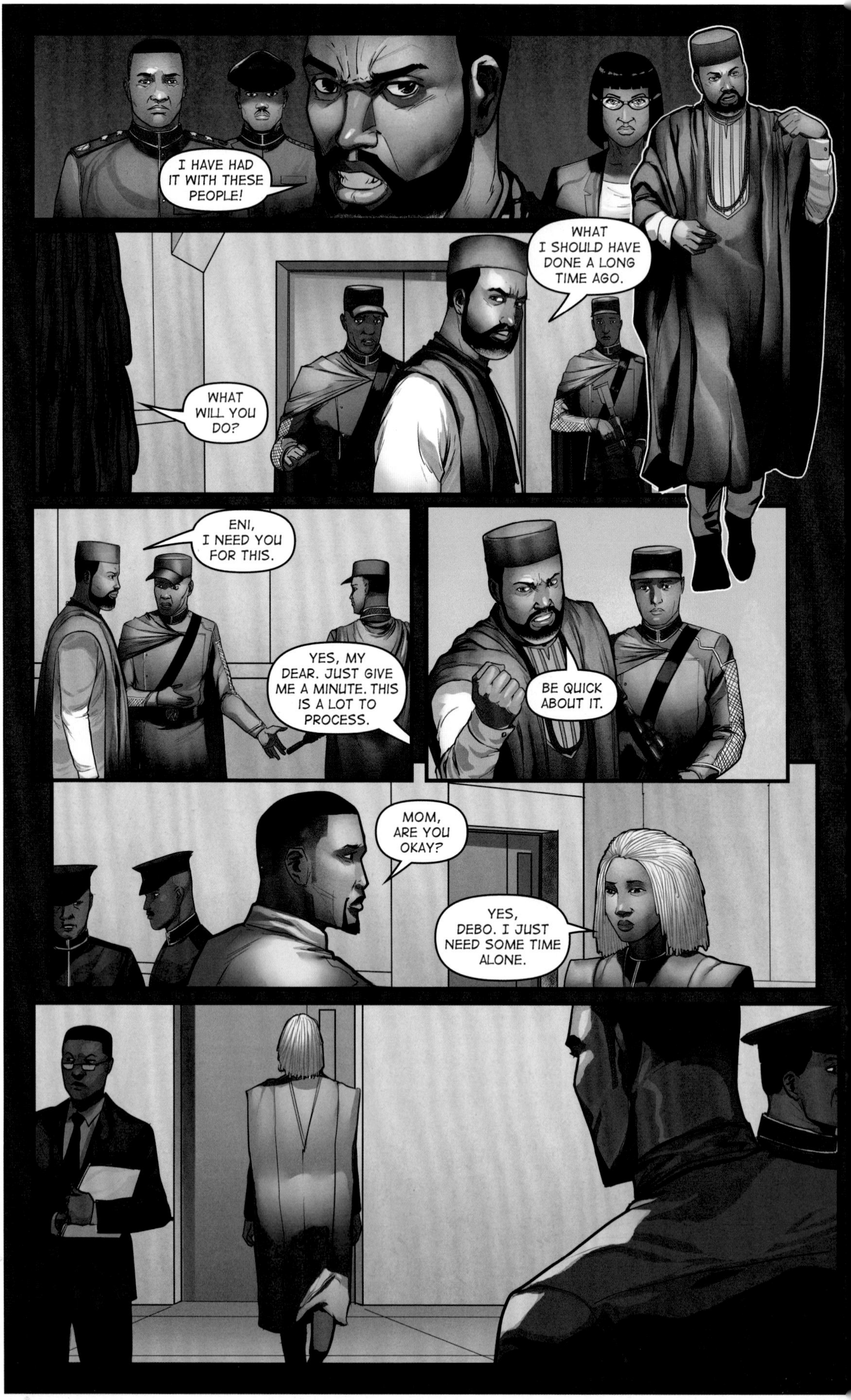
I HAVE HAD IT WITH THESE PEOPLE!
WHAT WILL YOU DO?
WHAT I SHOULD HAVE DONE A LONG TIME AGO.
ENI, I NEED YOU FOR THIS.
YES, MY DEAR. JUST GIVE ME A MINUTE. THIS IS A LOT TO PROCESS.
BE QUICK ABOUT IT.
MOM, ARE YOU OKAY?
YES, DEBO. I JUST NEED SOME TIME ALONE.

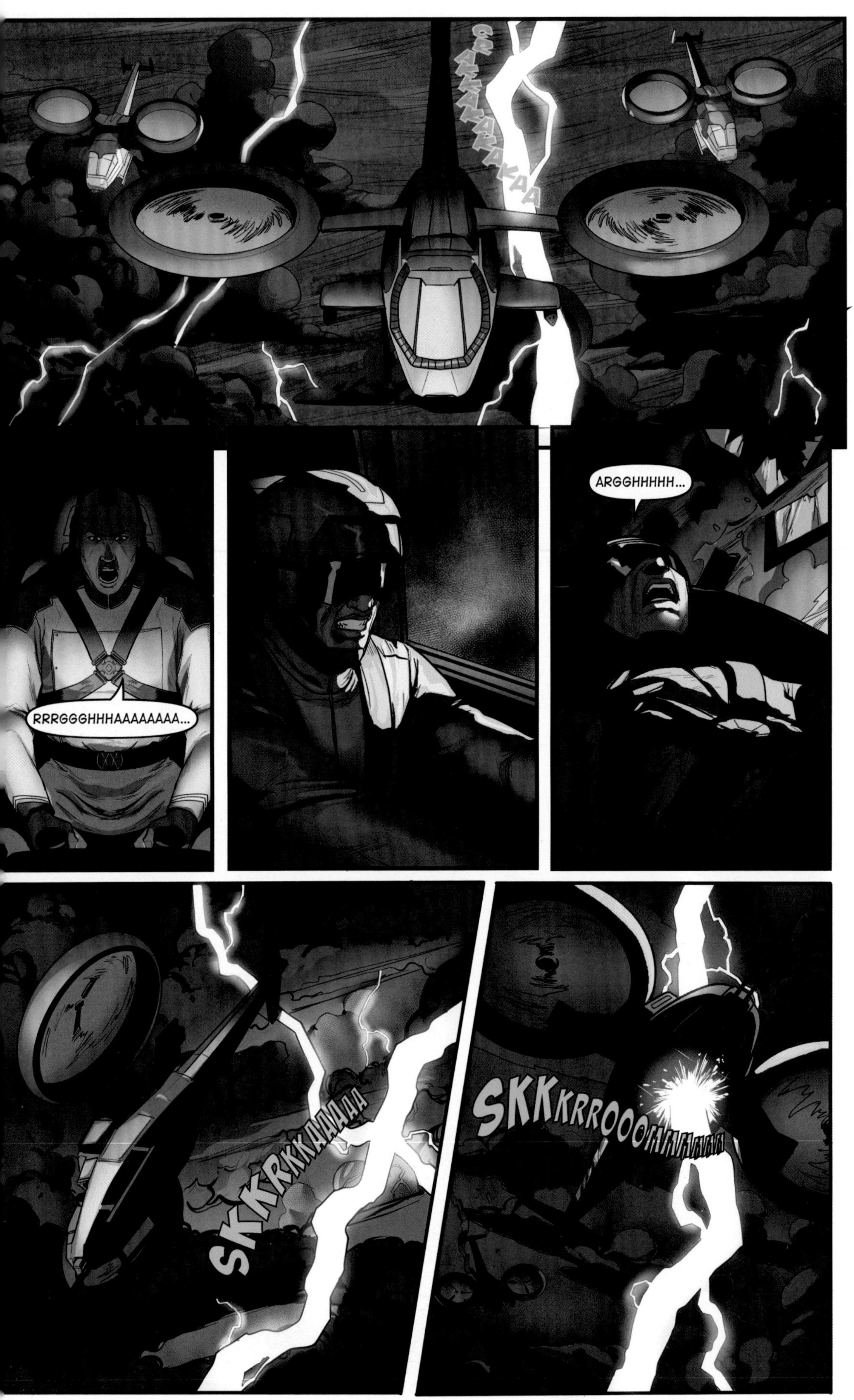
CRAKAKAKAKAKAA
RRRGGGHHHAAAAAAAA...
ARGGHHHHH...
SKKRKKAAAAA
SKKRROOOMMMMM

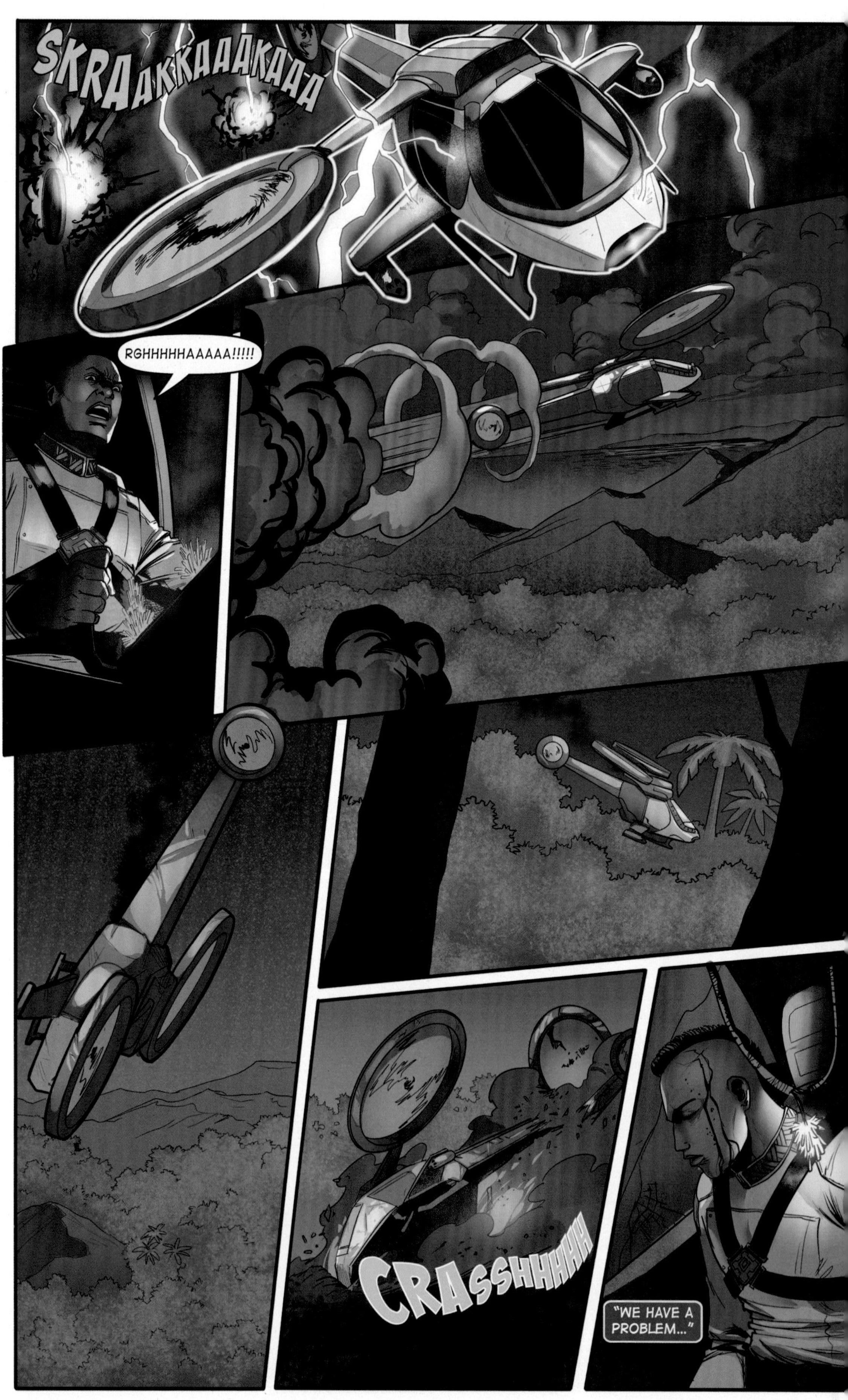
SKRAAKKAAAKAAA
RGHHHHHAAAAA!!!!!
CRASSHHHHH
"WE HAVE A PROBLEM..."

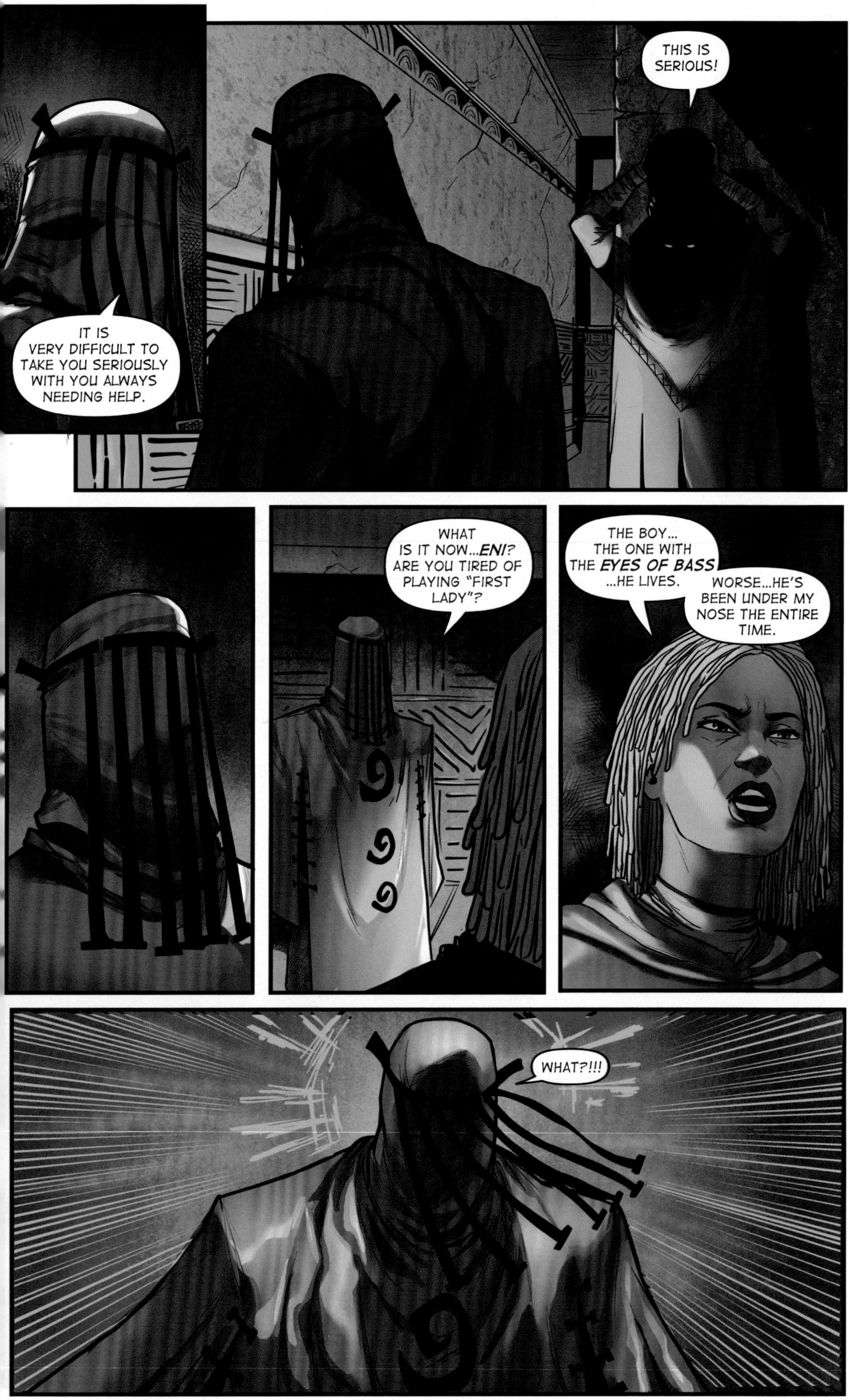
THIS IS SERIOUS!
IT IS VERY DIFFICULT TO TAKE YOU SERIOUSLY WITH YOU ALWAYS NEEDING HELP.
WHAT IS IT NOW...ENI? ARE YOU TIRED OF PLAYING "FIRST LADY"?
THE BOY... THE ONE WITH THE EYES OF BASS ...HE LIVES.
WORSE...HE'S BEEN UNDER MY NOSE THE ENTIRE TIME.
WHAT?!!!

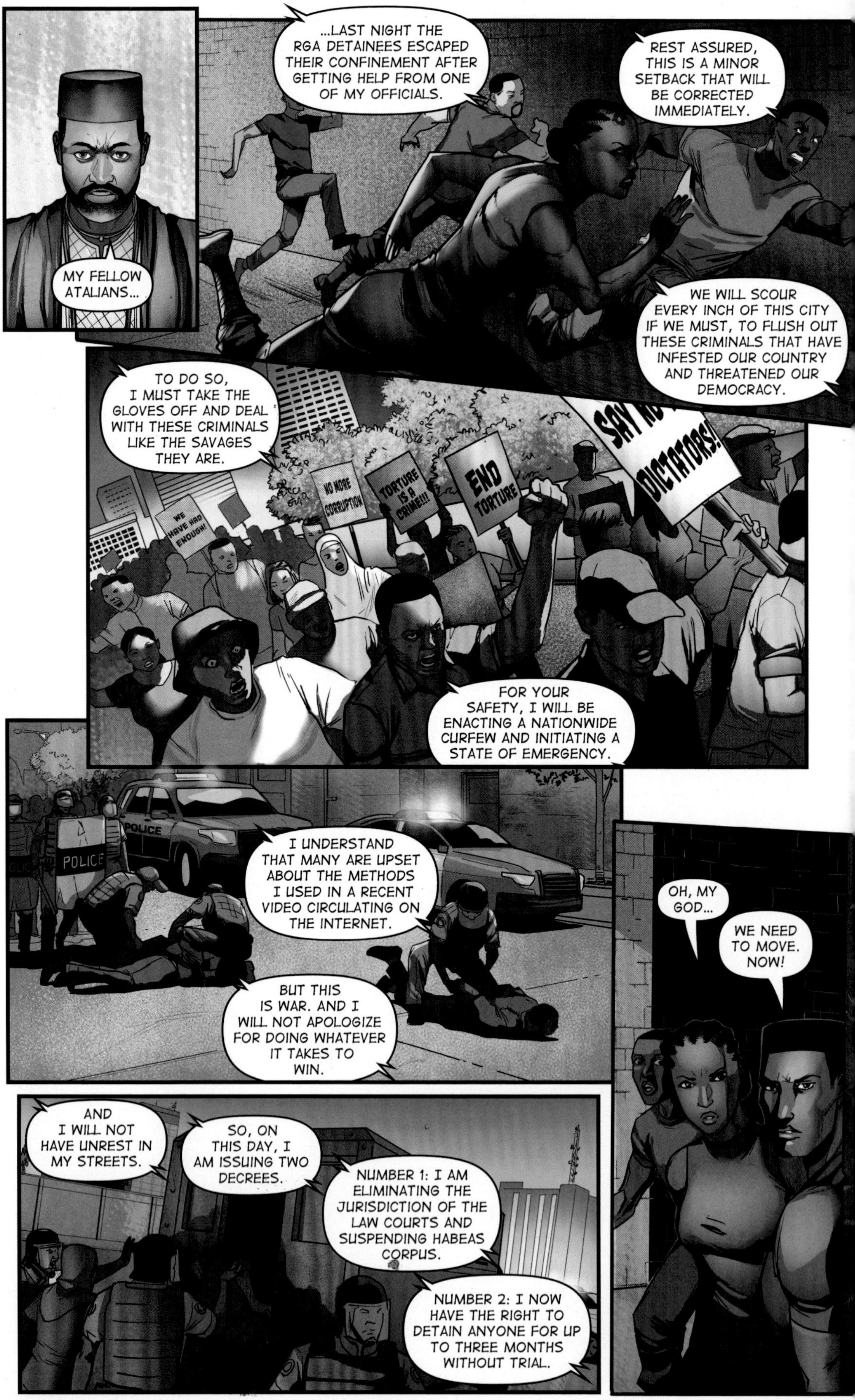
MY FELLOW ATALIANS...
...LAST NIGHT THE RGA DETAINEES ESCAPED THEIR CONFINEMENT AFTER GETTING HELP FROM ONE OF MY OFFICIALS.
REST ASSURED, THIS IS A MINOR SETBACK THAT WILL BE CORRECTED IMMEDIATELY.
WE WILL SCOUR EVERY INCH OF THIS CITY IF WE MUST, TO FLUSH OUT THESE CRIMINALS THAT HAVE INFESTED OUR COUNTRY AND THREATENED OUR DEMOCRACY.
TO DO SO, I MUST TAKE THE GLOVES OFF AND DEAL WITH THESE CRIMINALS LIKE THE SAVAGES THEY ARE.
WE HAVE HAD ENOUGH!
NO MORE CORRUPTION
TORTURE IS A CRIME!!!
END TORTURE
DICTATORS!
FOR YOUR SAFETY, I WILL BE ENACTING A NATIONWIDE CURFEW AND INITIATING A STATE OF EMERGENCY.
POLICE
POLICE
I UNDERSTAND THAT MANY ARE UPSET ABOUT THE METHODS I USED IN A RECENT VIDEO CIRCULATING ON THE INTERNET.
BUT THIS IS WAR. AND I WILL NOT APOLOGIZE FOR DOING WHATEVER IT TAKES TO WIN.
OH, MY GOD...
WE NEED TO MOVE. NOW!
AND I WILL NOT HAVE UNREST IN MY STREETS.
SO, ON THIS DAY, I AM ISSUING TWO DECREES.
NUMBER 1: I AM ELIMINATING THE JURISDICTION OF THE LAW COURTS AND SUSPENDING HABEAS CORPUS.
NUMBER 2: I NOW HAVE THE RIGHT TO DETAIN ANYONE FOR UP TO THREE MONTHS WITHOUT TRIAL.

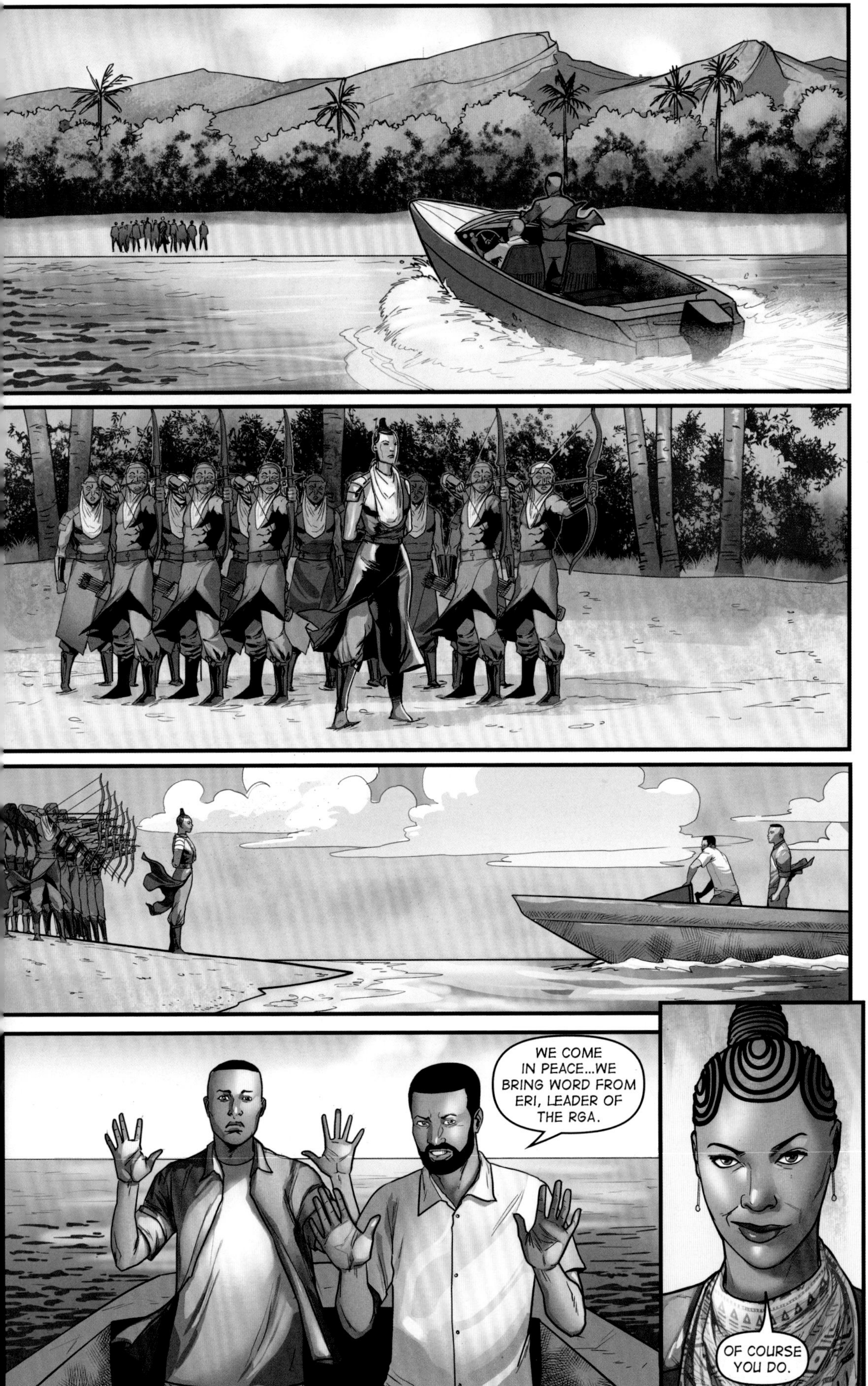
WE COME IN PEACE...WE BRING WORD FROM ERI, LEADER OF THE RGA.
OF COURSE YOU DO.
TO BE CONTINUED!

YouNeek YouNiverse Q&A

with CREATOR ROYE OKUPE

CITY OF AKONI ART BY GODWIN AKPAN

CITY OF AKONI ART BY GODWIN AKPAN

The last time we saw the Kingdom of Atala was in the *WindMaker: Birth of a King* one-shot (reprinted in *Malika: Warrior Queen* Volume 1). That story was set in the late Fifteenth Century, but this story is set in the Twenty-First Century in the now Republic of Atala. Can you tell us how things have changed over the last five hundred years of so?

It was so much fun reimagining Atala in the Twenty-First Century. Honestly, world-building is the most exciting part of the process of creating for me. The fun challenge here was trying to figure out how to pay homage to the Fifteenth-Century Kingdom of Atala while at the same time making the Republic of Atala feel like a modern, bustling West African metropolis.

To do so, I sat down with both Sunkanmi and Morby and what we did was extrapolate different motifs, patterns, figures, and structures from both the art from previous WindMaker books (*Windmaker: The History of Atala* and *WindMaker: Birth of a King*) set in the kingdom as well as from Yoruba culture—as base ingredients to design things like buildings, statues, outfits, vehicles, and so on.

A few examples are the air transport and sky trains/shuttles used at the Floating Palace. If you look closely, the red materials that outline the windshields for both are inspired by Yoruba coral beads.

AIR TRANSPORT ART BY TOYIN "MORBY" AJETUNMOBI

FLOATING PALACE ART BY GODWIN AKPAN

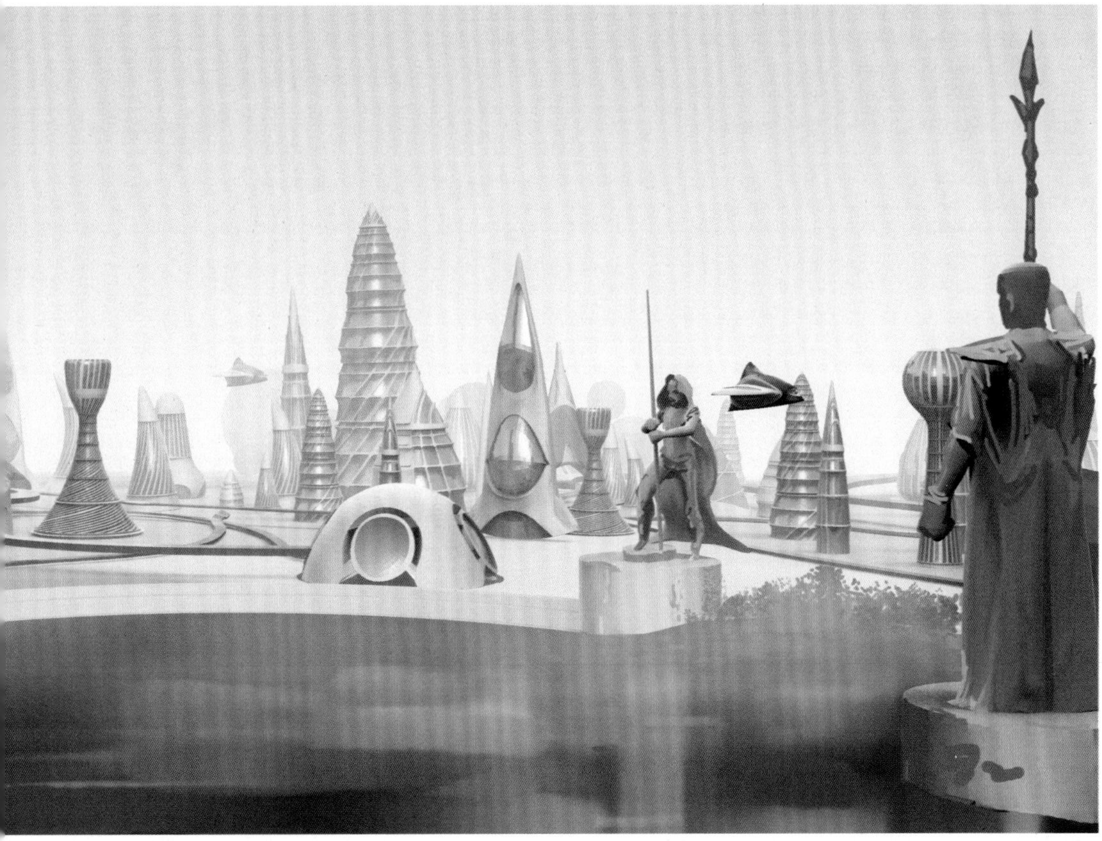

SKY TRAIN/AIR SHUTTLE ART BY TOYIN "MORBY" AJETUNMOBI

Option 1

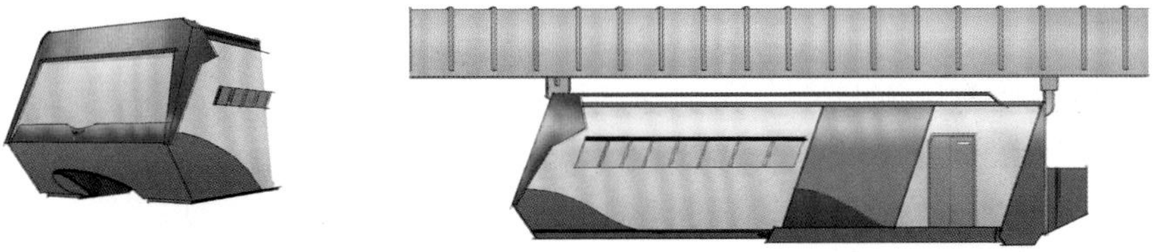

Option 2

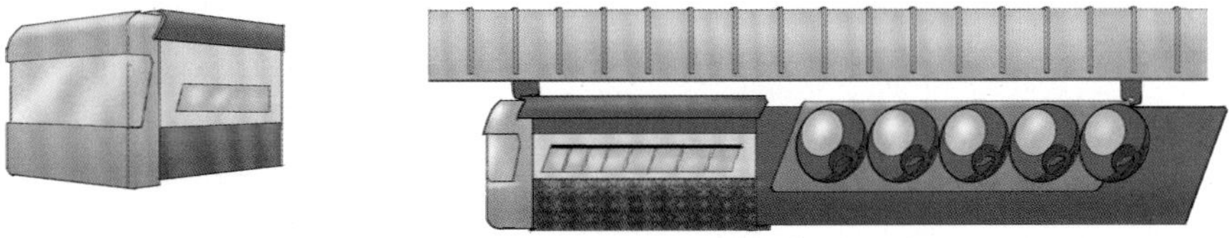

Option 3

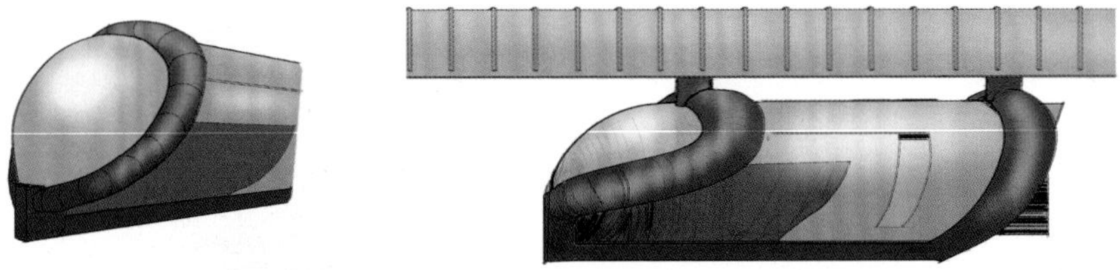

AIR TRANSPORT ART BY TOYIN "MORBY" AJETUNMOBI

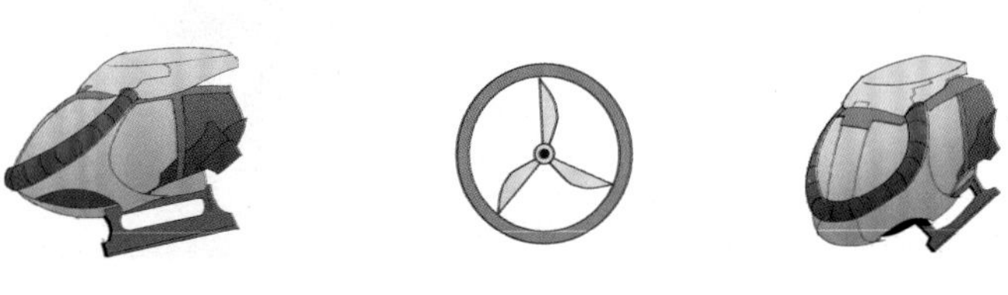

This is clearly a new story about a new WindMaker and not the original Bass Kazaar from the *Malika* series. Can you talk a little bit about your choice to start off the *WindMaker* series with a character that isn't, well, the original WindMaker?

WARNING: This answer contains minor spoilers from *Malika: Warrior Queen* Volume 1. If you haven't read that book, I suggest you skip this question. Or at least the first paragraph.

One point I've always wanted to (and hope I continue to) drive home is that in the YouNeek YouNiverse, rarely do you see characters that die get resurrected. As I've mentioned before, I really want readers to feel like the stakes are truly high in this world and that consequences can sometimes be dire. So while killing off a (fan favorite) main character like King Bass (a.k.a. the Legendary WindMaker) was incredibly tough, it opened the door for me to tell a "passing of the torch" type origin story with Bo.

My goal was always to kick off this new series with a passing of the mantle, putting a new "hero in the making" in a crucible that would eventually mold him into the WindMaker, a.k.a. the champion of Atala. That way, it truly feels like an origin story as opposed to a spinoff series. People come into the YouNeek YouNiverse via different series (*Malika*, *E.X.O.*, *Iyanu*, etc.), and I felt like old and new fans alike would appreciate this approach.

We hear the term "Eyes of Bass" used quite a bit in this volume. Can you elaborate a bit on what exactly that phrase means?

The "Eyes of Bass" is an ancient prophecy in Atalian history started by the Red Ravens—the elite military group of the Kingdom of Atala. It basically states that one day, in a time of desperate need, the spirit of King Bass, a.k.a. the Legendary WindMaker, would be reincarnated in an Atalian hero to set the people free. This hero would be recognized by the same glow seen in King Bass's eyes when his powers were activated.

WINDMAKER   ART BY SUNKANMI AKINBOYE

"EYES OF BASS"   ART BY GODWIN AKPAN

WINDMAKER ART BY SUNKANMI AKINBOYE

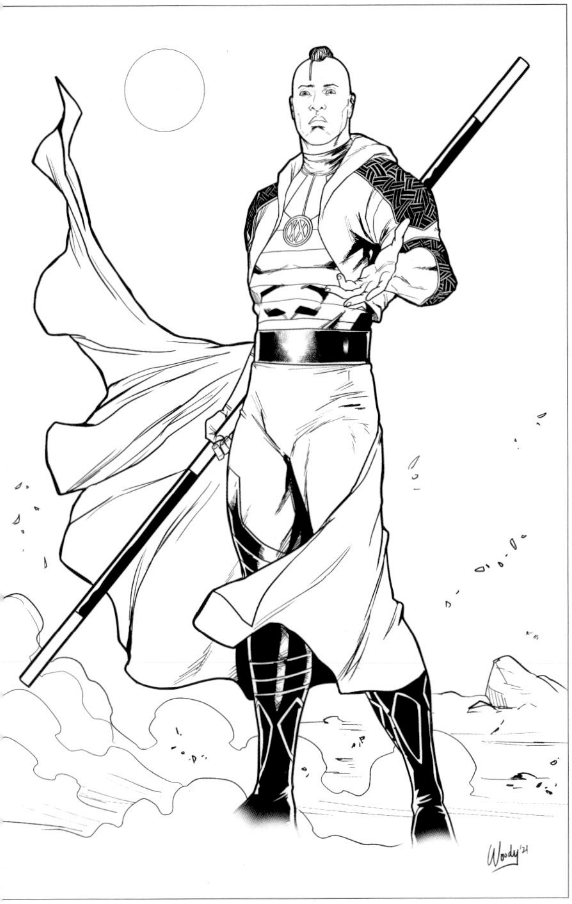

WINDMAKER ART BY TOYIN "MORBY" AJETUNMOBI

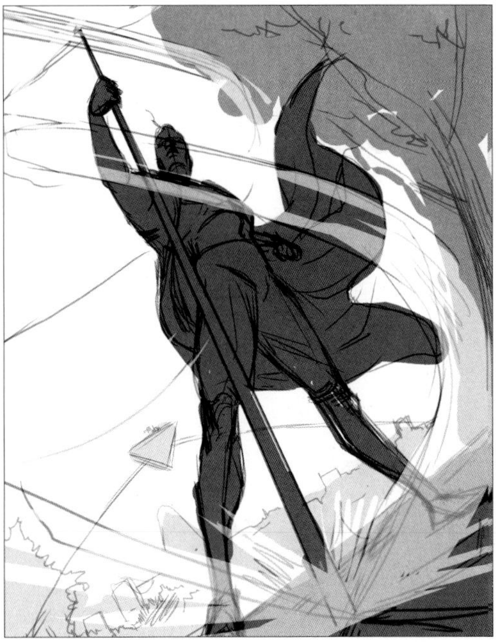

GRANDMASTER
ART BY TOYIN "MORBY" AJETUNMOBI

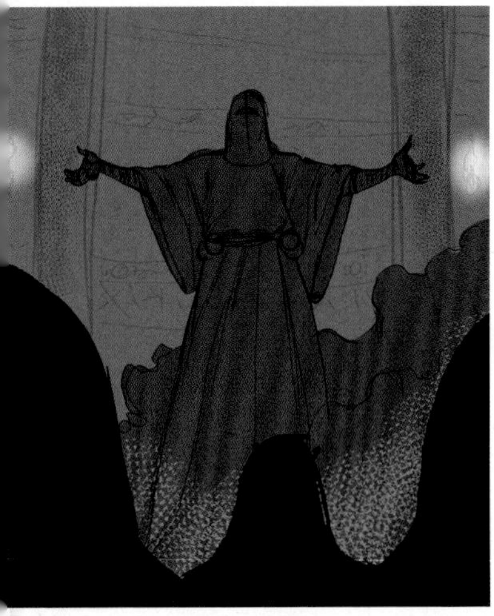

RED RAVENS ART BY GODWIN AKPAN

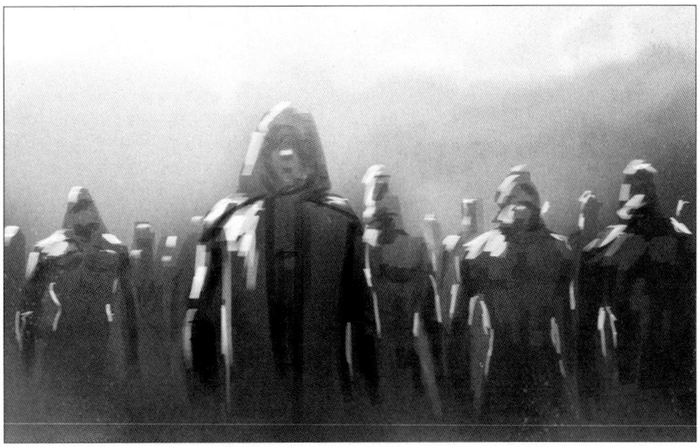

You left us with a massive cliffhanger. Once again, we see that the Olon Jin are pulling the strings behind the scenes. Just how dangerous are these guys, and how did Eni, the first lady of Atala, get mixed up with them?

If you look closely, the Olon Jin have had their hands in every major conflict that has plagued all the heroes in the YouNeek YouNiverse. They are essentially the constant and very dangerous dark cloud that hovers over the entire YouNiverse. And we've only seen a fraction of their grand plan.

As for how Eni got entangled in their intricate web, well, you'll just have to read volume 2! (Wink!)

Dark Horse Books and YouNeek Studios are proud to present a shared universe of fantasy and superhero stories inspired by African history, culture, and mythology—created by the best Nigerian comics talent!

Malika: Warrior Queen
Volume 1
(pronounced: "Ma-Lie-Kah")
Written by Roye Okupe.
Illustrated by Chima Kᵃlu.
Colors by Raphael Kazeem.
Letters by Spoof Animation.
Begins the tale of the exploits of queen and military commander Malika, who struggles to keep the peace in her ever-expanding empire, Azzaz.
Sept. 2021 Trade Paperback 336 pages
$24.99 US $33.99 CA • 9781506723082

Malika: Warrior Queen
Volume 2
Written by Roye Okupe.
Illustrated by Sunkanmi Akinboye.
Colors by Etubi Onucheyo and Toyin Ajetunmobi.
Letters by Spoof Animation.
Dec. 2021 Trade Paperback 280 Pages
$24.99 US $33.99 CA • 9781506723075

Iyanu: Child of Wonder
Volume 1
(pronounced: "Ee-Yah-Nu")
Written by Roye Okupe.
Illustrated by Godwin Akpan.
Letters by Spoof Animation.
A teenage orphan with no recollection of her past discovers that she has abilities that rival the ancient deities told of in folklore. These abilities are the key to bringing back an "age of wonders," to save a world on the brink of destruction!
Sept. 2021 Trade Paperback 120 Pages
$19.99 US $25.99 CA • 9781506723044

WindMaker
Volume 1
Written by Roye Okupe.
Illustrated by Sunkanmi Akinboye and Toyin Ajetunmobi.
Letters by Spoof Animation.
The West African nation of Atala is thrust into an era of unrest and dysfunction after their beloved president turns vicious dictator.
April 2022 Trade Paperback 144 Pages
$19.99 US $25.99 CA • 9781506723112

E.X.O.: The Legend of Wale Williams
Volume 1
Written by Roye Okupe.
Illustrated by Sunkanmi Akinboye.
Colors by Raphael Kazeem.
Letters by Spoof Animation.
The oldest son of a world-renowned scientist, Wale Williams—a.k.a. tech-savvy superhero EXO—tries to save Lagoon City from a deadly group of extremists. But before this "pending" superhero can do any good for his city, there is one person he must save first—himself!
Oct. 2021 Trade Paperback 312 Pages
$24.99 US $33.99 CA • 9781506723020

E.X.O.: The Legend of Wale Williams
Volume 2
Written by Roye Okupe.
Illustrated by Sunkanmi Akinboye.
Colors by Etubi Onucheyo and Tarella Pablo.
Letters by Spoof Animation.
Feb. 2022 Trade Paperback 280 Pages
$24.99 US $33.99 CA • 9781506723037

YOUNEEK STUDIOS

DarkHorse.com
Text and illustrations of Malika™: Warrior Queen © 2021 YouNeek Studios. Text and illustrations of Iyanu™: Child of Wonder © 2021 YouNeek Studios. Text and illustrations of E.X.O.™: The Legend of Wale Williams © 2021 YouNeek Studios. Text and illustrations of WindMaker™ © 2021 YouNeek Studios.

Press Inquiries:
pr@darkhorse.com

Sales Inquiries:
tradesales@darkhorse.com